The Middle Path

A guide for spiritual unfoldment

The Middle Path

A guide for spiritual unfoldment

E.W. Blighton, Author

Compiled and Edited by M.R. Blighton

Published by:

The Science of Man

First Edition

Printed in the United States of America

Library of Congress Cataloging - in - Publication Data

The Middle Path

E.W. Blighton, Author

M.R. Blighton, Editor

(Approx.) 300 pages

Library of Congress Control Number: 2001090495

ISBN 0-9672633-0-1 (Paperback)

ISBN 0-9672633-1-X (Hardback)

Printed by:

Sheridan Books

613 E. Industrial Drive, Chelsea, MI 48118

"No book ever carried wisdom; books carry knowledge.
The only wisdom you can gain is that which comes from within"

Father Paul

CONTENTS

FOREWORD

The author of this book, Earl Blighton, is no longer with us, but some of his words live on in tapes which were transcribed from classes and lectures. He was an electrical engineer until the final eight years of his life, when he devoted himself entirely to spiritual-religious work. During his working years he also took short sabbaticals in order to serve in an active way. The longest period was one year that he gave over entirely to counseling and encouraging young prison parolees, helping them to find work and otherwise get back on their feet. He financed these missions out of his own savings. Another mission involved working with colored light in healing.

Rev. Blighton was pastor and one of the founders of the Science of Man which was chartered in 1961, when services were held in San Jose and San Francisco. Some of the younger members wanted to form a residential order and this came about in 1968 in the form of the Holy Order of Mans. From a meager beginning, the Order grew in six years to almost 700 members spread across the nation as well as Europe and Japan. His students lived semi-monastic lives dedicated to spiritual growth and service. Several years after his passing in 1974, the original Science of Man was restored as a way of preserving his teachings and to independently carry on his work in whatever way presented itself

The teachings expressed here are timeless, reaching from ancient wisdom into the coming age, and they present a way that is neither to the left nor the right, that is not entirely western or eastern, but universal and applicable to all. They point the way from the outer material world to that of the spirit.

We have called this book "The Middle Path" because it shows a way between two extremes. In the words of its author, called Father Paul by his students, "we do not lean either to the occult or the mystic side of things but we go through the core. It is what the old mystic called the bootstrap method; you pick yourself up by your own bootstraps. This is a bit tougher, but it is still shorter than going around and around the mountain."

The teachings do not condemn other religious beliefs, but seek to present spiritual Truths which are essentially Christian but basically the same in all religions. Father Paul once said, "the teaching is not all in the words, the things that we tell you. It's in what we manifest and live." And again, "experience does not come in words."

We cannot explain a spiritual teacher in intellectual terms because his work transcends the material and the mental. To him the spiritual path is a great adventure, and Father Paul motivated others through his own enthusiasm and directness. He was not self-serving, and lived not for material advantage but for the vast reach of infinity.

INTRODUCTION

Father Paul, as he was known to us, his students, was truly a remarkable person. He did not look particularly remarkable, and his outward personality was not very remarkable, so that judging by all that most people think, he would not seem remarkable at all. When I first met him in 1969, he stood about five feet seven, balding, with white hair and glasses. He seemed like an interesting character, a little tough yet right there with you when you were talking. But what was remarkable about Father was what happened to you if you were open when you were around him. If you were open and seeking God, your life would be changed. If you were open you would be overwhelmed by golden light and the most beautiful divine presence, an ecstasy and bliss like you only read about in books, except that it was happening to you. These things didn't have to happen in his direct presence, but were happening all around him and could and did happen all the time. On the other hand, it could be excruciatingly painful to be around him if you were dealing with your own impurity or just some junky ideas that you may have picked up somewhere. The Spirit and the Fire would burn until all that was false was gone.

Father Paul didn't teach about himself, he taught God first, and Jesus and Mary as our real teachers. He taught the path of Mastery. He took his students to Jesus and Mary if they were willing to go there, and he taught literally thousands of students. There were never more than 700 students in the Holy Order of Mans at one time, but at least a few thousand students passed through the doors of his school, some for just a few days or a few weeks, others for a few months or years, but all were marked by the experience.

In this book are some of the things Father Paul said on various subjects, edited by his widow Mother Ruth. We hope that his word may prove an inspiration to you. Perhaps open you up to a greater experience of the Spirit. Perhaps even open you up to those great teachers, Jesus Christ and Mary.

Rev. Titus Hayden, November 15, 2000

ACTION

We should understand that action is a necessity if one is going to attain permanent spiritual development. You cannot attain lasting spiritual development without action. Your acts are your prayers. In other words, as you act and move and do, this projects and perpetrates a form and pattern of what you would have happen. That is our prayer, and it will be. Now it might not have been so six centuries ago, but it will be now, in this age, because the soul stands in balance.

We hear people say, "Somehow or other I pray and pray, but I can't seem to feel God. I can't seem to feel the Spirit." No, of course you can't, because you started from the wrong end of the horn.

You can pray and pray, but if you've gotten your physical life and action separated from your spiritual life and action, you're not going to be there. And until you take that spiritual life into your physical one, you're not going to see or hear the manifestation of the Spirit. You're not going to feel the presence of our Lord here, because you have distinctly separated them and said, "Well, I live a spiritual life, and I live a physical life." As long as you live two lives, you're going to live two lives, and there isn't any part of one going to be in the other.

Now, metaphysics and all these other things are a waste of time unless they're used. You have to do something or it can't do anything for you. There is only one reason on earth that a person would be interested in any metaphysical teaching or Bible teaching, or even in coming to listen to a lecture. Because if you are not interested in how you can control your own physical being, make your life happier and prepare yourself for a journey, a conscious and controllable journey when you leave this shell, then forget about it, because you're only going to agitate and disturb your own self. You're only going to keep on seeking for "what" and for "why". You're only going to keep probing for something, and it's useless, with nothing gained.

Of course, if you're just interested in being amused, well, it is a nice amusement. Sometimes the words are pretty, but not too often here because we don't read much poetry and such. And if you're not interested in doing, you'll save your teachers a lot of time and trouble if you just tell them so they don't have to bother, because people can spend many hours in discussion.

When the time comes to offer the results of your experience to others, you will always know the kind of people who are most in need, or the institution or group who would be most concerned. Mystically this principle can be entitled "the cosmic law of service", and if we could get your consciousness to the place where you could hold within yourself and your consciousness the things you have learned through divine inspiration and from revelation or intuition from within, you would take a look in the mirror and see how many selfless acts you have performed in the last week.

It is therefore a vain and fruitless inquiry to ask beforehand for the knowledge of any unpossessed matter. For knowledge can be yours only as sickness and health is yours, not conveyed into you by a hearsay notion, but by the fruits of your own perception and sensibility.

We could pretty nearly perfectly follow Jesus Christ and our Father in heaven if we took those two things: the First Commandment, and Emerson's famous saying—and I've said this over and over again—"Your actions speak so loudly, I can't hear a word you say."

I have gotten, over the years, so tired of listening to people's opinions, so tired of listening to people's dogmatic teaching. But I know the absolute cure for all of it, and that's always one thing: you don't have to contradict them, all you have to do is take them out to the kitchen and say, "We have to get a meal for these hungry people", and see if they'll dig in up to their elbows helping to clean and to do what is needed. Greatest little antidote in the world for all the dogmas. Take them out for a street mission and see if they will go with you.

Down through the ages the old mystics, long before our Master ever came here, trod that lonesome path trying to get people to love one another, and nobody understood them. Now don't ever come and tell me that "I love so and so". Let me see it. Let me see it, then I'll believe you. Because love requires giving and action. Don't tell me you love Jesus; let me see it! Because those words are just idle noises, that's all. Let me see the action, then I'll know that you know what love is. And then the Father will know too—not from what you said. It was what you did because of the power and the force that was going into action to demonstrate that love.

Now the thing you have to do is get right down inside yourself where you're just as happy to do a job that you don't like and you're just as happy to put your arm around a fellow who's doing something that isn't right according to the code of creation, and love that person as you would anybody else. Until you can do that, don't come around me with all your metaphysical books, because they're just the bunk if you won't use what they teach.

Reading, writing and studying never made a man of God, never made a teacher, never brought anybody into God-realization of the Self. You can sit and read from now until you drop this shell and you will not gain God-realization. You have got to work with the forces and the power. You can sit for five years with mantras and if you don't get out and get some action, it won't do you one bit of good, and that's being proved every day in the year. A thing has to manifest both in mind and in the earth plane, in action.

Slothfulness is a thing which brings a sort of retrogression in the individual. There is such a thing as motivation. Our actions motivate. And then within ourselves we gain the consciousness of things in life, and the spirit and consciousness of God's motivation itself within us, which couldn't be done through words that we would hear. A true experience can hardly be told by words. It has to be experienced. This is where the old cliché comes in that gives a minister the way out the back door when he says, "Oh, you can't know God. The Bible says so." True, it says so: because you can't know it on paper. I can't tell you, but you can experience it so you do know it just the same. You probably couldn't see it either, psychically or spiritually or physically, but you still can know it. Because after all, what is your physical sight but the most inferior part of your entire living organism and existence?

You can be 30 or 15 and be an absolutely mature individual. It is all a state and question of how much you can use of what you know. And this is a factual thing. How much can you use of all that you know? If you just have the words about something and you can't use it, then you don't know it, do you? You can go through school, you can get all the degrees in the world, and if you can't use it you still don't know anything, because words, without being able to use what they say, what they convey or communicate, are useless. They've no bearing upon civilization or godhood or manhood or realization or any of these other things. They're useless.

How would you like to meet Jesus here now? Would you do the same as you have planned to do in the future, if you were to meet him in person now? Or might you change your plans? It is here, present. We like to think we are Christians, but down at the core of it, are you? Or are you just yourself? Ask yourself that question. Do you really think that you're living to promote the Christian teachings and help other people? Or are you promoting Tony or Jane, or someone else? If you were ready to meet him tonight without any qualms at all, I'm sure some people's thoughts in this room would be different. You wouldn't be doing a lot of things that you're doing right now.

Your actions are a prayer. Yet not all action is physical. If you are not going out and marching down the street, you may feel that you are not doing anything. But you will learn someday that the most radical and most powerful changes that take place on earth or any orb are done very silently. Don't forget: as above, so below. That simple little statement says it all at one time.

AKASHA

If you were to come to me and say, "Father, I have a great yen to know what I was like two lifetimes ago", I would probably answer, "Well, how is that going to make any difference?" But it might in some cases, if you knew, because it might put upon you a greater burden of responsibility. Then in order to do this readily, unless it is a real emergency and some information did pop through right then, I'd say, "Well now, you have to let me go into contemplation and I may have to go out of my body, because I have to read it in the akasha, the Mind of the Father on the physical plane," which isn't on the physical plane here, but the akasha is the Mind of the physical plane, you see. So I'd say, "Well, I have to read it in the akasha to find this out. It's there but I can't readily do this without getting pretty quiet."

Now this you would understand; but when I say the Tree of Life is a pattern in the Mind of the Father, then you take it to be something else. Remember this, that the creation of all things are in the akasha. It is a matter of imagining from the form the reality of what it actually looks like, and then having a real desire for that to come into existence in the world. And it is through the desire for this, and through feeling, that the life force is brought into play, then we start the creation of whatever we have imagined or whatever form we have used in that creation. And without question you also have the power to dissolve anything that has not been fully created already. If you look outside and see a tree or a rose, it is there, but the basic form is in the Mind, in the akasha. It is part of a growing, living thing.

The akasha is linked through the fundamental substance like a great ocean in which all forms are waves. It is linked between the elements of fire and water, between the water and the air, and between the air and the earth. It is the connecting medium uniting the various forms of cosmic activity. And you will find this is true when you get into the understanding of the alchemy, when you get into the understanding of the use of prayer.

Now you have to gain the greater realization, and this realization may go on for many, many years, for a lifetime or two. But the akasha is open to you, and it depends on just how much you get rid of yourself and how much you are in control. It works just like any other electrical circuit. If you can become absolutely quiet and negative—so to speak, inactive—the force will flow to you.

If mankind, in some terrible holocaust of fire, lost all the books and ancient writings, he could still regain and rewrite all the great teachings of the world. I hold that the meditations on all subjects since the beginning of the world have been brought forth and spread through humans, entirely by God's revelation or through the help of angelic beings or spirits of those beyond, or through understanding and long observation. By this could be re-laid the foundation of new sciences as well as new monuments of truth for life here and hereafter.

ALCHEMY

Very few people in this world today know anything about alchemy. The books you can find are written by persons who know just one little thing about the subject, and this is why so many people are misinformed. When you see a book on alchemy that tells you all about how to do it, you can just label it as false, because any person who knows it won't put it in print, that way.

When you read one of these books or pick up a reprint of some old book about some of the ancient artists of alchemy, the old men of wisdom, you immediately get a picture of somebody who goes into a very mysterious chamber, through a sliding door or something, where he presses a button and lights a flame here and another flame over there; and you get a wondrous picture of all kinds of things.

But, you know, where the alchemist works truly is right here, within himself. And here is where he creates the things in the material world. Or he moves out of this vehicle and goes to work in the other world. There is no mystery about this.

The alchemists and the mystics of old knew that man's greatest stumbling block in the use of mental and spiritual powers was his lack of faith or, in other words, his lack of confidence. This is one of the hurdles you have to get over. You not only have to have confidence that the Word will work, but you have to have confidence in the Master, in the works of the Father and the laws working through you.

You who are in spiritual work are contributing to the way of life of the new earth, and your day is like the alchemist's day in his laboratory, only yours is wherever you are. We often misjudge the simple things that we do. They look so unimportant, as though we were not accomplishing anything. But that which you do every day is in accordance with alchemic law. It is a simple form with tremendous power and tremendous life that it creates.

ANGELS

An archangel is a great being that is of service to the Father and creation, one who has developed and gone to a state of reality far above anything you can imagine at the present time. And I think that's as close as I want to define it. There are ways of seeing these beings, and some have done so.

Let's see if I can give you a little better understanding of those great heavenly creatures who were created by God as messengers. Angels are spirit, or what we call spirit. Because they are less dense, we cannot see them with human eyes as they really are. But they have at times assumed bodies and appeared to men.

In the Genesis story of the ladder, Jacob could see hosts of angels ascending and descending from the heavenly or spiritual world. The Testament says that a soul has a personal friend, a guardian angel; in other words, members of God's court, the Host, have charge to guard each one.

And then, of course, there are other beings who were the result of greater attainment, who have definite parts to play in the scheme of the evolution of man on this planet, and about whom we hear very little. First of all, we want to make it very plain that until we become conscious that angels are in existence, how is it going to be possible for us to really know anything about them?

ASSUMPTION, COMPREHENSION,

REALIZATION

We learn that man has the power to assume certain roles and certain things in his life, that they will function and they are real; and this is not play-acting. Now I know people who will go on and explain the mental science to you as a play. They will tell you that all you see in front of you is not real, that it's part of the play. And they live every day that way, as though in a play.

Well, I'm going to tell you one thing, my friends, when they wake up after they've left this vehicle, they're going to have a real sudden shock, and it won't be an act or a play. It will be very real, believe me. And they'll wish they'd found out more about the reality of it. Because when you wake up and find that you have nothing but your mind to control the energy and the powers around you, you'll wish you'd listened a little closer to what Jesus taught.

There are three things in man's life that have to do with his advancement and his spiritual reality. One is the attaining of his independent knowing. The second is illumination, and the third is realization of God. From the first to the third of these major concepts—or I should say major realities—he may study about them, he may work on them, he may get to the place where he has light, or to a certain extent has broken through into the light. But until he starts to function with it, he hasn't got it, because he hasn't accepted it.

I know of people who have worked very hard to attain the God Self. But until they accept this and go to work with it, by the assuming, the acceptance, the reaching out, the moving with it, they'll never have it; because you may see all kinds of fantastic spiritual phenomena, but until you use these powers that are God-given, you haven't got them. You've only seen something that is a manifestation of their use, but they have not been used by you; therefore, you don't have them. You have to work with them, step out on it.

It is as the Master said, "Arise, take up thy bed and walk." Why? Otherwise more or less the same sins return unto thee. He didn't say, "Maybe you can get up, try and pick up your bed, see if you can walk," no. He said, pick it up, walk; but mark my word, don't go back and do it over again, because it will come back to you. Now the man had to assume that he was well, didn't he, or he'd never have gotten off the bed.

The church very often calls this an act of faith. Well, it's far more than what the usual interpretation of faith implies. You are actually assuming and taking on the condition that you were commanded to do, and you are acting on it. And after leaving earth you must function on other planes where the same law holds. The very first act you're going to perform on the spiritual plane will be assumption.

You can be nothing unless you assume that role, and do so with logic and understanding. An actor does not start with footlights and clothes. He has to start with elocution and long hours before a mirror, and develop feeling, to practice the part and live it before it is even presented to the public.

Now there's another factor necessary in here, and that is comprehension. You have got to understand what you're working with, or at least what you want. Can you comprehend Jesus, can you comprehend the great Son, can you comprehend the statement that he made when he said, "Only through me shall you see the face of the Father"? It is possible for you to do so.

You must reach the point of comprehending that this is a fact and you know it is factual before you have seen it. Otherwise you wouldn't move anything. We have assumed it will work and have comprehension of the form. Once it is solid within yourself, you don't even have to think about it.

Then there is the realization of this: to realize that this is, and to accept it and work with it. Now I can see wheels going around in many heads, because three concepts such as these—assumption, comprehension and realization—you might not run into every day, but they're very simple. These are three points of understanding and getting things to function.

This comprehension is a very serious thing. It will move more things in your life than anything else that I know of, because this is the halfway point, so to speak. It is the point at which the fork of the road occurs. From ignorance or no understanding to comprehension: this is the halfway point. And the whole earth is at that point now in its decision, in this way to the fulfillment of what the Testament said, that there shall be a new heaven and a new earth.

The term "faith" as used in the Christian philosophy is a blind acceptance that something is or is going to be, or that something will take place. But when you assume something, you do a little more than that. You know that it is going to take place. You know that it has already taken place. Now, that is a rather ridiculous statement on the face of it, but when you start to analyze it, it isn't, because anything that happens, first happens in the mind, and in the Mind of God—because it happens simultaneously there.

What is in your mind is in the Mind of God, isn't it? Now, that may make you shudder a little over some of the things that you've thought of in the past. You wouldn't like to feel that you had put this in the Father's Mind too, would you? Well, you have; so watch out what you think about. If you assume something, you assume that it already exists, and this is true, because it does exist in the Mind of the Father. It exists in your mind too, because you are the creator of it, you are the one who has given your word, which is the word of God, that it is going to happen down here in this world.

Now you may not say this audibly. You may not make it a distinct statement, but you may repeatedly accept something as a fact, and therefore it will become a certain condition or fact in your life. You may accept that you have arthritis or stomach ulcers or something else, and it will be. I'll guarantee you one hundred percent that you will develop them.

You know God never failed to answer a prayer, never. A true prayer has always been answered. And the answering of them does not always bring nice things, because people don't pray for nice things always. So when you assume something, you are actually going the full extent of faith. You are accepting the fact that it already is, and this is an act of assumption. It is something that is taking place now. You are now in that state of assuming, and therefore it is.

Another factor which enters into the picture here is comprehension. A person may be able to understand certain things in word pictures, but can you comprehend the exactitude and the reality of your prayer, how it could be? Can you comprehend the reality of it happening? No true Christian can say that he merely hopes God will answer his prayer, because then he is doubting the Testament, and a doubter of the Testament is not a Christian. So to comprehend is to be able to assume something and fully understand that it has happened. Comprehension of Reality.

The third step is the realization. This is the materialization of it, realizing that it is so and that it comes through the source and the power, revealing through its channels that there may be many people who had to do with the bringing about of this one prayer into reality.

And then realizing that it is and accepting it on this basis. The realization of it exists when we start to work with it, when we start to realize— in illumination, for instance—that this is light, it isn't imagination, and you start to work with it. These are not mental concepts.

It makes no difference what you call it. It is the recognition of power, of the Supreme Power and Intelligence which is the Root of all things. And you don't realize anything until you work with it and cooperate with it, in a sense. When it answers your questions, when your prayers are answered, when you have gotten results, then you'll have truly realized a thing, a prayer, or the Self. You have not only comprehended it is so, but it is so, because the Self is all there is. Until you can think in no other way, you cannot have realization. You cannot have a mind in Christ and still think through mortal means.

And this is our great trouble in this life, not only with philosophy, not only with the teachings of God, but a lot of other things. It is the trouble with our modern education, because no longer are you taught to have confidence in what you have learned, and to use it. They take you down a narrow channel of learning and tell you that you have to find an expert in order to get it to work. That's a little bit silly, because I'm the expert and so are you.

Until you have made a prayer and gotten an answer, you don't know God. We must learn to know things. A teacher of old has told us that one of man's greatest sins was in not doing something. He said you may do, and you may be wrong, but you have done and that is the lesser sin of the two. If you don't do, you can't know, and if you don't know, you are not sure.

This is what each one is faced with when he goes into the spiritual channel of things. He can work and study and go on for years learning, but until he gets his feet wet, until he does something with it, he doesn't know a thing. He may have letters that long after his name, but he does not know anything. There is only one way you can know, and that is when you have gotten yourself out of the way, and you've let the power of the spirit work; and when you've done this, then you know. It becomes a reality when you let it go, and let the Spirit work.

I am emphatic about this because the keynote of every man and woman alive is their happiness. And the moment that they know, there is no more fear. Fear has gone out of their life forever, because they know that the Holy Spirit is a real thing, and there's no more fakery or imagination about it. That is why the answers to people's problems and their need today is to know! That will remove all need of the rest of things.

Now that doesn't mean that you shouldn't get an education. It's nice to get an education because you have to be able to converse with people. It won't change the action of the Spirit or the power of God a bit, but you can understand more and appreciate more of God's creation by it. So you see our keynote, our work—and not just our work but that of every person on earth—is to know. When he does, he'll ring the bell every time. The answers are not in the book, in the reading or the studying. The answers are in the practicing. Do you know?

ASTRAL ENERGY

In older writings forget about the times and the periods mentioned, because nobody had a watch or calendar in those days. Only
the priests or scribes kept track of anything of this nature, and their
information was put together by astrologers, those who studied the
stars.

*Q: Is the God of this solar system also over other systems in the
universe?*

A: Possibly. I never got that big. This is one of the things that
many people get into, but until they've reached the point where they
can conceive of a Being functioning without a body, it is well to leave
that sort of connotation alone, because they don't know and they can't
conceive of the thing. But there is physical evidence of the universe
which God created and there is evidence of the relationship of those
planets to the organs, which we know through astrology and through
experiment; because there are certain times when healing can be
brought about much more functionally and pronouncedly than others.
The entire astrological chart is a map of the potential influences of the
planets out there on us.

*Q: What determines the different ways the illuminated body func-
tions?*

A: Chances are it is the state of mind or the pattern in which the
individual thinks, the things they accept.

Q: Does it have anything to do with the zodiacal aspect?

A: Well now, that's another question which I keep out of most of
the time, but in some signs there are certain prevalent possibilities that
are stronger than they are in others. Every sign has its, should I say,
weak spot? It isn't a real weak spot, but it's a probability, and it has its
particular type of disease that it is susceptible to. They don't have to get
it, but they're susceptible to it.

*Q: Doesn't that weak spot eventually become a very strong spot,
after the individual gets straightened out?*

A: Well, when you rise, if you've gone through illumination and
through realization, then you get beyond the horoscopal level, so to
speak, the connotations of the horoscope, and you become master of
your own body after awhile.

Q: And at that point the sign really doesn't mean anything at all?

A: Nothing, except that if you're a wise man, you will learn the strong facets that you have and use them. Remember this, the characters used in astrology are only there to symbolize the functional part of that orb – the real planet and its influence on man, its electromagnetical influence. Now, this is not pseudo-science, this is astro-chemistry; someday we'll understand it. All we need to know and understand is the symbolism and its general effects.

Now you can take astrology – the real science of astrology, not this bunko – and use it for diagnosis and for other things of this nature. This is possible; it shows the probabilities. In other words, these forces are in action. Now, are you going to let them influence you or not? Born under certain aspects, some might say you have everything against you. But there's no more influence over you than if you were born next door to a drunk. Just as much sense in it. He certainly didn't vibrate very well either, I'm sure; and there are some people who were born and lived and were brought up in some pretty shaggy places, but that doesn't hurt them any.

The influences are there and if you want to let them happen, why, all right, that's up to you. But if you use your own influences, your own will, all the powers in the world are there around you that you can use all you want to. And you can use the good side of this indication and multiply its power by knowing so.

Q: How do you multiply the power?

A: If you know that a certain part or aspect of the sign you were born under is a good influence, and you also know how to use the Word, and if it's to some advantage, why don't you multiply it? You've got the help of the planets too. You've been thinking of words again. Just forget the words; you have planets, you have atoms moving about a nucleus. What are you going to do with them?

Q: Use them to advantage.

A: All right. Now you're getting someplace. You know what their electromagnetic influences are, don't you? So you're going to use them. Wrapped up within the confines of your body is the totality of the vibration of every planet of the universe, of this our solar system, every one of them within you. And if you went into it as a science, you could test the formation and pattern of this great molecule, our solar system, and you could predict the next epidemic years ahead of time, and the nature of it, and what organs of the body it would affect, if you let it.

Q: Man's vibration would affect everyone and everything that was around it?

A: That's right. In other words, it's a pretty good bet that the reason we have such persistent visitors here in this atmosphere is because we're not behaving ourselves or keeping things straight, and they want to make sure that things are kept straight in some way or another, so as not to affect their planet and their life. Do you see that?

If we change the influences on this planet, we've changed the influences on the whole solar system, because the relation to the Sun, the first-born, and its polar attraction to it, affects all the planets. And these have a definite electro-magnetical relation and spiritual relation to us—the radiation from them—which definitely changes the relationship of all of the planets and the people as a whole. Let any one of these planets become extinct and we would have a radical change in the rest of this solar system, or in the Body of God.

As for our playing around with atomic bombs and one thing or another—sure, they are terrifically small in comparison to the size of the earth, but there is a definite field relationship between ourselves and the sun and the other planets. The earth has an influence on Venus, Mars, Jupiter, and so forth. And so do they have upon us.

We're talking about this solar system—the only thing we're ever concerned with—and before creation took place here.

Do you think that everyone that is in this solar system started their life span when this system began?

Q: You mean the soul, or the personality?

A: There's only one thing you can talk about when you speak about a man—you mean him, not his legs and arms, or whatever he has. You don't think that all of the people that are on this earth came out of this particular place, do you? If you do, you've got another think coming.

Q: You're talking about this world, or this solar system? This orb, this little world right here?

A: This one. There are quite a few that have come from here and many that didn't too. There are a lot of people on this little globe. If you get a cosmic view of this place, they look like just a lot of little peach fuzz moving around. And yet wrapped up in them is enough power to move anything you've ever seen.

It's just a normal situation. You see, you haven't learned to think cosmically with symbols. Cosmic conception, it has been called by some. The reality hasn't come home yet, because if it does, then you'll be able to think this way.

ATMOSPHERE

You are a light unto yourself. You are a system of your own and you have an atmosphere around you just like the earth. Each individual cell has an atmosphere and later, when you come through illumination and as the body grows more in light, the cell becomes illuminated. The same thing holds true on all levels. Your atmosphere is something you have to determine. How do you let in more light? You have determined you want it there.

You can control the shell of your atmosphere, and you can choose what is permitted to pass through it. And if you practiced it, you would know that no one could get within five or six feet, or better than that, of a man who is living the way of Jesus Christ, without being affected by it. They can't do it, because everything that comes into your atmosphere is changed in frequency and vibration according to the quality of it. And there are no barriers to this because they are not conscious of it. In other words, you're tapping them on the shoulder, very subtly.

What causes [spiritual] light to be cut off from the earth? Because the earth has an atmosphere, and man's thinking blocks it out.

ATONEMENT AND REDEMPTION

R edemption is not the atonement or the forgiving of past sin. Atonement is for those things of the past, whereas redemption is an existing thing now, a redeeming of the physical being into the spiritual reality, and into the spiritual heaven world. Rebirth, being born again.

It's pretty hard to get hold of this, which is why I keep dwelling on it. Because as soon as you can get hold of this idea of the universal things and their function, then you can open up and get away from your littleness, because you can see your extreme smallness in its greatness, you see? And this is the answer of redemption, bringing man into his own greater reality. Thus the power and the force brings on the regeneration, and you become what you should be—a spiritual being. The flesh becomes of the Light.

Q: All these years I've been hearing that word redemption. Forgiveness of sins. Then actually there are two things in it, there's redemption and atonement.

A: That's right, there is. Atonement is for the past, but redemption is bringing forward into the normal spiritual state. The redemption brings us to a point where rebirth can start to take place, you see. And through the sacrament of the Lord's Supper, we gain the spiritual essence, so as to begin to take on the new life and the new light. And when the new light starts to come in really, why then we start on our period of regeneration. Why did God have to give us Christ Jesus?

Q: To absolve us from our errors?

A: That's it! Because man got himself behind the eight ball, and Jesus had to bring the atonement through bringing the Christ to earth. We always duck that. I've been in class after class, and when it comes to anything that has to do with the atonement, we don't want to lay it at the door of the Master and say that he is the one that was able to bring it to us. For some reason man does not want to bow and accept this as a gift. You know, that is the hardest thing in the world for people to do, to accept gifts. Even socially, it is quite an art to be a graceful receiver; even there it is very difficult.

What would be the difference whether the error or sin was a little one or a big one? It would not matter except for one thing: the little one has got less energy, and the big one has more energy. If I were to rate sins or errors, call them what you may, I'd say that about the worst error that man can commit is to misinform somebody about his God. Now this isn't in the books, but this is my angle about it, because when you cut off the Source of the light, it is pretty hard to have any light. And if you get a misconception of your Creator or the Christ, it is pretty hard to get the light there. It is hard to understand Him or to understand yourself.

Now, it is these things that are the barriers; it isn't when you break house rules or sneak in after hours. That isn't the great sin, such as when you get in the way of other people and prevent them from raising their vibration. I hear people say, "But you know the things I've done, the misery I've caused in the past." And so on and so forth. This immediately builds up a barrier, because he is still trying to do it. He doesn't stop to think what Jesus went to the cross for, that he was crucified to eliminate that. So you look at your past and say, "Now that experience was entirely wrong, but there is this: I know I've been forgiven, because that is what Jesus did for me."

One of the most detrimental things to anyone: while he is hard-headed in listening to direction, he is just as hard-headed about forgiving himself for what he has done. This statement, "let go and let God", isn't just a matter of things you own, or money that you have, or some girl friend or boy friend. It has to do with your own errors of the past. You hang onto those things just as ruggedly as if they had some value. And I've seen people work for five or six months to try to let go of a bad experience, and they'll fight like little tigers to hang onto that, you know.

Well, that is what Jesus went to Calvary for, and that is what we celebrate in the holy days. But if we'll just look at those experiences as something we went through then but know that it hasn't anything to do with now, then we will gain the perfection and function of the Self in God. You can't tie yourself up to an old life and then turn around and expect to function in a new one, because you're not living in the new one yet. You're not living in that new life until you've let go of the old. And there's no other way of doing it.

AURA

We know that there is electrical energy around the human body. And we know through experiment that this radiation from the physical body, or the mixture of radiation from the spiritual body and the physical body both coming together with the electromagnetic forces, produce that tremendous, what some call that very mysterious, that all-inspiring aura. Shhh–this is supposed to be the height of all spirituality. Well, haven't you heard it like that?

No! This is created by the emanation from the physical body in what we call the process of metabolism and its cellular breakdown. The radiation from the Self giving off light, coming through the vital or spiritual body, and the electromagnetic currents which go crosswise to this, where these lines intersect in the space around you, produce this visible–or, to the human eye, partially visible–aura. And it will change in accordance with your thinking and the level of consciousness which you are using at that moment in time.

This aura, of which so much is heard in metaphysics, is a magnetic field around any magnetic body, including even some mineral life. But in order to make a true observation of this it is necessary that one have spiritual sight, for the physical eyes will observe only the radiation from the physical, while part of what we see with the physical eyes is of spiritual quality and from spiritual sight. It isn't until one becomes truly cognizant of this and has opened up to the light and developed true sight of spiritual and psychic things that he can really observe with this sight, for the spiritual quality of the aura is in reality only noticed by spiritual sight.

Auras have no actual color but they are radiations of the spiritual body passing through magnetic emanations produced by them. They are electromagnetic in nature with exceptionally high vibratory rate beyond the vibrations of light in the ocular range of spectrum, and the human eye's optical nerve is not sufficiently sensitive to produce the sensation we know as color.

The auras of objects are affected by persons handling them. Aura, mind, and so forth, are colorless unless they're functioning. Other organs give off colors consistently according to metabolism and function. When lines of force cross they create a color which you can discern with your sight. Two different people wearing the same garment would register differently on a spectrophotometer. Why? The machine has no likes or dislikes, but the person's atmosphere acts as a filter, and the color is screened through this atmosphere.

The aura can be measured, and I have measured it. It can be photographed, and we've seen that done. So there is not anything about it which is not happening scientifically, and no one has produced anything very strange. The aura is a perfectly natural thing, and you could even see this if you used different types of magnets within a certain area of a body of some kind – not a living body, but within the area of a box or anything like this. You could see that they would produce cross fields if there was a difference of frequency and intensity in the magnetic field. They would produce a light which you could see with the spiritual eye or with spiritual sight. And this isn't so tough to understand when you realize that the earth currents are used by man and his physical body for parts of its function.

You can never detach yourself from your own enveloping aura, either in body or in soul. Jesus taught this when he said, "Let your light so shine before men that they may see your good works and glorify your Father which is in heaven." Your light, remember. That word is not used as a figure of speech but as a statement of fact.

A positive light surrounds you. It is produced and expressed by your physical and moral being, and those among us who have cultivated their inner organs of vision will see it before they see you. It can be of the purest radiance, or a mere nebulous film. But whatever the moral and physical condition of the man or woman concerned, it is always shown in the aura which each individual emanates from himself or herself

AWAKENING, RETURN, FEAST

The awakening, the return and the feast were taught by our Lord Jesus Christ in the parable of the prodigal son. And these, along with epigenesis, are really the foundation of the process of illumination, both of mind and body, at which point the light may be received, can come in, and can become an existent part of our physical being. For until this takes place, the regeneration and the fruits of the Spirit, which are really the epigenesis, will not be existent and will not be known. It will not be seen or experienced. And those things are experienced not in the physical but in what some people call higher mind, or I would call it the lower heaven world. They are in the upper psychic world, so to speak.

The awakening we are talking about happens at the moment when the individual starts to become conscious of the fact that he is a living being which is partly god and partly man. When he comes to the state of understanding that he has a personal divinity which is a part of the Whole, then he begins to come to a point where he knows that God exists, and that he exists with Him.

As to awakening, you'll know when you have succeeded. It is usually after you have gone through a certain portion of life, or a short period at least, where you swear that every person you ever knew has turned his head away from you and doesn't want anything to do with you for some reason or other. You thought you had friends here and there, but you find out that you haven't got anybody.

Then you start to look around and wonder if there is a Jesus Christ someplace. Because I have never seen it to fail that most people just can't be bothered with any spiritual advancement until they get down to the spot where everybody else has turned their back. They're hungry, and their heart is hungry too, when everything else has failed them. And then they'll turn to see if there's anything left, really, that will help them out. This is an experience that every person goes through sometime or other. Now, the people you are calling friends may still be your friends, but with their every action it doesn't appear that way to you. And this happens.

The return to God is the letting go so that things can happen. And this is where we lay everything on the altar. You lay it all on the altar and ask nothing. Now, when you do this, you are letting go and letting God. Until you do, you haven't done anything, because that is the moment at which you have returned from strictly mortal consciousness to a point or interim of where you begin to start to have what is commonly known as God-consciousness—cosmic consciousness, or a consciousness in the higher mind. Without this you are, as the theologians would say, still Adam in his prehistoric state and have not yet earned the right to enter the banquet room of the feast. You have not returned to the Father, and therefore no feast is possible to be had. This is when you start to receive the Light of Christ, when the body and the face begin to change. Your body starts to take on and go through the rebuilding process.

The feast doesn't come until after you've gotten a full dose, so to speak, of that Light within you, when you have a real honest-to-God illumination—and I'm not talking about you sitting there in meditation and seeing one of those little white balls running across, you know. It is when you really have got it so you can't miss it, so that you are never in darkness again.

The feast in reality is only made possible because of the crucifixion of our Lord Jesus Christ. And we use this in a blanket way, because this tells the whole end resultant of the great cosmic play, in reality. For only then will epigenesis exist, which has the power to let the illumination take place. Man in himself could not reach illumination. Man in himself would not have earned it. This is a great cosmic gift. It has been made possible by the Father from the first, but in this age and in this day it is distinctly, more than ever before, a gift of God.

We were designed from a cosmic standpoint to have that Light, and we rejected it once, or maybe a hundred times, but at least once. We rejected putting ourselves, our "all", upon the altar, or we refused to let go and let God. And I can say it in a few more ways too, but it's all the same. And so now we need the grace, the epigenesis, the power, that extra gift of the Creator, the evolving life to push us across the line to get us really started.

CHARKAS

Now, people in many schools will talk to you about the kundalini, and they'll talk about the control of the chakras and all of these terms. And then you could read a whole book about meditation on the centers. Some will tell you that the power of the soul rises to the brain, and they speak as if the soul is being relocated in the brain, and then man starts to see in a spiritual way. Well, this is not true. There's quite a little that goes on before this happens.

Now the soul of man is around the Self and is located in what you might call the rear of the abdomen, because this is where it would appear if it could show up in the physical layer. But actually it sits in the spiritual body of the person. Due to the fact that the entire solar plexus and the nerve endings of all the autonomic nerve systems of the body end in the great chakra, or solar plexus, here is where the spiritual energy is picked up as it travels up through the nerve system. One thing which has gotten more people in trouble than any other is the vagus nerve which leads through the center of the body and goes to each one of the organs.

Some people, when they go into deep meditation with very weak bodies, have a great deal of trouble. But as this energy radiating out of the Self—being screened by its type through the experience and, you might say, the memory of the entire lifetime—is picked up by the nerve system, it then moves up the spine, and as it comes in contact with the locations of the chakras, they respond in their appropriate way.

We prefer to sort of disregard the chakras and leave that up to Something that knows a little more how to work with them and how they will work than we do. So we allow these chakras to be run by the intelligence of our soul, and we keep our hands out of it. We don't meditate on them, we don't concentrate on them, we don't try to spin them, and we don't try to control them that way. We let the light and the Christ Intelligence, that comes through the soul and through the Self, control these things. And consequently many of those who come through into illumination have never even read about a chakra and they haven't had very much trouble either, getting through. So you see, Nature and God, the Creator or the Great Intelligence, have provided a foolproof system, providing you don't stick your fingers into it.

The chakras are there, there's no question about this, and they have a purpose. They are part of an electromagnetic field balance, and they have to do with the heart, the thyroid and the medulla where the sorting mechanism goes on for the thoughts coming in and going out. And in this way, when we leave them alone, everything stays in balance and what takes place is a bridge between the pineal and the pituitary, and then we have a light which comes in. Some people speak of it as a light in the head; other people say they see it somewhere else first. Some say they see it out in front of them. Well, a certain amount of this is a matter of their consciousness or where they're projecting their consciousness, so to speak. But it can be seen where it is natural, in its normal place of location, and they will eventually get there during their development.

So you see, this spiritual framework of function is just as much a part of the physical control of the body and it is just as orderly as our autonomic nerve system is, or our motor nerve system. And it has had created into it certain methods of safety, and ways of moving and controlling them. That's what is meant by the soul force changing and moving upward, having been hitherto relatively quiet. This is really not a conscious function; but in some respects it was, and so a certain amount of absorption took place and was thrown into the physical and into the consciousness of the individual from the spiritual body.

We have heard someone speak of the force rising from the base of the spine upward. Now, this person saw something, but he didn't go quite far enough. Concerning the base of the spine, well, there is some that feeds in there from the coccygeal nerve, of course, but he stopped there. He just wasn't able to go back into the spiritual body of man and see the actual original contact and the source. He didn't follow it to its source; he only went so far and then stopped. And it is true, there would be energy coming there at the base of the spine, but it would be through the coccygeal nerve, and here you would only be picking up a very little bit, and he might find a little light there, this is true.

Q: What goes through the spinal column?

A: Electric nerve energy. The energy does rise, but if you stay and work on the solar plexus entirely, you are going to eventually have some real problems because your emotions will become uncontrollable; whereas if you allow yourself to "let go and let God" the forces will rise to the heart, to a certain extent, but in the normal way. You don't have to play with it.

The throat center, the thyroid center, is very definitely a functional part, because it is the balancing valve between the physical and the spiritual body, and it is the thing which feeds the cells as they break down in their normal function of the muscles and the tissues, in living action. That is why this center is so important. With some people who come along you can figure right away that they've got a thyroid that's out of balance, because the metabolism isn't working properly, and digestion, and probably the pancreas, is out of whack.

Then you'll find somebody who is hyperthyroid, and you know that the thyroid is out of balance in this case because they're sped up too high and there's too much flowing in there; they're activating too much energy all the time, so there's no balance between the two functions. In other words, the demand of the body is not being balanced by the spiritual flow into it; there's more flow in than is actually needed. And this is what we mean by a balancing valve within the being, it will balance itself out.

And here is where the person, when he finally becomes conscious of God, allows the energy to come right in directly through the crown chakra at the top of the head—the place where he had a soft spot when he was born. Here the energy will come in and you will supply yourself as you need, once you have gained a real consciousness of the Father and His creative Force. And you won't have to worry about anything else.

In the course of training, people have listened to many quotations about "let go and let God", or "get out of the way". Well, they didn't realize just how functional these things really were and what they meant, because as they let go, they released the blocks that were in the nerves, in the spine, and in the other centers, and they immediately began to supply and to set up that bridge so that they did start to get a little light, a little understanding, and a little sight. And this, you see, is a great reality.

It is much easier for us as we start down the path to understand someone saying to us, "Well, get out of the way and let it happen", and so forth, if we have some idea why we should be doing this or what it is for, because otherwise we couldn't do it very well. It would be hard just through discipline and exercises to do this, but when we understand what is going on, it is a much easier thing to do.

Now when these two glands, the pineal and the pituitary, are brought into a balance where there is a spark or bridge between them, we then have a male-female function going on. And when the body and the soul, the physical body and the soul, come into contact, there is a spark between them which takes place—that is an inter-changing field,

31

in other words, takes place—when the pituitary and the pineal are bridged. Then it is possible for light to be realized. Realized and seen. Why? Because the soul is feeding that light out of the Self, and it's coming into your body.

Now when you start to gain this control, and you're drawing in the magnetic forces beside the spiritual, this is what the Master meant when he said, "If thine eye be single, thy body shall be full of light." When the person keeps his eye and his attention on one particular facet of creation and function, and also the two glands become one in function, then the male-female aspect of the individual comes into perfect balance and the illumination or the golden wedding takes place. And the energy from the Self moves into the physical structure as the spiritual body is completely filled with this light, and there is no question about the illumination. This isn't something where you have to go into deep meditation to find out if it exists. You'll know it and it will show all over you when the physical body is filled with light.

CHARITY

We talk about Christian charity, and immediately somebody thinks about putting five dollars in an envelope for the United Christian Fund, or something or other. Well, that is not charity, as such, and most people forget and lose track of the reality of what charity is. Charity is not something where you give your money, but where you give the purest form of—what? Compassion and love to the other individual.

And you know, charity begins at home! It begins right here. Now, we give to this other kind of earthly charity too, you know. We feed them, we clothe them, we house them and keep them out of the elements; we do all these things. But I wonder how much charity is really going on, sometimes. For charity is the first act that is required of man, to reach the reality of that pure fire that comes through the purity of the individual, of the seeker.

We don't want to get so wrapped up in philosophy that we forget the realities we have to deal with here. Charity is something most people pass over as being a sort of nice word, but not meaning too much in this world at the present time. It is how you do or perform any service that determines whether it is a service or whether it isn't.

Charity isn't a matter of giving a dollar. Now, a dollar is still a dollar, I'll grant you that. But the way in which you give it, your mental attitude and your spiritual cognizance, is going to determine whether it's charity or not on your part. We hear a lot of talk about selfless giving, and all that sort of thing, but a great many people who talk about selflessness are about as selfish as anyone could be, because they never forget themselves.

Charity is one of the qualities most lacking, even in the advanced. This is a quality we cannot assume; it is a value built in by your personality. It is the sum total of your personality, and it has to be there or it isn't there, one way or another. There's only one way I know that you get it—well, there are two ways. One is your very definite soul-searching missions before the cross, before our Master. And the other is through long suffering. I don't advocate long-suffering for a person, because I've got too much to do. So it is my personal recommendation that anyone who does this soul-searching and finds a lack, that that's what they should get busy with and get it over with.

If you go on to study the Master, you'll find yourself balancing up the facts of his life with that which you are doing yourself, and you'll find out whether you are charitable or whether you aren't. Now charity is that sort of thing in which you must love the person. This is the very kernel of charity. Tolerance isn't enough. When you tolerate a thing, you let it set because you don't like it. Tolerance isn't enough to bring another person close enough to you to work with them on their spiritual problems. There's only one way to work with them: you love those people, with all their faults.

You cannot always help a person by giving him something. Now, you can feed him the way we do. It's an emergency, to keep him alive, give him a chance one more day. Yes, that's fine. Give him some clothes when he doesn't have any to wear. But you'll never help that man until you put him to work, working toward a goal that he really wants to work toward—though some of the goals of men, we couldn't put them to work on, because it wouldn't be right for us to do. You know, you can work toward any goal that you want to. You can work toward a goal and you can reach it, good, bad, or indifferent.

But at the basis of all this is your attitude, your feeling, the way that you give to that person. Here is the basis of charity. You've got to give it with the attitude that you are not stepping down to that individual. You've got to give it to him the same as you'd give your own son or daughter some oatmeal for breakfast, because they need it and because they are part of your flesh and bone. This is charity; you're doing it because they need it and because you enjoy the privilege of serving them. You get them clothes, you do these other things for them, not because it is a duty, but because you love Jesus who died on the cross for their sins, and to bring this earth back to a place where they could gain from his experience. This is charity, a result of your own attitude, your being.

But if you act through fear, because you are afraid not to, then it would not be an act of charity.

There are many people who do these beautiful things, and they do help humanity, and their deeds certainly carry the stamp of noble individuals, but they have not reached the point where they live and do because of the Cosmic reality that exists. And they don't reach that higher level of inspiration. Jesus said, "Father, forgive them for they know not what they do." This is one of the greatest manifestations of charity. And even after the resurrection, his first consideration was for their welfare.

We've seen that actually giving money to people for charity is all right occasionally. But to be put on a poor list is not good, because that will not help him to be not-poor. You have to teach him. You will sometime be at a place where you will have to pick yourself up by your own bootstraps, so to speak, to raise yourself up. And this is part if it, you see.

CHRISTOS and the SUN

I don't know anything further than the Christ or the Father. I was not here when He first created the earth.

If you take a cell or just a common molecule, or a common atom, you'll find that they all have a center. And right on down the line, everything runs the same way. It has to have a center. The Christ is there, the Christos. And I'm sure that you're not going to find anything that's contrary to the laws of creation and the laws of science in this creation, because it is God's creation.

It is inevitable. It's like the Law of cause and effect. You do something and it is going to have an effect, and that's all there is to it. You can't help it. You short-change somebody and it's going to rebound, has to. But when you've risen above these things you won't bother to short-change anyone, and you'll have all that you need.

All the way down through, from the old Hermetic saying, "as above, so below", these old rules are all true. They show themselves throughout the whole structure.

CHRISTIANITY

Love God with all thy heart, and thy neighbor as thyself. Now you take that and analyze it and you will find all other forces and action in it. Now these aren't things that you haven't heard before, but they are things that have not been used in relation to the powers and forces of the universe and, like it or not, they are going to work that way, and you are going to succumb to their use or you are going to break. So you have two choices, one way or the other. There is no other way. The love of God and one's neighbor is the motive of the Christian will, the Will of God. This is the very foundation of all the Christian teachings.

COLOR

There is a mystery surrounding the nature of color and its effect on human life. It is an intriguing manifestation of spirit energy. Colors associate themselves and blend, so to speak, in our physical vision; but a part of our vision is, of course, spiritual vision. This is why what we call "sensitive" people are harder to please with their surroundings than those who are not. It is purely because within themselves, they have become more attuned to the true creation of God, and therefore are more sensitive to the combinations of vibrations. Thus they will not accept something which does not work rightly together. It isn't necessarily a personal thing. It is usually because the wave lengths of these two colors could not blend, possibly, in the way that they are being used—in relation to form, for instance.

Color is a reactive thing of the retina, which becomes a way to define substances and the things we see. Higher frequency is less visible, so various colors register even if not consciously seen. We will see colors differently due to our own color radiation; we can scarcely distinguish our own, because it is one with us.

In the color triangle, we have three basic hues, blue, yellow and red. There exist no other colors in the universe; that's all there is. Anything you can think or see in any created form is created of those three colors. There are shades and there are tints, but that's all the colors there are.

For the God symbol at the top of the triangle, we use blue. The second point of the triangle, for the Son, is shown in yellow, and this also represents the form and pattern. The third point of the triangle refers to the Holy Spirit, and this is in red.

What is the foundation of every man's carnal color on earth? It is red. One who radiates mostly the function of mind, radiates yellow. The color of this Age is blue; and if you have spiritual sight, you can see blue. The entire encompassment of the whole is the blue of the Father. Yellow is the purging light of Christ. Gold comes out of the whole thing.

Minerals and plants affect the human constitution also, according to their colors. Thus a yellow flower yields a medicine that affects the constitution in a manner similar to yellow light.

Blue is cooler, because it has short wave lengths with so little time between the impulses that you don't notice it, and there is no emotional impact.

Red is warm because of its long, slow wave-length. It has an agitating and heat-giving effect.

White radiates; black absorbs. White multiplies and projects the power of light; black negates and absorbs that power.

We read of being "surrounded by the royal purple". What do they mean by that? What is the royal purple? You leave this earth! There are no answers that don't refer to Christ power and God Force, the powers and forces of creation in action. When you go through and have the veil removed, you leave this earth. You go behind the blue veil of Krishna, as the Easterners say. That is the royal purple. You have left materiality.

COMMUNICATION

We sometimes feel that we have to convince the individual that we're talking to now; that if we cannot do that and are not successful in convincing that individual, that if we don't get him to come into the church or the Christian community, or somewhere of this sort, that our mission was unsuccessful, that we have wasted some time and have accomplished nothing. Now this is not so. And this is not the real thing that happens, for many things that have been said a long time ago—not by us, necessarily, but by someone—are just coming to life.

And we must remember when we are talking with the individual to find out somehow what kind of language he uses—I mean his profession, his job, or maybe he has a craft of some kind. Let's find this out and then use words and understanding that will reach him. Now, he may not agree with you, he may say that he's not interested, but this doesn't make any difference. Don't let it disturb you, because it may be a year or two after you have seen him that these things will bear fruit.

I have seen many things happen of this nature, people that had been to a class of mine years ago, and when I see them again ten or fifteen years later, something has happened. There has been a distinct change. And they'll come out with: "Well, Father, you remember what you told me?"

So you had better not change your ideas to suit somebody. You'd better keep those ideas consistent with the teaching, because you never know when you're going to meet them again. And believe me, you can meet them again. Over a period of time you will meet many things that you have said, and sometimes you're going to have to scratch your head a little bit to find out why you said it in that particular way, because there are times when you might shade something in order to get it across, so that the other person might understand it. But you want to keep it pretty close to the line, because you're going to have to meet it again. It may not be tomorrow, or for two or three years, but it's terribly embarrassing to meet something that you've said and not be able to agree with it. And I've seen this happen.

CONTACT

Q: How can anyone contact Jesus, if he has not the high consciousness to reach up easily?

A: Well, if you have enough faith with prayer it is possible to draw him to you. You can ask him to come in, and a great many times he will.

Q: Well, but then he'd have to get dense, wouldn't he?

A: No. All he'd do is just project his own image, that's all. You could see it. Most of the Master teachers don't use a solid form, but you can see them just the same.

You must remember one thing, that the great Masters do not come down to earth every time they manifest to somebody. This would be a terrible burden, because they have too many to manifest to. And it would take quite a little time.

If you at the present stage of your development couldn't conceive of an individual as he really is, the only hopeful concept I could give you of this would be that of a Self; if you could imagine a being whose Self had reached proportions big enough to envelop the earth, why then, you're someplace within a few miles of it. This is ridiculous to say, but I am just giving you a trifle of an idea. The further we go in this, the more we realize that we don't know very much. Then when somebody says that the Master came down and spoke to him personally, in most cases, why, he usually just projects something and keeps a good distance away.

Communication between two people separated by distance is a vastly different thing, because you can communicate with anyone if you know how to project your consciousness. If you have gained the ability to put your consciousness at any one point, there you can see, hear and be heard. You are. And this is from one realm of vibration to another which is much less dense.

Q: When we contact someone in the heaven level, are we building up life within us and then releasing it?

A: Oh, no. We are working strictly through the mind, you see, in this case. The Mind of the Father and your mind are one; and so we can stop off any place we want to on this deal along the way, and there the message will be conveyed, wherever we put it. And the way this is usually done by those who know how is that they know someone they want to contact, and they make that specific point and call that individual.

CONTEMPLATION

Contemplation is meditation and concentration together. The art of seeing comes as a gift. When you really receive the Light, truly, then you begin to see.

Contemplation is a very special art. It is the setting-up of a meditation or principle, a point of information sought, and then keeping one's consciousness and concentration on it; just keeping it in mind that way, and waiting for the results to come from within—or from without, maybe. Some of the Brothers might answer, too. You know, someday you're going to get the surprise of your life, when you're going to ask for something and somebody is going to answer you from above.

Mind control is essential. Not this emotional fou-fou that goes on in some churches; just good, solid, clean, well-formed thinking. Then when you go into meditation, you can get some results because you're in control of what is going to happen. You're not leaving it to some blind, drunken idiot of the psychic world that wants to contact you to give you some emotional buzz for their gratification. But you're in control. You are not indulging this emotional stuff or going off and "doing our thing", you know; but you have feeling, the same kind of feeling that Jesus Christ demonstrated at Calvary. That's the kind of feeling to have and that's the kind of feeling that will make this world so that the Christ can manifest again.

CREATION

I'm going to talk to you today about the Spirit and the energy that carries that Spirit, the Personality of God, and how He created this universe. The Life-force that is carried by energy from the Father is a personality and part of God, through the Son, the Christ, the First-born. It is the Light; it is God in action, the action of the Spirit on itself.

You are using energy every moment of your life. You could not live without it. It is manifest on every plane and in all of the multi-colors, motions and things about you. It is all there is; it is God being seen in the physical world.

When God created this solar system, He set down certain laws by which it would function. It was through His will that He collected to Himself that power from within Himself from which the creation was made. And therefore, as He set the pattern for these things, it was by His will that they were so done. The laws of creation as set forth at the time of creation, and the Word which was passed on to man through our Lord Jesus Christ, were the will of God. And when we act in accordance with the laws of creation—the basic ones—when we are moving in a positive, creative manner, then we are acting in accordance with the will of God.

When we are trying to do it ourselves in our own stupid way, and trying to get away from the creation, we are still going to be using the will of God, but for a non-creative thing, which is bound to have repercussions.

Q: What do you mean by a non-creative thing?

A: Something which is destructive, which tears apart and breaks down the normal path of evolution as set in the original creation. One of the functions of the priesthood is to work with the path of evolvement, so that man can follow the processes of evolution and so that these should be in accordance with the creative Law and the will of God. And we do this so that the races and the people can be brought together, and so that they can go through certain stages of development and can live within the framework of creation.

In other words, they are that which is known in the Old Testament as the handmaidens of God, you see? And the closer we get to being nothing, the closer we get to having no personal will, no desire for having our own way, the closer we get to the will of God, to following the things that come through the Self and that come out of the Eternal Mind.

Now remember that no sacrament will function that is not in accordance with creative law, and it has to be done through the basic alchemic process, the same as all other things in creation, and it is always very, very simple.

Now what happened in the first chapter of Genesis? God started the first creation, didn't He, and got the world created. And where was that creation performed? In the Mind. After God saw what He had created, He approved of it, didn't He? And what did He have to do in order to create it? He had to love it. Right?

In these chapters of Genesis, you hear of six or seven stages of the seven days of creation; and in those seven days you will find the four elements of creation, that is fire, earth, air and water; and you will find the three parts of the Trinity also existent. You say that is a symbol? Yes, but not a symbol on a flat piece of paper. This is in the Mind of the Father.

Jesus said, "The Father gave me the Word, and I give it unto you." This Word He spoke when He created, when the sound went out, and it is in this Word that the pattern exists.

What was the state of things at the beginning of Creation? There was a matrix there. There was a form there. Before you could create a man you'd have to have a form, which is the vital body. And then you can put the chemical consistencies in it. You see now what I'm talking about? As above, so below. It has to be created up there first before it can come down here.

"Let there be a firmament in the midst of the waters"; and then He divided the waters from the waters. So what was it He did? He took some of the "stuff", the substance He made the form with, and brought it to a little higher density, didn't He, so that He separated the waters. It is the only way He could have done it; He had to change the vibration of this.

If you want to talk about scientific things, here you are, right in the first chapter of Genesis. Well, you'd have to put something between, wouldn't you? When you separate a room, you put up a wall. He separated the waters from the waters, so there must have been something besides the waters, in between; and it had to be of a different vibration. They have got to change the density of that substance because it is the substance that's coming closer to another world.

"Let the dry land appear; and it was so." Regardless of translations or errors in these things—moving maybe from Aramaic to Hebrew and back into Greek and somewhere into English—you can actually reason these things. You can know simply what had to happen if you understand the laws of attraction and repulsion, of chemistry, and the difference in vibration of things. You talk about it all the time: in the chapel you say, "My, what a high vibration". Compared with other places or times, it is higher or lower, one or the other.

But remember, when you talk about consciousness, this is one place where you will keep yourself out of confusion if you will just explain in your own mind that you're talking about living in another world, another sphere. It's totally different. You go into meditation and what happens when you raise your vibration? Things look different then, don't they? And in fact the things you will see when you are in that particular level, that sphere of vibration, are considerably different than they are in the dense world.

So while you are in that particular function of meditation, you are not in this world. When you have lost consciousness of the body and have seen things that looked different from those of this world, then that must be another world, mustn't it? So there is another sphere, another world.

All things are constantly creating, constantly moving and progressing in a spiral sort of shape, but always coming back to the same place, a little above. When you look down on the creation, you see the perfect loop or circle, but when you get off to one side and get out of that circle and take a look at it, you'll find it looks like a spiral spring, because nobody ever came back to the same moment, the same time or the same place; then you can take out the terms "time" and "place".

In God we learn that we have a new faculty, one that is spoken very little about, and that faculty is imagination. It says you choose the way to light or to darkness. This is your privilege. Now imagination is not the idle toy of a child playing with a buttercup or a butterfly, and imagining some sort of playfellow. Nothing is more free than the imagination of man, and through it many things can come. In fact, without imagination you cannot create anything in your world, no matter what it is. Though it cannot exceed the original stock of ideas furnished by the internal and external senses, it has unlimited power of mixing—this is the agitator— of mixing and compounding, of separating and dividing these ideas in all the appearances of reality, as you envision the thing that you accept.

For it is your imagination that cements your vision so that it may be filled with the spirit to motivate it, which will accept the Power of the Father and bring it into a reality. It can bring a train of events, with all the appearances of reality, and give them a time, a place, and so forth. But this is not fancying something, because when you imagine, you have placed your feeling in it, and this must be motivated by the Spirit.

This whole thing of the Spirit is the key and kernel of creation. Unless you're working with that, you might just as well forget it, because it is the only system of communication through which things can be motivated.

CROSS

The cross which we wear on our breast represents the body of man and his trial in seeking to master the animal being, through the Self within him.

Now we know that when two forces cross, at their point of interim or crossing there is bound to be a resistance to one another, and thus light results, regardless of their frequencies, regardless of their realities. If they are two different forces of energy, there will be light of one type or another produced at this interim of crossing.

When the force of the kundalini, the creative force or fire, rises, and across it moves the force of the Word and the will—which is the Will of God, if it is properly oriented—there is going to be light. When the Law is in action within us, and we readily know and understand and accept the Word of God, that Word will manifest. And when we are using the Creative Force in the many channels for creation, then we know that there shall be light within that being, for the two forces then come together and the result is light.

This is why one of the preliminary steps to the illumination is elimination; for as we eliminate the dross from out of the temple and open the way, as we get rid of ourselves, as we set aside all our likes and dislikes, as we set aside all the personal desires, as we become true brothers, then the light really starts to manifest and the flesh takes on that one and glorious thing which is the rebirth. And Jesus told us very distinctly that "lest you be born again, you shall not enter the kingdom of heaven."

CYCLE

Everything completes a cycle, it doesn't make any difference what it is. Everything travels in a cycle, whether it's energy, the movement of people, education, the acceptance of an individual, or whatever it is—it always travels in cycles.

That is why very often when I feel a crowding of something I'll just go out, go someplace and do something that isn't so religious, maybe, like golf or going to the movies to see a Western, or something like that. That's to give me a chance to go through the down cycle without any particular care about it.

And what I usually say is that it breaks up the combination and I relax. But actually what's happening is that I'm just taking away the negation of the down cycle and letting it work, not interfering with it, and letting it go on about its business till we get the up cycle. You see, if you work with nature, if you really work with God, it's an easier way to go. It's an easy track; no problems.

In reading Genesis should we use the word "millennium", or should we say "the next day"? Because actually in that realm of understanding, there is no such thing as time. It doesn't exist. There are cycles of the sun and cycles of the earth around the sun, and there is a cycle of the moon around the earth, and so forth. But time does not exist in the cosmos. And therefore everything is here and now.

You can trace out the various forms which have to do not only with the physical body, but also with our solar system. They have to do with the electrical fields that we live in, with the energy that comes to us from the sun, the compensation, the return, always the return circuits with all things.

DISCIPLINE

The use of discipline is, of course, one of the first orders of training, no matter what level you are on. Discipline is absolutely essential, not only to the ones that are being taught, but also discipline of ourselves. Self-discipline is a most potent tool in our work. It doesn't necessarily have to relate to something that is in the teachings of the Master. It can be applied in most anything that we wish to designate as a discipline, that will do some good. This is the old, old story of repetition, used on a higher level. Now I don't care if you want to give up cake, and you do this with the purpose of disciplining yourself, and you set a time that you are going to give it up for, say, two or three months, and you do this with the purpose of disciplining yourself.

Discipline is a very powerful tool in learning. It strengthens the will, and it strengthens your decisive qualities. In other words, a decision requires both the intelligence and the will to accomplish, but in doing this we are making the ego subservient to our will and purpose. This is very important, because it is placing the will and the ego in balance, and this is the first step toward being strong and being able to work without any self-purpose. It is the first step in selflessness. It is the first step toward learning to function because of the function, and not because we particularly want to, or because we particularly like something. These are tools we develop.

You have reached a point in development and training where you have to manufacture the tools, and you use these tools for certain purposes. Your will-power—and your "won't-power", as someone has said—must be developed so that it will bring about a higher and a much cleaner level of operation. In other words, the will then starts to work on straight, clear, clean decisions, not as a matter of any emotion, desire, liking or disliking. It will operate cleanly and very straight, because you desire to have it work, and that only. This is, in reality, the approach to a higher level of operation where people can be taught to make decisions under discipline. Because they will then learn to make a decision without getting in the way.

Discipline is not a matter of just your life, or mine. It is a matter of your aid, your cooperation. Discipline aids in your cooperation with your brother, so that his life and his reality of God can be revealed.

DREAMS AND REVELATIONS

Most people would say that you had to be a bishop or a very highly evolved individual before you could have a revelation of any kind. Well, it is only through revelation that you really learn anything that is a lasting reality within your own being. Not out of a book, because you can study all the books ever written and you'll never know a thing about this.

Until you have had a spiritual experience, you have learned nothing. And only through our spiritual work can we reach the point where we can gain a true understanding of our own path. As to what you need in accordance with the cosmic level, I can't give orders that way; I can't lay the path. Only you can lay that path through the revelation within yourself. No one can interpret your experience for you.

A person's intuition is the result of the connection existing between his soul and the spirit, the One Spirit. The stronger this union grows, the greater will be the intuition or the spirit of knowledge.

Not all perceptions of the soul are of a divine character. There are also many images which are the products of the lower activity of the soul and their mixture with the material elements, the consciousness which exists of that which we do not know.

Out of the Self comes truth and direction, that is so. But most of us, even with our most accurate understanding and getting our human self out of the way, may still get some little miscue in there somewhere, even when we receive something out of the Self. So it is necessary for us to find a way, if we are going to advance to the point where we will know something within ourselves.

We talk about revelation, we accept the fact that there is revelation, but you know honestly, right down deep in our hearts, we're not really sure that there is such a thing. To think about listening to someone speak from the other side who doesn't have one of these bodies to carry around, is a little bit preposterous now, isn't it? If you said yes, it would not surprise me, because you could go out and take an inventory or a poll of most of the priests or ministers you choose, and you'd find that very few have experienced such a thing.

This is a great thing which we accept out of the last book of the Testament, but we seem to think that it only happened back there when good people like Moses and some others existed, who wore long beards and white robes, you know, and prayed all day long and didn't do anything else. Well, they did as much work, if not more, than we do today, because if they hadn't they wouldn't have lived.

There are a lot of prophets who spring up in different ages, in different times, but the trouble with the prophet often is that he'd like to get his name on the prophecy, just in case it was right.

Q: We are told that one should write down things which come in some kind of revelation or dream, or a vision of some kind, and I'm curious as to where these originate. Do they come from the Mind of the Father?

A: Well, you might be receiving a revelation, and if you kept track of them, they might fit together. And you might be receiving a warning or a prophetic dream, but I don't go in very much for dreams. There are people who sometimes have a prophetic approach to dreams, but I find that you can get too far off the track, and I like to keep the Master in view most of the time. I do say, take cognizance of what comes to you in this way, and perhaps what you're thinking was a dream was not a dream at all but a revelation. And then when they start to fit together, you begin to know the reality.

In other words, no matter how far you go into this work, you need to know, and you need to be governed distinctly by caution, even though you have absolute faith in the Master and you get to the point where you really function with the Self. Until you've done that for a long time, until you have set up a consciousness of "this is right", and "that's wrong" from your inner being, you need to go ahead and proceed with caution, and to work with it.

Of course, you cannot both accept and not accept, either. But always remember that we're given these tools to use, and we are also given a mind to use them with. So in this way we will keep away from the endangerment of getting hold of things that people might wish us to believe from the other side—that is, the psychic world. We are in a period right now where this sort of influence is quite strong, and we have to guard against its use; because I've seen many people who have been sent off on the wrong track, in the wrong way, by using it as the absolute God's truth because they saw somebody and that somebody told them something. God gave us a way of working with these things, and it is up to us to develop these tools and use them as any other tools.

We must learn how to have our mind attuned to receive at any time the impressions which the Cosmic Mind can make on our human mind. And if we take the easy way, letting in the light of the Christ will provide the energy and the way to eliminate the difficulties so that our functions will work on a spiritual level.

EGO

It is probably an error that the word "pride" has usually been attached to the mundane action of the ego, and the ego has been set down as something which is formidable, dirty or evil. Now that is not so. The ego is something we need, providing it is balanced with the will. Without the will and the ego you do not forge ahead to take responsibility, and you cannot step out on it.

Down underneath here, hidden very subtly, is our pride in what we do. And spiritual pride is one of the worst things that you can attain. Down underneath we have forgotten those who have paved the way for us to enter into this age, who have for thousands of years paved the way. There is absolutely no necessity for anyone's going around being loaded down by the ego, being loaded down by any form of that sort of disturbance in these days, with all the things that you're given in the Way. Of course, this gets to your ego a little bit.

You know, a person needs the ego. He needs the Self. He needs the will and the wisdom. If you were to go and see the Masonic temple, for instance, as a physical manifestation of this you would find two pillars on the front of the building to represent the will and the ego. They are the gateway to the inner temple.

I have known people who could use the law of prayer and use it effectively, yet down underneath, in their own inner being, there was still the taint and mark of the ego, what we would call over-striving, and this, lots of times, brings on troubles within the individual. We are not willing to open ourselves and receive what is really coming to us because when we do this, we know that "we" didn't do it. It is coming then through the Law and through the creative force and pattern which was created many eons of time ago; and this hurts us because we have to let go of the words and realize that we are only being when we have let these things work through. There are some cases where the will is essential, but not too many, unless it is the will to do the Will of God.

When you start getting angry about something, remember, you are only angry because you are not confident of your position. The only time a person gets mad is when he is afraid of being hurt; and fear exposes him. "Perfect love casts out fear". Love is the giving of light and life through the personality of God, through the personality of Christ. It is the power of God, through Christ, given by one human to another. And love cannot be given unless it is accepted in return.

Q: By the Christ, you mean Jesus?

A: The Christos, not Jesus Christ. Oh, he gives us lots of love, yes, but we're talking about basic principles. You can't overcome fear, you have to let go of it. Man has never overcome one thing. He only lets go of it.

The more you know, the harder it is to get yourself out of the way. The more you know the more you feed your ego, and the harder it is to get yourself out of the way so you can reach the Self and Truth.

Now you are always asking, "Well, how do you let go?" And I would say, "Stop hanging on." All you've got to do is stop "possessing" everything and watch how fast all this other junk goes out of your life. Because it is just excess baggage you're carrying, and it actually has no weight at all. It has no actual use and you are going to drop it anyway as you leave this earth. It doesn't count for anything anyway, and neither do you—not the part you are looking at. What you see in the mirror is worth, let me see, I think it is seven and a half cents—maybe a little higher at today's prices, but it is practically nothing. Like any vehicle you might have, it is according to what use you can make of it.

All you have to do is stop "possessing" things, things of all kinds, and don't worry about them. Then your ego problems and all these varied and sundry things that happen to you, all these diseases and terrible catastrophes that you have, and everything of that nature, will disappear because there won't be anything to hold them. You're going to shuck them off anyway before you leave this earth—as you leave this earth.

EVOLUTION

You have a responsibility which is not only to yourself and to God. We have been talking all this time about the individual—the soul, the Self of you. Let's get away from this selfish talk, and get to what we call brotherhood, but on a higher level, the evolution of the race of man in this form. I don't know whether you realize it or not, and probably some of you won't like it, but you have a responsibility to the evolution of the human race. Every time you come into incarnation, or just before you come, you usually do a little work along this line with those who can help you. And as you go down through the years of incarnating on this particular orb, you are evolving the form and the function of this body. Down through the ages, you've discarded this organ and changed that one, and changed this reflex and that, until you have come down to the present age where you have a body which is functioning as it does.

Also, the racial forms of thinking are part of your creation. They're part of your selfish personal thinking. You needed races at one time, in order to gain certain functions and a certain understanding of creation. I'm not going to talk about all of the things that were acquired through this, but one which you are trying to acquire, and so far haven't made a very good job of, is being able to look at another brother who isn't the same color as you and still not be conscious of the fact that he is any different than you are.

One of the reasons for races is brotherhood! That has a fundamental bearing upon Christianity, because if your brotherhood doesn't surmount color, you're going to have problems when you get to other places, believe me. Real problems.

With regard to this particular vehicle, at one time we had a form that was much more gross, it is true, but we dropped it away because we no longer had any need for it. Mankind through the years has created his own vehicle thus, because as he goes from life to life, he carries with him the knowledge and the formation of that vehicle. Otherwise we could not remember the past and what we were.

A human is a being who is occupying a body which has evolved from the lower animal form, and when that vehicle got to the point where it was a perfected vehicle, then God breathed the Breath of Life into it, didn't He, and it was emancipated in the soul. This vehicle and being which was brought up through evolution on the earth plane is the "hu-man", whereas the "El man" is one who was highly evolved when he came here from well, from some other place.

Q: Is this where the sons of God married the daughters of earth?

A: This is the El men, the sons of God, yes, the evolved ones. Somewhere along the line, in this age, there are many pathological changes to take place. The new Way will change the human body, to what extent is not known, but the pigment of the skin will change, not right away, but there will be intermediate changes. The vital [spiritual] body of man, instead of etheric blue will become a golden color, of copper almost. The chemical content of skin will change.

Q: God made me in His image and likeness, so I must be like Him.

A: You are, but this is a vehicle that you have accepted and created before you came into this particular cycle. You might find that if you went on to Mars, you'd have a different type of vehicle, but the function would be the same. The body ten thousand years ago was quite a bit different. But through evolution man, carrying the record of his evolution in his soul, has changed those organs which he no longer needed, because he has risen above, and is able to use the powers which he was not able to use before.

Now faith, as we look at it from the physical standpoint, and as taught by the Masters, is actually the reactive pattern which brings about what we call epigenesis and what in the Bible is called grace. But this has been misused and misunderstood, for faith was taken to mean something accepted without any personal reaction or personal understanding, absolutely blind. Epigenesis or grace is that which triggers the spirit and is part of the evolutionary pattern. This evolution begins in all things when the impulse of a new or higher order or purpose is manifested.

In other words, what we are saying is that evolution is not just a thing of man, but if you create a new idea and set it into motion, and you say, "Dear Father, I accept this idea in my life, and I would like to see it grow," and you have the feeling that draws the spirit into it and gives it life, then for that idea, for that principle, that is the moment when evolution starts, and it will grow. And as it grows, you will grow too, in the understanding of it, while it becomes fully matured and developed and functioning in the material world. In evolving it will absorb certain things, and as it does this you will learn, and if it is good, you will get a mark on the black side of the ledger. This is epigenesis; in other words, on and above that which you have really earned by your own actions.

Evolution begins also with the sensing of an ideal state above that already existing. Now man, for some thousands of years—well, twelve thousand that we know of—has been looking to God as the great All-seeing, All-knowing Being from whence all good came. You see, they were sensing an ideal state here and thus started to evolve toward the realization of it. This then exists and builds according to the use of faith, and the use of the spirit in matter. Now this is evolution, moving toward an ideal state or pure form. This is matter as created by the Father in its original way, in Mind. It is the ideal in spirituality.

This is the form, you see. This is the way in which form evolves, and man is the one who gives it life and the one who determines whether or not it shall live and become part of the earth and part of this universe. He is the evolver of the physical body and its form, from life to life, and he is also the evolving one of the race and of this cycle of evolution, the greater cycle into which we have just entered.

FAITH

Faith is knowing that the Law works. You have heard a great deal about the Law and we have gone into many ramifications of its use. We've taught quite a bit about the Word, but there are some things we haven't gone into very deeply, and one of those things is faith. Not blind faith, but faith in the Law and in the fact that the power of God exists and that the Intelligence is there. That's where confidence comes in. You act in accordance with that which you have declared.

When we have faith in something, we know that it works. In other words, we have confidence. One of the greatest stumbling blocks of man, in his use of mental and spiritual powers, is the lack of faith. We pray and if we do not have faith, it does not work. Man does not know his powers, and he has had no confidence in them till now.

You cannot sit there in a state of questioning and say, I wonder if it does, I wonder if it doesn't, maybe it will, I hope so. You see? You have the divine right. The Word is with you. Use it with confidence, in a state of faith. Do you see the difference? You don't wish it; it's there the moment you have visualized or formed the divine idea—because it is a divine idea. In Mind it exists! It exists right then, though you don't see it in front of you in the material world immediately.

How many people say, "I haven't seen Jesus, so I don't know". That is one of the weakest excuses I know. What was it he said, "Blessed are those who have not seen and yet have believed"? The great majority of things today are done without you seeing them. You ride on a plane and you don't have anything to do with the control of what goes on; you give yourself over totally, your life, your safety, your future, everything, to a man who has been trained mechanically and aerodynamically to run a plane. And yet you can't give it over to Jesus Christ. And that's all that's required.

Faith doesn't grow, it comes about through doing. Every time you use it, you either have faith in it or it won't work. You have to know it. You don't test to see if it works because, you see, if you make that test, you have a doubt in your mind. "Do not try the Lord, thy God." In other words, He's given it, but don't test Him to see if it will work, because when you do you're in doubt, and you're doubting the Word of the Testament itself.

Faith is the knowing that these things work, and that your prayers are answered. Then it becomes an automatic thing. When it gets down deep enough into the reality of your being, then it becomes part of the soul growth, an ingrained part of your consciousness. Remember that faith is the element that stabilizes and divinizes our future. It creates our future, for each one of us, to the measure of our salvation and our own calling, or our particular chosen destiny.

Q: Could you explain the difference between faith and conviction?

A: With conviction you know that certain things do exist; they do function. You're convinced of it. This is your conviction that this is so. But faith is an active framework of power which is the energy of God and Christ moving through the Law.

Q: People ask, do we believe this and do we believe that. But faith is knowing, not believing.

A: That's right. It is not blind, it is active. But there is no faith existent until you have acted. The comprehension and the existence are simultaneous. I'm going out on a limb here because this is something you wouldn't understand unless you really had worked with prayer, unless you'd felt God. Because when you pray, it doesn't exist until you've finished the prayer and you know it, but the moment you know it, it is done. It's the instantaneous interception of that cross period, that periodicity, as we use the word. There is faith at the moment it functions.

Q: That would kind of explain about the meaning of faith as the substance of things hoped for.

A: Yes, it's just like another demonstration of this in mathematics. You can run a random line around something to describe it at certain interval points, as in a chart or a map. You say, this is so many feet east, or north. Here's a point, and here's a point. Now, you've taken and calculated this all out, and find there's a bearing of north 43 degrees east. And you might find this on a navigator's map too. You've charted it all out, and when the navigator gets to this point, he's going to change his course. Or when the surveyor goes out and surveys the piece of property, he puts the stake in there. Well, you've worked it all out on paper and it's right, but it isn't until you go out there and survey it and put the stake in that it exists. You get what I mean?

Q: Is that the stepping out on the prayer?

A: That's right. Otherwise nothing can exist. Nothing has happened. You can go on for hours with a prayer, make one fifteen minutes long, and when you get down to the end of it you haven't done anything. You can give glory to God; yes, wonderful, that's fine. But you haven't created anything except a rapport between God and you—which is the most beautiful thing in the world; but you've really got to give when you do that. You can't go halfway, you see?

But when you want to create something and you want something to come into this world, you've got to get right down to that point where you really step out on it. Then something has happened right then. Not the past fifteen minutes, but now. Now is the moment that the pattern and the force which comes in is motivated by the Spirit, the feeling of your word, of its existence. That's the Fire of the Spirit.

GOD

In the beginning God created the heavens and the earth: the first sentence in the Bible. There are many names for the same great Being, all understood in the same way. It makes no difference if you say God or Allah, or It; and in the ancient orders this was always called the Nameless One.

The subject of the Creator is one of the things which causes the greatest difficulty with the mass mind out there, because they say, "Well, yes, I'll concede that there is a great Intelligence out there someplace, and there must have been Intelligence that created the system of orbs that exists. But I don't seem to sense anything like this. When someone preaches a sermon, I have some emotional feeling, but I don't get this when I try to think of God." And this is perfectly natural, because they rationalize everything possible right out the window.

Now, you can show the reality of this by symbolism, or you can prove it by staying on your knees long enough until you make a distinct contact. But try to give me all the words in the book and you have given me nothing, as far as the Father is concerned, because you are living and functioning within a body which is transient. You are flying around on a whole lot of little things, with all this great "security" which most people are looking for and which is not there, and which you never will have until you get out of the physical body. And yet you are looking to understand and to sense something so great even in proportional size to yourself that you can have no concept of it.

Pictures have been taken of the moon and other places in space. But there they are able to center on a small area and take a picture with movement involved, something you can look at and accept. But this Being that we're talking about, the Father, is of a state of being which we don't even know about and could not conceive of even if we tried. We have found it impossible to do so because of our narrow-mindedness. It is difficult enough for us to deal with everyday things on the street, to say nothing about reaching out to conceive of something this large and this perfect.

In former times people believed in many gods, and in evil powers or devils. And here again we have a misuse of something their priests apparently told the people, that these gods and goddesses were separate entities. But they didn't tell them that these represented the personified characteristics of One Great Creator. Then later when the people came to the acceptance of One God, they also accepted that there was one devil. This, like the story of the Tree of Knowledge, brought in the belief in duality, of two opposite forces. Since a house divided against itself cannot stand, there must be One God, all-inclusive and all-powerful. But within that Being there is both male and female, the positive and negative polarities needed for creation, not good and evil as opposing forces. Negative does not mean bad.

An interesting thing happened a few years ago when an Eastern Teacher called me from India and said, "Master Blighton, I wonder if you would take care of a certain person for me there in your city."

I said, "I'd be very glad to, but you know I'm afraid that I wouldn't do very much good for you because I happen to be a Christian. It would be unethical."

He said, "What, have you found another God?"

I said, "No, I haven't, but some people feel there's a difference."

He said, "Well, you and I know better anyway. Will you take care of it?"

So I said, "All right, I will."

There is evidence that people for centuries upon centuries back have accepted God. Now there must have been some time and some place where this started. Somebody had to come across the Divide or from some place and bring this forth. I'm not saying that there was a specific time when the world began as we know it today, but there might have been an era which started things as we see them now. And this we recognize by the cycles of man's movements and his workings in matter, as well as his workings on the other side, both of which are very important.

We learn that the circle is a symbol of God. And then we find that the atom is a little round sphere. "As above, so below." At other times we look at ourselves and find that we have a round atmosphere, more or less, and when we look at the atmosphere of the earth, it too is round; and we see these various things that follow right straight down from the macrocosm to the microcosm. And when we look within ourselves, we'll find the very cells of the tissue of our physical body are identical with those of the solar system within which we live. Now it must have taken a pretty smart Being to start this system, and He certainly must have had some very definite idea in His Mind, because wherever this worked, He used the same form over and over again, repeated Himself.

In speaking of the macrocosm, I mean the whole of God, you see; that is the Macrocosm, as far as we're concerned.

Q: What is the microcosm?

A: Well, if I had a microscope, I'd show you. Man is the microcosmic god, as mentioned in the ancient works.

Q: Man created in the likeness of God, in other words...?

A: Well, that is the Self in the body of man. We hear in lectures and in books about people wanting to unite with God, to become one with Him. Well, if this happened, I'm afraid they wouldn't want it, because most of them couldn't stand it, to begin with.

As for the Trinity, we'll take a little example of the Three in One. We have a room here on the earth plane. Then, in the next plane of vibration, up here or down there according to who you're looking for or whether you go up in vibration, there is another form and another entire sequence going on. And at the base and foundation of this, God is All, but it is all of the energy, it's not nothingness. It is the basic force of the universe which within it carries the Spirit that comes through the first-born of the Father, the Christos, that which came down and was born as a little child. All three of these things are present in this room, aren't they? God on every level, All-present. All are different levels of vibration, but all present in the same vibration, consciously. That's the way it is with the Holy Family.

Now, there's nothing so mysterious about the Word. Whether good or maybe not so good when you give it, it carries with it the breath of life, but it probably carries some of your indivinity with it too. So this is then the spirit of what you said. Truly, is that so complicated—in this technological age? I don't think so. Anybody should be able to understand three different levels of vibration all in one. Don't we use hollow telephone cables today and have seventy five or a hundred messages going across at the same time? Nobody makes a date with somebody else's wife that they didn't mean to, I'm sure. And all the messages are kept straight at the same time, all at the same instant. Why should we wonder so much about having three in one; what's the mystery about this? We do it technologically; why can't we understand it? We use this every day.

Q: Father, you said we couldn't really get God consciousness, but we could reach to the Christ consciousness. If they are already the same thing, three in one....?

A: I didn't say they were the same thing. They are three different actions going on, but they are all one. You have one telephone cable, but you have a hundred messages going through it. They are all one communicator, aren't they, part of the same thing? Didn't you ever take and put some, well, oxalic acid maybe, in water? It's all in the same container, but they certainly aren't going to mix.

The Spirit of God is the personality of God manifesting by the force of the will through the power and energy of creation, of His Mind, of His body. It is that simple. Because the Spirit of God motivates all energy, all force, all matter, through the Law. It motivates it and it will function wherever you are, whether you're here, on Venus, Mars, Jupiter or anywhere else, it'll work the same. It might work a little quicker, it might work a little slower, but it will work.

GRACE - EPIGENESIS

"Epigene" means upon or after—after the origin. In other words when God created us He saw the probability that we'd need a little more than cause and effect would give us, so He provided epigenesis; and Jesus provided the grace. In the human body we have grace and epigenesis both. Grace, the intelligence of God working through man and giving to man a gift which he absolutely did not earn; and epigenesis, where man devises ways to overcome physical deficiency. Now, you can earn grace and you can also have grace which you haven't earned, and there is no part of creation where this grace and epigenesis do not exist.

So if you've had a fifth grade education and you've been given a sixth grade job to do in this stage of evolution, your epigenesis will carry you over that rough spot of what you lack, and with the grace that has been brought to you, you'll make it, without question. So consequently you have gotten the sixth grade education without going through the sixth grade. You see how wondrous God's creation is, every little thing compensating for the other?

Grace does this: it serves as a conveyance for the light and the love of Christ, a gift that we have gained over and above our own motivated action. And this shows us that there is something more than just actual cause and effect; there is cause and effect plus.

Some religious systems have utilized the Law as the foundation of a faith, but it tends to become very, very mechanical, so much so that they lose the opportunity of the grace and the beauty of this, the seeing of it, and the appreciation and the joy of it. They have lost the zest of the spirit, you see, because of their mechanical actions and approach to the laws of God and Jesus Christ. Quite true, it is very orderly and it will quite definitely function thus and so. But though it does function, that should not take away from you the fact that this was done by love and sacrifice that was ordained and set up, and it was not an accidental happening. It is distinctly a gift. There's no law that says our Lord has to give you grace. He set it up voluntarily.

I have to say, don't lose the sense of the divine grace, because if we do, then we have nothing but the cold function, and so don't gain what we should by it. Because the grace in itself, with knowing, does bring us epigenesis which is the real grace. In other words, be able to feel it, be able to know it, be able to accept a little room for miracles.

Let us realize that even though we're talking about grace, we are still talking about the understanding of the power and the force that is real! It is in action. This is what we're living with. This is not a static state, in other words, it is a reality. And though we use some of the terms used by the conventional church, it is a reality, not just a philosophy. There is a wide difference between the two, and if you lack this state of grace it is mainly because you do not know it is real, that grace is a reality, and what comes from it is a reality.

Epigenesis is your effort plus God's gift, let me put it that way. It is your effort plus God's gift of grace, the acceleration on and above the ever-creating Force working through your acts. Did you ever study mathematics? Well, numbers accelerate. There is no such thing as becoming static. You cannot stand still and live. You either gradually and determinedly accelerate or you decay.

Epigenesis is a word that covers a lot of things. It is the process by which grace is produced, and added grace becomes a reality.

Q: Could you explain about epigenesis being a process?

A: Yes. We talk about the Law, that it says this and that and something else. Well, the Law is the general overall process which, when you put the words into it, brings something forth, doesn't it?

There is electricity. How does it manifest? It manifests through a very simple law of what we call Ohm's law. E is equal to I minus R, meaning the current flow and the resistance to it, that tells you how much force you're going to have. It's like a human being, isn't it? You know, as much spirit flows as you don't have resistance.

Epigenesis is the way in which you attain grace, you see. Grace is a granted thing, a gift of God through our Lord Jesus Christ, but epigenesis is the thing which starts it moving, and it is an ever-accelerating thing; it never comes back to the same point. You don't come back to the same point.

You need to know this is a reality, because if you don't, you won't have the grace to pull through; it isn't going to work for you. You aren't going to receive the grace until you know it is so. Remember what he said, "he that believes and has not seen is even closer to me" (I'll put it in our words) "than he who has believed and has seen." In other words, any fool can believe what he sees in front of him. That doesn't take any initiative on your part, or any love or anything else.

I've been told this: "When I see Jesus Christ, then I'll believe it."

If you want to bat it out with logic, that's fine with me, but I want the grace. I want the epigenesis working for me. You know, I want that bonus payment that I don't have to work for.

The Testament says that God is a loving Father, doesn't it? Jesus Christ came so you could receive that grace, but until you know it you aren't going to receive as much. It isn't going to fulfill as much. The Host many times has reached down and saved people's necks and pulled their chestnuts out of the fire, because they had enough grace coming to them. But the Host are that kind of people, you know. Until you get wise, why, they'll every once in awhile use some of your grace to pull you out of a predicament and kind of give you a boost.

Q: Is it stored up for when you need it?

A: Yes, for when you need it. Oh, it's put on the records, just the same as your interest is entered on your passbook or bank statement for the interest on your deposits. Likewise, your assets and liabilities are shown there; they're in the soul. And your grace is stored up there. When you look back on your life, you know full well that some of the things you've done should have knocked you off a long time ago. But there was something or other that kept you together and you got by. Right? We all hate to admit it, but we need to. That's why we say, "confession is good for the soul". It is. If it weren't for what the church calls grace, for the interest we draw through epigenesis, we'd be in a bad shape because we'd be paying off a lot of karma for many years to come.

But epigenesis comes, and it manifests in grace through many channels. It isn't all from going out and giving somebody a meal. That isn't the only thing that does it. Our thoughts about other people build up a potency. The way in which we approach a person that is in trouble, the kindness which we show to other people that we know are not going to acknowledge us or do what we advise them to do, or who maybe don't even believe as you do, and say so; and you're still kind to them. This also brings us grace. Our reactions and our relationship with our family, these are all things that gain us grace, very silently in most cases. So also does our very attitude toward mankind as a whole. Now I can say that they're totally wrong in their thinking, but that doesn't mean I don't love 'em, the rascals.

Q: Was epigenesis one of the original laws of Creation?

A: Yes, it is a law of God. That is His way of the return cycle, so to speak. But I want you to understand that this is something that works on and above the Law. It is the acceleration of the motion of the Law. Life always changes, you never go back. Today is today, today is leaving. When this day is gone, it will never return, and the conditions under which you lived it, and the conditions of your thinking, your imprint upon the sands of time, as the poet would say, is set. It is done with and gone, and will never happen again. This period of time will never return.

Now you may live other days, but you will not live this day or another day like it. You can't, because the planets of this solar system for eons of time, if they go forward from that, will never be the same. The combinations of relationships are too multitudinous even to calculate. That's where the constant rising and changing force of epigenesis lies, and the grace that comes from it, the grace that comes through it, as given by the Father.

One of the things we must learn to do is to receive these things and to work with them. You have to step up, go on. The only thing that's going to get hurt is your ego, because you couldn't do it your way.

Paul said, "Sin shall not be your master, for you are not under law but under grace." Cause, effect. Cause, effect. It begins to seem a cold mental thing, and it isn't, because in addition to this we have the grace of God through our Lord Jesus Christ. This is love expelled from Him and given forth to all mankind. It is not a cold factual thing. It is a very great and loving thing, a very warm thing. This is the way the Master gave it totally to man. This is the whole key to Calvary. Don't just read about it, study it. You've got to feel these things if they're going to mean something to you.

HEAVEN WORLD

Most religious writings have made it appear that the spiritual world called heaven was a separate kingdom or condition located in the skies or space above us, and that we either had to pass through transition to be lifted up or, in order to think about it, we had to lift our thoughts up and away from ourselves to that place. But Jesus preached no such thing. He taught that the spiritual world is part of ourselves and not located in any part of the sky. He said, "The kingdom of heaven is within you," and that whoever seeks may find.

Now, that's a fine statement, but most people never heed it, really. Sure the kingdom of heaven is within, because that's the source from which you're going to travel in it; not in this physical body. It's the Self you're going to move in, your own soul body and the Self with which you're going to move into and through the heaven world. This is within, and it's the only way you can get inside the kingdom of heaven. I'm sure that they would not let you in with those boots on, that's for sure. And what's more, you wouldn't want to carry that much weight. The more you just take these things simply and don't try to get yourself complicated, the more easily you'll find the great answers and wisdom in these teachings.

The various religions all the way back for five thousand years have been looking forward to going into another land, another place. Now I want to ask you: you've been learning about reincarnation. Where are you going to reincarnate from if there isn't another place where beings live? You can't teach about reincarnation, and not teach about anything in between that and your last life. Do you think somebody puts you in a vacuum bottle like you put your coffee to keep it warm? There is no way of teaching a complete cycle of life without studying the reality of the hereafter.

It always goes back to that one thing, your mind, your whole being and consciousness. You have all the words, and there isn't any question that you are intelligent. You may be able to tell more about the philosophy and the Testament than many seminarian students, but that won't do you any good, because it isn't the power and force moving. That's just the story about it. And if you haven't got the reality of it, to be able to move that power and that force, you are going to have an awful time getting around. How would you like to try to move a jet airplane without any jet fuel? Wouldn't get very far, would it? Well, that's what I'm talking about except that your jet engine is your mind and the records are in the soul. That's your way of propulsion.

For years people have tried to side-step this issue of heaven and hell, but you can't, because it's part of the life cycle. And you can't have an uncompleted life cycle and accomplish anything with it. Fortunately, the White Brothers are a little more lenient sometimes about these things, and then sometimes they are not.

Q: When they say there are seven heavens and three levels, where does that come in? How does it fit together?

A: We haven't said anything about seven heavens, have we? You see, we've got such an awful job getting up to the first one that we don't worry about the rest of them, because we know if we can just get one foot on the bottom rung, why, we'll be all set. We'll make the rest of it. We're only worried about getting our foot on the bottom rung. That's why we skip the chakras and this other paraphernalia, because we're worried about just one thing—getting the Christ light. We're pretty simple, you see, and we get it because we stay simple. We haven't so many things to get, so we take it all in one little package. You understand what I'm saying? It's true, and this is part of what the Master did for us, in his coming here.

In teaching how man is going to approach heaven, I sometimes say, "What kind of a heaven do you want when you get there?" This may be an unusual question, but over the years and the centuries to come, you're going to have to face that question in the inner council, and that is a positive thing. You are going to face the reality of Christ Jesus, or you are going to face the possibility of going nowhere. Now, would you like to send your brothers nowhere? Well, I wouldn't, but this is what you're doing when you do not teach heaven or hell. Now, after a certain length of time, we know that something's going to be brought in the way of help, that's sure. But are we going to leave an incomplete cycle of life, or are we going to complete the cycle and try to make up for what has not been done?

There is an absolute necessity for putting some rungs in the ladder by which these people can work with it and follow it through so that they won't be left adrift when it comes to dropping the shell and going on. Because otherwise, you've got from here to there, and then what? I'm not saying that we should set down a scale of judgment or anything of that sort, but should give it some connotation through which these things can work and which they can look forward to, which will create the path and method of getting there. What the Boss does afterwards with them, well, that's His business, and it's none of mine, in that respect. In my mind it's just as important to get them right up to that place where He takes over, as it is to get them through this part of the road and the initiation here on earth. We could eliminate an awful lot of suffering and trouble if we could instill within them some idea about something that they would reach.

Q: Well, that depends on the level of consciousness at the time you leave the physical body, doesn't it?

A: Yes, it does to a certain extent, that's true. But you will be able to hear and see just the same from there, and consequently you need to know a little bit about things. And if we can get it across, we'll have broken the chain of ignorance; they could be picked up and straightened out. That's what I'm talking about. It's very important that they have a goal beyond the earth; otherwise why go through all this?

Q: Could you clarify what you meant by "what would seem to some people to be heaven"?

A: Well, I have heard heaven spoken of and described as streets of gold. Now, it will take them some time after getting there—if you were to figure it in man's time—to learn that there is more to it than just this, you see. I know some believe that we go up and play a harp all day. Well, I can't think of anything more discouraging in the world than to play a harp all day, because that would get real monotonous.

Q: Especially if you didn't know how to play one.

A: Yes, that's my trouble. Heaven is entirely a different place than this, and it is entirely balanced in every way. And you can, if you are willing to work at it, get to the point where you can determine where you will go and what your next life will be like.

Q: Do you believe in reincarnation?

A: Oh, no, I don't "believe in" reincarnation; I know it's a fact. I don't "believe-in" anything.

Q: Father, as long as reincarnation has been brought up, these people that refuse to accept it as a fact, and refuse to accept that it is existent or even possible, when they go through transition are they trapped on the other side until they come to the realization that there is such a thing as reincarnation, and then come back?

A: Well, now, do you mean someone who has created a heaven for themselves or their groups? Of course, when they get there it's going to take a little time for them to absorb the truth, and for them to get to the true realization of what this solar system, both in the physical and in the

Mind of the Father, is like. And then they will start to learn and to prepare themselves for reincarnation, under the guidance of a teacher, of course. You don't have to stay in heaven too long if you know your stuff, because you can go directly from here to another orb if you wish to—this is true too—with a very short stay, very short.

Q: What if you don't believe in heaven, and don't believe in God?

A: Well, I'm sure you'll have to learn just the same as the rest. You've got to go someplace, unless you just want to wander in waves of something or other, in between.

Q: You're saying then that I've got to believe in heaven?

A: No, I didn't say "heaven" as somebody else might say it. But I say that you are going to have to determine what you are going to do while you're off the face of the earth, or out of a physical body. This has been known and prescribed for thousands of years.

Q: When those with some attainment go through transition, what happens?

A: The Brothers will meet you, yes, and they have to do something with you. They can't just leave you there floating. There is a place between here and heaven, of course, but I wouldn't want to see anyone get caught halfway. You have to go someplace. Well, where would you like to go? I don't want to send you to where some people have told me to go, I'm sure.

Q: I don't believe that exists either.

A: Well, that's all right. There is a borderland that is a very confusing and disturbing place, that is for sure. And the psychic world is part of this, of course, a level of it.

Q: So then I have to set in my mind an answer?

A: Well, decide—what are you going to do with the rest of your life? You've decided what you're going to do with this life, part of it anyway.

Q: I may have been here many times, but if I don't realize it while in the world, how am I going to think of where I'm going to go? All I know is that I'm going out of my body, but after that, I don't know.

A: You'll know after that. But you will know before that if you keep plugging, too.

Q: What about these people who figure that once the physical is through, that that's the end?

A: Well, then they get earth-bound. And that's what we meet in these spiritualistic circles, those that return to earth, and you will see spirit manifestations or whatever you care to term them. These are the people that are sometimes contacted. They will manifest because they use the psychic forces to do so, in an effort to make contact with individuals and to gain the feelings and the emotions of those who are in physical bodies. Just because they're out of the body doesn't make them any more intelligent than you and I, as far as that's concerned, and probably a lot of them not as much.

Q: What happens to them then?

A: They stay in the borderland until they finally wake up and then they will be picked up by some of the heavenly host and steered around until they get to the place where something can be done with them. They will be taught some things so that they can get back through. They'll begin to understand and absorb; and then they'll get ready for reincarnation. Not necessarily here, but some other place, maybe. This isn't the only place in the universe.

When we emerge from the world of sense and its three dimensions into the heaven-world—some people call it the supersensual world, the psychic world, and so forth, but heaven-world is good enough for me— we then become conscious and functional within that world. The fact is that it isn't a plane of consciousness, it isn't a state of consciousness; it is a world. And when you speak about a state of consciousness, you are talking about another world, because that is what it is. You pick up a lot of metaphysical books that talk about the lower heaven world, the second heaven, fourth and fifth heaven and so on, and who understands them? But if I told you that you went to another world that is finer than the earth, and less dense, you could understand that, couldn't you?

HEREAFTER

Man should be (I don't say he is, he should be) preparing for his future. You know, religion used to be a case of trying to keep yourself out of—well, out of hell, you know? It was sort of an insurance policy that you were going to go someplace that was halfway decent. And some people even got to the point where they sort of loved the Lord and became conscious or cognizant of Him and His work, those who got a little closer to Him. And they were sort of preparing themselves for the afterlife.

But someplace along the line, our long-haired metaphysical friends forgot all about the rest of the trip. They forgot that there is more to life than what they are experiencing here, that this is just a wee drop in the bucket even of some people's conscious life, and that this is not a case of just learning how to do something. What some people's religion or metaphysics amounts to is learning to see how well they can perform, how they can do things that some others can't. Can they get illumination and be able to brag about it? Well, now that doesn't go down too well, as you'll find out sooner or later, because that doesn't put you beyond the reach of either the Law or the hierarchy above.

You'll find out that there are still divine beings that have something to do with your life and mine, just the same as they have always had something to do with it. And if you think for one moment that when you drop this shell and walk away from it that you're finished, and that regardless of what you have done in the past or anything else, that is the end of the score, well, you're very wrong; because that's just another part of the interim of your progress. Another part, another stage of movement in life will go on just the same no matter whether you are in this physical body or whether you aren't.

All of the teachings to help man attain, to change his way of life, were pointed toward one thing. There is no particular reason why you should be interested in being good if you weren't looking forward to a life beyond, eternal life, because it wouldn't make too much difference, would it? We could get what we wanted and never mind, really. So the life beyond, continuation beyond this cycle of life, is really the ultimate idea of spiritual training so that you can handle this and get the most out of it. This is the same as persons who study engineering because when they get out of school they want to work at engineering and continue along through life in this field.

Likewise, when we try to help you toward attainment, this is so that you will know how to run your vehicle and be able to do other things so you won't have difficulties in the other world. Thus you are really not only helping other people here, but helping yourself afterward.

Because there is another place. There are other worlds, there are other levels of life, and there isn't any question about that. It isn't some sort of story that somebody wrote, and I don't have to take it for granted because, as I've said before, "I've been there, Charlie." I have seen it, and have seen people that were living there. I have even seen people manifest here, from other places, and I have tested these events and experiences. I have seen those places—some of them. I never got good enough to get up at the top, but that's another thing. That'll come, I hope, in time.

Now let us elaborate on this a little bit. I wanted you to get the idea that this isn't just because somebody else wants you to be good or because you want to help somebody else, but you too have a reason for getting yourself under control and for learning many things about the function of mind and soul, for yourself and your own means of travel.

When you go to live in the other world—that is, if you even get to believe that there is another world; and until you get to believe that there is another world and know it, you are not going to go there either! You know that? Well, you'd better find out, and before long, because you know your word is going to manifest just as perfectly in that way as it will in any other. Just as perfect. And if you don't know by the time you leave here that there is another world, you'll find yourself out there floating around nowhere, and it may take a long time to find out where you're going.

There is life hereafter. And you'd better think about that, because you should be starting to learn about your own physical vehicle, and your own spiritual vehicles, and you should start to take it seriously, so that what you do now will help to prepare you for the rest of the trip. And there is one, believe me. If you think that you have ever experienced anything in the way of strange phenomena or things of that sort, you have just been in kindergarten until you start to have some real spiritual experiences, real ones. Then you will begin to know and sense the reality of things. And some people have wondered what happened when they started to experience it, because this has got everything else all backed off the map, totally, believe me.

This is what you have to prepare yourself for; or else what—back to kindergarten? But that kindergarten isn't quite that simple, because people who do nothing to prepare themselves or bring back their memory, at least of former times, very often lie for a long time around the earth, until their consciousness finally comes to a point where they can begin to use their own vehicles the way they should know how.

They should be told what to do when they drop this shell, if they don't make the full illumination; what to do, or what is going to happen. The only thing on God's earth that they've got to move around with is the control of their body and mind. There's nothing else that will move them. Now, for those who have gained some spiritual attainment, perhaps this is a salvation to them because they will be approached. But those poor ducks out there that have not had enough teaching, when they pass over that's where they're going to go.

Some people might think I was talking about spiritualism. Well, I'm not, nor am I saying anything against spiritualism either. But this is done solely by the transportation of your own vehicles through time and space. It is not a brand new sort of thing just invented. We're speaking of the spiritual world and it was all done before we got anywhere near to it.

We have failed to mention the purification of the soul which has to do with the life hereafter, after transition—the other half of the cycle of life, the complete fulfilling of this life, not only on earth but in other places too. To this end, our Lord Jesus Christ preached repentance.

You've got to get away from the idea that there is confinement to a physical form like this. This physical form is nothing but a tool, a way of living at this level; because you'll take on other forms when you are on other levels. You have to have a vehicle, no matter what level you're living on. If you were living three levels up you'd have a vehicle to function in there or you wouldn't be there.

Q: Isn't there a place where there is no form at all?

A: No, not in reality, because no matter where you'd be, there would be the form for that level, even if it would appear formless here.

Q: Can you have any of these experiences while in a dream state, when your body is sleeping?

A: You're trying to say that in the lower heaven world you could go through the experiences and avoid the physical world? No.

Q: What about experiences on the astral plane? Are they genuine experiences? Are they on your soul?

A: That world is just as real as this one is. Never create the idea that when you're there, you're going to be treading around on clouds or something like that. You're not! That world is just as dense to you in reality, when you're there, as this is here, only in a much different way, that's all. But it's a very solid, usable, experienceable, manageable world, according to the same laws, more or less, only more of mind than otherwise.

Q: Is karma working up there also?

A: Well, you don't assimilate karma there as you do here. You might get rid of some of it. When you go there and before you come back you are always in, should we say, better shape than you were when you came back the last time. You have always risen. That's one of the laws of chemistry, of course. By osmosis you can't help but pick up the influences of the world in which you exist. Even people who are very wonderful and perfect have picked up something through osmosis, even though they didn't do anything radically bad, so that coming into the world they would still have some of what the churches call venial sins, things about their thinking, and so forth, and various little things that they would have error in, just by osmosis. You know the old story, one bad apple in the barrel is going to influence the rest of them.

Q: Do we evolve on the other side?

A: I think our word "evolving" has us sort of at a disadvantage; and I mean by that that we no longer have a physical body then. But you must remember that the record of those lifetimes is there. You must remember that you're not going to do away with the marks and the scratches on the soul encasement or on the soul, which is the case of the Self, because that's there. And when you go into the other plane, you will go where you have the ability to function, and no other place. And this is why we say that if, for example, you are a good Methodist, remember the good Methodist heaven and then you'll have a place to go to work it out, so that you can get there and be there awhile anyway before you find out that it really doesn't exist in the way you expected, after all.

Now you will function as you have gained the ability to function. This is why, in the process of evolution, or in the process of spiritual evolution, I should say, that man learns to control his vehicle. This is why you have your old teacher always yelling, "Can you control your mind?

Can you control your thought?" And you think it sounds like a broken record. But if I kept you at it for a whole year, it wouldn't be too long. Because your thoughts and the control of that mind are the only things in the world that are going to do you any good when you get out of this body. You've no other control. You just let one thought slip, and boom! You've had it. I mean, things act just like that: you're there, period!

Our three bodies come into what we call the Universal Vehicle of Man. And it truly is that, because when you leave this physical plane at what they call death, you will drop this one, and a little while after you've left, you will drop that one, and that's when you get to the point where you have enough understanding and enough control of your vehicles to understand and not be frightened. You then go on until you have dropped the other spiritual body totally, and its emanation, and you go on in your own being—the soul and Self—for they two are together. The soul is the shell of the Self, and you'll see that one of these days. You won't have to have anyone tell you this.

THE HOST

There is a Host, or "followers of the Way", and they do exist. In the Bible they have been called "the sons of God". The White Brothers are another part of this great Host, and they too exist; we have seen them. The Host is a real thing. And it is a fact that there are angels, there are those who have special jobs, so to speak, in the hierarchy. These are actual beings, not nature-spirits of any kind, and these are not of, nor do they belong to his satanic majesty, that's for sure.

But we are reaching a point now in this new heaven and new earth, while it is being created under our feet we are reaching a point where these things are evident. These beings are becoming more evident, even to people who are not as well-developed or as sensitive, because the substance of the earth itself and that which is upon it is becoming less dense. Therefore our sensitivity and sight reaches a much higher level. And as the new heaven is being created, it is much closer to the earth and more of these beings, in their movement and their service to humanity, are at times being seen. Some of these are seen in the form of a teacher in his mission to help people, others just while they are doing something else which has nothing to do with the individual who sees them.

And of course, when people become conscious of higher beings, it is something which they are a little afraid of, because they don't really gather the understanding of it. We need to learn the reality of these things, of other beings and even of those things which have to do with the psychic, to a certain extent. At least not to be afraid of them and to know that we have complete power over them, as far as that's concerned—if we're not afraid of them—through the Word and through the existence of the light within us. And then to become cognizant of the fact that these beings, the Host, are people who have once lived.

The White Brothers are not something specially created by God. You might say they're the earthly epitome of the perfection of the Path. They are people who have taken on certain obligations while still in a physical body, and have fulfilled those obligations. They have taken eternal vows at one place or another and fulfilled them truly, and have joined with the Host. So they are the end product of the Christian way that Jesus spoke of. And they have had to come back a few times, maybe, to attain that state of purity. But there is no criterion; by their works you shall know them.

When you look at this from the standpoint that they have been living beings in denser human form, and they probably made the same mistakes sometime or other that you have made, you lose some of that fear and are able to communicate with them much more easily and will learn something from them. That doesn't mean that we don't test things to find out who or what they are, so we won't be fooled. But it means that we are going to take these things in stride, the same as if we were out in a forest someplace and saw an animal that we didn't know very much about. We'd be a little cautious and see if he was ready to jump on us; but we wouldn't necessarily have to kill him just to make sure.

And it's the same here. We're cautious, we test to find out whether this is really the truth, and then we can listen. But don't just take for the high timber because you see somebody that is not in a totally dense body. That's a little bit foolish. You may have reached a point where you don't do that, but nevertheless you should gain a little more consciousness of this. And by learning that this is the end product of a truly civilized Christian path, the Way, you would be able to gain a great deal from these beings, because I'm sure we don't have enough teachers. People are always looking for guidance, and some are not as yet able to reach the Master and listen to him, so they might get some valuable guidance along the way.

Once we have made a test and find that this person is truly a Teacher or part of the Host, there isn't much chance that we're going to receive any false instruction. But we have to make sure that this is so, and that it comes from a higher spiritual level. We don't start out by trying to reach them or to do it ourselves. If we have a need that they can fill, why, they'll fill it; they'll be there to give us that guidance. When we reach a point where we become of this consciousness where we can converse and work with them—in other words, by the time we have gotten our little selves out of the way and our big Self has taken hold—then we are starting to function. For we will have learned one great thing: that in absolute humility there is tremendous power.

When you go through certain initiations, you are told a story about an Invisible Host. And you find that as you walk down the street, after you have made this declaration to yourself—not necessarily to another person, but you've made the declaration—you'll find that you meet people and you'll know immediately that that person is seeking too. You'll think, "Ha! Here is one of my friends," though you've never seen him before in your life.

THE HUMAN BODY

Part 1

There is no greater, no more true, image or likeness of God on the face of the earth than a healthy, radiant, normal body and brain. When you read that true spirituality depends upon the weakening of the physical body or on the negation of physical or mental power, you should know that you are listening to a false teaching.

In the body of man, or the vehicle of man, as we call it, there has been found evidence of the existence of a spiritual body—we know it's there. The physical body would not hold together if it weren't for the fact that there is a spiritual vehicle there. Although it cannot be seen with the naked eye, experiments can be conducted which prove the existence of this spiritual vehicle. Most findings in science, the fundamental ones, concern things which are not visible to the physical eye. Many of these have been found and proven to be true which could not even be seen in the microscope; just as some of our planets were known to be there long before we ever saw them in the telescope. Many people say, "I can't see it, so I don't believe it." Well, this is no longer a valid argument in this day of nuclear physics and many other branches of science.

If this is true, then how much more is there to man and his vehicle than is now known? We are endeavoring to understand the body that we are driving. And many people today are doing just that without really knowing how to do it. They are driving a vehicle which has tremendous possibilities and a tremendous and unlimited source of power, but they don't understand it. And so they put it in high gear when it shouldn't be in high gear, and they wear it out pretty fast.

Instead of understanding and learning about their vehicle, and learning how to refuel it, not just with food but otherwise learning how to take care of it, learning how to use it and its unlimited powers, they go on blindly shoving it into high gear when it should only be running in low gear and letting something else do the rest of the work.

When we look at the circulatory system, we find that a great deal of the function of the entire human system is an electro-chemical function, not just chemical but electro-chemical. For around this body—I'm not talking about auras now—around this body circulate the electro-magnetic fields that come from the functioning of the vehicle. The circulatory system, which you might call the distributing system, is the part of man that, when it is not functioning properly, some organ within the vehicle is going to pay the penalty of working below normal.

Now if you do not get enough air in the lungs you are, first of all, not going to be able to carry in these small blood cells the amount of oxygen and certain other qualities—which are not always definable chemically but can be defined electrically—to the cell system of the body so that they can be recharged, so to speak. Not from what is in the blood, but they will set up and stimulate the system so that from this other structure that holds this together—and it does—the cells will be recharged and brought back into strength and vitality and the body is then rested and ready for use.

The condition of man's body is the mirror of his mind, about eighty percent at least, and I'm being extremely conservative when I say this. But we live in a strange world in the midst of tremendous electrical fields. This building, for instance: it is a rather small and insignificant place, but there are numbers of wires and cables running through the walls that are radiating electrical fields of energy that we are exposed to at this moment.

When you go down the street, you're exposed to millions of volts of electro-magnetic force, and each one of these cells is exposed to it; so that is why we have to say that the body is only eighty percent reactive to the mind, because there is another quantity here that it reacts to, due to the external conditions that we are passing through.

If the person is in a state of depression, the pulse of the heart changes, along with the metabolism, which is the breaking-down and rebuilding of the blood system, allowing the food energy, the vitamins and things of this nature, to go into the blood stream. Our entire physical vehicle functions on a basic principle that the function of the body itself is motivated by either external or chemical shock, in reality. Coming down to the fine points, all things function from this basic form. In other words I'm saying that when there is a change of the external pattern that you are living in, when there is a sudden movement in which the body must protect itself or move in a different direction, there is the impulse of this that runs to the brain and then there is reaction, and adrenaline is poured into the system, in accordance with the essential quickness with which you must move or change. It isn't always because of danger, by any means.

These are the things that control motion, alertness and the nerve tensions of the body, both reflexes and the motor systems. On the other hand, we have chemical shock where excessive acid and toxins are gathered in the structure, and they lodge due to what some of the bio-chemists call blood-sludge, and other things of this sort, and they stimulate nerve ends and nerve systems; and again there is a moving of the adrenaline in the system, and you have what would be a nervous condition.

If this condition exists it is a mental thing due to lack of control of the mind itself, in that the mind wanders, it gathers fears unto itself, most of which are imaginary, and immediately this starts to affect the circulatory system. You say, but how? The heart is pumping, the normal flow of adrenaline is there which is necessary for function; the person has eaten enough food, he has had enough rest. But as quick as there is a dropping, a depression sets in, you have a fear. And when you have this subnormal fear which is strictly on a mental plane, in the mind, you immediately have a slowing-down of the circulation. Because all of the nerves have contracted around the arteries of the body. There is a pulling together. I won't go into the details of this, but the whole arterial system is full of little holes, all the way along, and these are all controlled by the reactions of mind, as well as automatically. When we get our thinking into it and mix it up with the normal natural pattern of function, then we start to interfere with nature and its function.

Now what has this to do with, let's say, our attainment, our godliness, our ability to know God or to receive the light of Christ?—and I mean light, as spoken of in the Bible. It is simply this, that when a person and his body is not fully functioning, neither is his own spirit functioning normally. I'll call it spirit. I'll call it Self, because it is the Self. It is the you part, the part that is you. It is the part that does not die and never will. And after all, anyone who comes to a church or a teacher certainly should be seeking to know a little bit more of themselves. The ultimate goal is to prepare yourself for that long trip later on, after you've dropped this vehicle that we're talking about; because if it isn't for that purpose, then a person is wasting his time.

When we start to worry, we start to get depressed, we start to slow down this circulatory system, then we are inviting all of the diseases which are derived from this. You can call them by dozens of names, but fundamentally they are only one thing: they are the lack of circulation and light in your body. They are the lack of coordination between your mind and the function of your physical being. For the mind does control the physical body.

If a person not only thinks he has a complaint, but he also believes it, then what can nature do about it? His entire body and circulatory system is not functioning properly, therefore his mind does not function up to snuff either. He is losing the divine right that was granted him by his Creator. Jesus said, "Thy word shall become flesh." And, "As the Father gave it unto me, so also I give it unto you." Now, this is not a parable; this is a reality. This is a straightforward statement.

A mystic studies the body taking the heart as the center of his development and his approach to illumination. Then there are those who study man and his greatness, because man is either a great being or the Father fell short in His creation. Indeed there is no reason for man to be here at all, except that he may glorify God, because this great Mind created him; and he must have a great many possibilities to reach the level of conception of living and moving in a great Mind with unlimited power and force.

Part II

Nerve System and Radiational Field

The nerve system is constantly pulsing with life and energy. The arterial system is caused to function, not by the driving force of the heart pump alone, but also by the light motion and pulse that is within the body itself; and it is there.

Life is a strange and beautiful thing, and it is as scientific as anything that you can find. Because life is, and this is a force that comes from the Sun of God. The life-force isn't something which just runs down through the various blood cells and lymph, and so forth, that feed through these arteries, but there is a distinct electrical pulsation that moves across the trunk of this body in which the principal organs lie, and that pulsation is just as regular as can be. It is an electrical pulsation and it goes about seventeen beats a minute—in the neighborhood of that.

Throughout this body there are electrical reactions and electrical fields. Now these fields are created by the spiritual body of man and its reaction in the physical, in what we call metabolism. It is the breaking down of cell structure and the use of this energy in motivating action and heat, for light. It is through this and the cross-pulse of the physical body that we have a constant awakening and a constant rebuilding of the cells—if we will let it!

And this is the sad part, that we do not believe many of the things that have been taught us—at least they were there in the Bible—and

therefore we suffer the lack, and are unhappy because this body of ours doesn't function properly. And of course then, if we do not know how to take care of the body, it is necessary that we should go to a doctor and get emergency help. And the next thing we should do is start to find out that God really provided a way for us to be healthy.

Of course this brings a big question. First of all, do you believe in a supreme Power, a supreme Reality? And second, if you do, then it is time to get with it and start to study something about it, and to learn some of the things that control it, because your mind does control energy. It makes a difference on what level you think, you see. It changes the strength of the electrical fields of the body that you function in.

In an experiment where physical strength and radiation were tested with various professions and ages of people, those who were working on the higher level of things, in the spiritual and in the professional fields such as the engineers and the chemists and so forth, had stronger and more pronounced fields of energy and electricity around their bodies than those who were working with more material things, such as the salesmen, and so forth.

Now the salesman uses his mind to sell from a psychological level, but he is not forced to use his subconscious as much, and he is not forced to reach out for the higher level of consciousness and God, as perhaps the minister or the chemist who has to use a great deal of imagination. In other words, the closer you are to the higher level of thinking, the stronger and more powerful is the radiational field around you, and therefore you have a better chance for good health, if you know how to use it.

I mentioned the sympathetic nerve system and its reactions. The sympathetic nerve system has connections between all of the psychic parts of man. Now we use the term "psychic" in this case, instead of "spiritual" body. It is shown that this is actually an impulse system of living wires, so to speak, that our entire body functions on. This not only carries the messages, but it also sorts out the messages. It causes the contraction and reaction of the muscular tissue and structure.

We have spoken of the effect the moon has on trees and plants. And here again in the body we have electrical reactions to the energy which comes from the moon. We know it moves the tides, and likewise has an effect on the human body, seventy percent of which structure is made up of water.

The sciatic nerve that runs up the leg and connects at the base of the spine is a feeder of electro-magnetic energy, as well as the spleen that picks up the electro-magnetic forces of the earth. The spiritual force comes down through the head, through the great chakra, and through the entire body. This way, as it drops through, it feeds the whole body with the forces of light.

Now the spiritual body is not an imaginary thing. This is a real thing and can be demonstrated. And that primarily is the reason for this human form. It is not only possible to feed the body with life-forces, but it is also possible to feed every part of it so that man is independent in his choice and he has something to use to stand up, climb, sit down, lie down, do any of the things that he pleases to do. And at the same time, one step further, the Master said that this body, if it is full of light, becomes eternal. And I mean that literally as I said it.

Q: Do you suppose there is as much force in a populated area as there would be in Siberia or the desert?

A: If it were in the northern part of the globe, you would find that the electro-magnetic fields were more intensified in that area than they are here, that's true. Population would not make any difference in the strength of the fields themselves, but they would not be as easily accessible, due to the external fields within which you are living. You see, we have so many power fields that we live in. Just imagine all the radio stations that are booming out these waves of energy all day long. You live in them and you sleep in them. A hundred years ago, you didn't. So you have a tremendous effect that breaks up these electro-magnetic fields. Of course, some have learned how to draw on them just the same, and get the same results, but they don't unless they have learned how to do this.

Q: I have a question also. Isn't it that the electro-magnetic forces we have around us in the city are an interference force, not like electro-magnetic forces which are natural and which we would get, say, if we were up in the mountains where we'd live without this interference?

A: Oh, that I agree with. In other words, you're saying that you have forces that are natural fields of the earth. Well, you're standing here and you have a power line running across overhead and another one underneath here. This is going to interfere with the natural field of the earth, absolutely. Because you get enough crossing of these fields, and this is what sometimes causes flashes of light and things that appear that are put down as phenomena. But they occur where the elec-

tro-magnetic fields become intensified enough so that where they cross they create illumination.

The electrical structure of man and his radiational field, here [drawing on a board] as the metabolistic breakdown takes place and the radiation goes out like this, then the fields that are there around the individual, when they cross, this is what makes visible what most people call the aura, and makes the vibration of it visible.

And you don't have to be particularly psychic, but if you shut your eyes and just open them a slit so that you're looking through the eyelashes, and look directly at a person through them, you can see this rim of sort of half-illumination that's around the edge of the individual, if he has any strength or power in him at all in his radiation, and this is due to the same thing that we're talking about—the crossing of fields.

Part III

Cooperative Functions

The brain is divided in two each way, so there are four parts of it representing the four elements of creation; and I could go on for hours showing you where God's mark is on every single part. If you could get into the world of the microscope you could see, even in that infinitely small world, all the revelations of these symbols just the same there.

Wherever the creation exists, wherever life exists, even in the crystal or mineral life of the earth, there is growth and there is a consciousness there. I've always called it just a mineral consciousness. It's like being asleep without dreams, you might say—not unconscious but in another state of consciousness, another state of being. Existing, not non-existing.

Meditating on this will give you a sense that no matter on what level you find yourself, you are alive and you always will be. So there is one discouraging factor about this: there is no way of escaping God's creation, and you cannot escape your duty. Neither can you escape the development of the individual toward his heavenly state, from whatever you want to call it. So the person who gets discouraged and says, "I'll commit suicide", is just a great big kidder. He's kidding himself, and it's just plain stupid, that's all, because there isn't any way for him to get away from it. It's absolutely inevitable.

Now most people will tell you that they have a very normal mind, and there's nothing wrong with it, fully developed and adult. Well, I've got a great big surprise for them. That mind is just developing, because it is learning to sense the different vibrations in consciousness of the things which they have not seen and have not experienced. The longer they live and the more they experience, the more spiritual experience they gain and the more they sense, so much the more are the cells energized in the mind and become conscious of one another. These cells have to be conscious of one another, because if they aren't they are not going to work together; no part of the human body ever is successful in its operation of this vehicle if it does not perfectly cooperate with all other parts. And I'm sure Doc here will support me on that.

There has to be absolute cooperation or there is not what we call health. Now why? We learn we have three factors in the body, and these are light, life and love. Now there aren't any other words for this, because light is the basic energy of matter, life is the development of the Spirit in action, and love is that pattern through which the God-force works, that gives us cohesion and adhesion and which brings about assimilation and dissimulation, the breaking down and the building up. So these three things, the three "L's", are the very foundation of the perfect body working with perfect assimilation of food and the spiritual power. These three "L's" are the projection of the Christos, or the characteristics of the Christ, and they are related to the three bodies of man. These things are fundamental; these are things that you need to understand something about.

The only wisdom that you can really gain is that which comes from within, along with what is motivated by factual material from things experienced. And it is the same thing with the human structure, the flesh body, and all its great divinity. You have to see it for yourself. You have to know it for yourself. You have to experience it. Your body has to become your companion. Your being has to become your companion. And when it does, then you begin to put your foot on the true path of wisdom and illumination.

You can get light spasmodically for years and yet never become an illumined being, because until you know your own body and become master of it, until you have gained realization of the things that come from within and the mind of the akasha, motivated perhaps and stimulated from the teaching which is given to you—and you do assimilate a certain amount of things through osmosis, through the mantle of your Teacher—until you are of that nature that you do nothing of yourself, you have not started on the path of wisdom, or as the poet says, to "tread the path of the stars".

The body must not be worshipped. It is a tool. Don't get wound up into worshipping material things or personalities. This is where we get off on the wrong foot. Persons start to adore somebody and then they are completely "caput". This is where they get sidetracked all the way down the line. There's only one answer to any problem, only one answer to your being here: "Love the Lord thy God with all thy heart and with all thy might." Unless you want to do this as your first objective, skip it, because you're not going to get anywhere on the spiritual path. You might just as well go out and raise whoopee if you're not going to do this, because otherwise you cannot get anything out of it. This has to come first and then, "all these things will be added unto you". There is no other way.

The automatic processes of the physical body are in the soul, because over long periods and eras of time, as man incarnated and reincarnated, he gradually changed the physical body in accordance with what was needed at that time. He—and others, of course—changed the universal pattern of the physical structure so that they would gain the experience necessary in accordance with the times. So that ingrained into the memory of the soul is the function of the species of body which is used at the time of incarnation, if they are changing.

This is what happens sometimes, and we're going to see some of these things happening. We will see people come into the world who will not have entirely normal function in their bodies, because as the physical body raises its vibration and the reaction factors, should I say, change, they will be more used to slower functioning bodies and minds, and conformity to the laws. Therefore some of them that start coming in may have difficulty, because they will not be used to that fast a reflex; and you have seen people whose reflexes went too fast for their experience. They call this thing a disease, but this is superimposed function. In other words, magnified action, because they were used to a slower functioning body with greater resistance to it.

Q: With spiritual striving, are you basically developing all three bodies so you can develop your consciousness?

A: You're developing one, because it reflects through the others.

Part IV

Spine and Balance

The body is divided into four parts really, and the dividing line is across the lower rib cage. The spleen picks up the magnetic forces basically of the earth, and electrical forces. The liver is on the other side of the body, the opposing organ, and the life pulse goes this way across the body. You have a pulse of the blood and a pulse of the body, both, from one side to the other.

Q: Does the heart pump in unison with this?

A: No; two different pulsations entirely. Nothing to do with one another.

Q: Are they in harmony?

A: The multiplicity, mathematical multiplicity, is there. Sixteen to thirty-two.

Q: Yesterday you said that the spine and the radial nerves were important to spiritual growth. I wonder if you could elaborate on this a little bit? How are they important to spiritual growth?

A: Well, the spine is important to spiritual growth because it conveys and conducts the fluids and the gases, and the force and power which is generated in the body which is necessary to conduct the spiritual power. And it conducts also the impact and vibration which comes through the centers of the body and keeps them in perfect function.

These things come also from the mind. And the same energy and force that are used for thinking by the brain— as a tool or medium or reflecting prism of the Infinite Mind—are conducted through the spine. It is the trunkwork of the reflex system through which you can function, not only in a physical vehicle but you also use the reflexes in psychic perception and the sensory functions, the feeling and emotion.

The nerves of the body and the radial nerves of the arms should be very well-functioning because they help you to sense through the fingers and the hands those things which are useful to perception. You shake hands with somebody and if your sensory nerves are functioning properly you immediately get the picture of the individual as he really is at that moment.

Q: What's the purpose of the coccyx?

A: It holds the coccygeal nerve, of course, and extends the spine directly toward the earth. And if you start to—well, sometime or other you'll start to learn to pick up earth forces, and when you do this, it will work. Yes?

Q: It reminds me of a divining rod.

A: You will pick up energy off of that too, when you get to really functioning. If I stop to think about it, I can feel it. But I don't think about it usually, and naturally I don't feel it because it's functioning properly. If anything went wrong, why, I'd know it, you see.

Q: One time you said you were so tired that you could feel it drain...from the spine. What did you mean by that?

A: Because I wasn't in balance between the life forces and the electro-magnetic forces of the earth.

Q: So you drew from the earth.

A: Yes. Now, learn to breathe through your belly. Don't breathe through your chest, breathe through the belly because this stimulates and keeps all the organs very much alive. And then the air goes right down to the bottom of the lungs, you see, into the lower lobes—diaphragmatic breathing. Yes?

Q: Is there any other reason why it relieves tension when you breathe that way?

A: Well, you get more air in your lungs, more life force. Life force is in the air that you breathe, you know. You get more of the life force in, and it transfers into the blood.

Many people talk about the Tree of Life, what it represents and things of this sort. There is also the tree of life here. It can be traced in the body, and we will do that one of these evenings. But the principal thing that I want to bring to you tonight is the fact that every single part of your physical being is adequately supplied with channels to maintain and keep it alive.

Part V

Divinely Human

"Look upon thy body as a holy thing, and know that it shall obey thy word." This is probably one of the most important directives that we've had. Although you may not have the consciousness as yet at this present time, you look at the body as a holy thing because the original archetype, the original pattern of the body, was designed and created by the Father.

Now science will tell you that through many centuries and eons of time, the body has changed, that man has changed his body through use, through his application and different kinds of work, through the changes in his environment, food, and different climates that he has lived in, and through the evolution of the earth. Your body and every-thing in it is the same to you—to the Self and the soul—as the earth is to the solar system. So here we have the macrocosm and the microcosm

103

again; because man sure is an awfully small, little being, and yet here is the whole holy pattern of creation.

The body of man takes what is called human form, and because man is divinely human, it is very beautiful. But one has to take on and realize within his own mind, within his own consciousness, the fact of the divinity of this human form. Not to go into great detail on this, but every aspect of man's body is divine, because it was created, it was thought of and it was the Word of the Father made flesh.

It had nothing to do with you personally, the general form. You could use various shapes, length of nose and size of mouth, length of chin or leg, shortness of torso and various other things like this. But the basic form was laid down by the Father in creation. This you could not change. Its variations and its picturing you changed, and you made it in accordance with what you needed when you came here. What you did with it after you got here, that's another thing. But basically it is divinely human.

Now this doesn't mean you have sprouted wings. It means you stayed with the pattern of human being, knowing, feeling; experiencing happiness, joy, sorrow, various attributes of the creation, and they were not bad. What you did with it that might have debased it, this is the part which might be called carnal. Every time that you do something or get yourself out of whack in any way, you immediately express it and show it on the outside of your body. Every illness, every bit of deformity, every bit of disturbance that exists on the outside of the body, in the form of disease or otherwise, is because inside you have changed [not necessarily in this present lifetime] that divine human aspect of your life. And then it manifests on the outside.

Some teachings do not, except in the higher work anyway, get too much into the function of the body. They kind of forget this, thinking of it as sort of "a dirty thing". But that isn't true; it is part of God's creation, and if you don't have a good body, you could have a more difficult time getting real spiritual development. And that is why the misuse and disregard of the physical body is just as sacrilegious, in reality, as a disregard for your way of prayer, regardless of what it is, or your disregard for the Creator.

The flesh body we think we know, but actually know very little about, because that can be changed. But you can't change the spiritual body; and you can only improve the soul so it winds up with the understanding of the outer body of man in the physical world, and so that he becomes master of that and is able to work with it and live happily with it, regardless of what he thinks about it now. It's a pretty wonderful thing to realize that we can control any part of this body anywhere, at any time we want to, if we know how to use it or know how to use the energy and the power.

The body of man has in it the consciousness which is of the Creator. Isn't that a wonderful thing? To think that after all the misuse we've given it, after all the corruption that we've exposed it to, after all the willfulness we have shown, after all our violations of the laws of Creation, there is something which we can't remove, and that is the consciousness that was of the Father-Creator. Because if we did that, our transition would immediately ensue.

This physical body we all see, but most of us do not realize how much more intelligent it is than we are. Although each cell has a divine consciousness and intelligence built in to do its work, and under normal conditions would work efficiently and without any special training, the fact remains that each cell has to contend with the physical body around it, and with the objective intelligence in the human body which often interferes with the cells doing their work perfectly.

Then man has his spiritual body, or electrical body, and this term is descriptive because that's what it is; but it isn't seen, except by those who have the sight to be able to see it. This is the structure which holds the chemical cell structure together, and through which the basic energy feeds the cell structure, through what science calls the nucleus of the cell.

This structure might be called an electrical matrix. In other words, each organ of the body, each muscle and nerve, is first formed in the electrical body. If this were not so, they would not be found in the dense physical body. If this were not so, it would be scientifically impossible for many of the elements to be together, because as they are chemically opposed to one another, they would repel each other like two magnets with their like poles toward one another.

Then we have the soul body, as it is often called. This is the vehicle which goes with us when we pass through transition, and it carries with it all the intelligence of the life span. Only man and animals have souls. You can know the soul only through its functioning and manifestation. And of course, you would not see the soul body unless you were able to see the Self. It cannot be perceived objectively; it must be sensed.

Light has to do with the spiritual body. I'm not going further into the spiritual and the three bodies of man now, because it requires too much time to give a picture of these without misinforming the individual. There should be a preparation on the side of the physical, and some knowledge of the flesh body of man, in order to understand the spiritual body, really.

These three bodies will, of course, all come into what we call the Universal Vehicle of Man. And it truly is that, because when you leave this physical plane at what they call death, you will drop this one, and a little while after you've left, you will drop that one, and when you get to the point where you have enough understanding and control of your vehicles to understand and not be frightened, you then go on until you have dropped the other spiritual body totally, and its emanation, and you go on in your own being, the soul and the Self; for the two are together.

Part VI

Spiritual Matrix

If you could see the spiritual body really, you'd find that the formation of this body was actually an electrical structure. And by that I mean you could say that the cell structure in the body was a series of interim points or, if you want to go back to crystallography, you know how they set it up in the cubes and squares, and they'll show you so many interim points to a certain type of crystal.

Well, the spiritual body is set up very much like this, if you were to make a man in that same way, and then fill that man with chemical structure for each particular function that is in the memory of the soul. But the body and its form, its cell structure, the organic structure and all of this sort of thing is in the spiritual body itself. And the cell structure is filled with the lower vibrational substance which makes it visible. Now you have skin in the spiritual body the same as you do here. These things are all the same.

The outer sheath around the Self is denser than the Self because it is of a lower vibrational nature, and you can test this in a laboratory or a test tube. If you take a certain number of cells of anything, whether they're living cells or not, but especially living cells, and place them in a substance of a longer wave length, you will find that a formation comes around the outer rim, and the outer skin of those cells will become tough, be harder to penetrate. And it's a perfectly natural thing to happen; it all works on the same plan and the same way.

No man lives that doesn't have light within his body. He could neither breathe nor could he function with his nerve system or the metabolic system if he did not have the light within his body. Light is an essential, basic energy to human life. No man lives that doesn't use the magnetic forces of the earth. Because if he didn't, the structural material form would not be reacted upon by the spiritual body which is the energy matrix, or you might call it the spirit of earth. And it is through this that we have the balance in the body. Because in what is called the normal state of man, the flesh in itself could not stand the light and the Christ. It is too powerful and of too high a vibration.

One of the things that has not been clearly understood is what I mean when I say matrix, or when we say that the spiritual body is the prime body. Now "prime" means first in power and form. If I could take a person standing in front of me and remove the flesh, say, of his outstretched arm, and you had spiritual sight, you would still see an arm there in every detail; because the arm would be there.

Until you understand the spiritual body, there is no necessity of trying to go any further, because it must be understood. You must realize this, because it is the vehicle through which the energy produces light in your physical vehicle. Light energy cannot come into the physical body directly. Some laser beams, of course, will penetrate, though someday we'll get wise to the fact that if a person had enough understanding and control of his mind, then a laser beam could pass right through him and never mean anything. This is because the laser beam is up in the frequencies which mind can control. And if a person really knew his atmosphere and worked with it enough, a laser couldn't pass through it.

Now every single organ in your physical body is dependent upon the spiritual body and its strength to hold it together. Every nerve system and every muscle, every bone is there because the spiritual body is present in every one of them. But with only the spiritual body holding this physical-chemical material together, you would not have feeling, because feeling is a thing which is like a sheet of lightning on the face of the earth.

In other words, the nerve system can convey a shock or the reaction of a stimulus to the brain and cause the necessary reactions for protection, and you may have pain, but this is shock. This is not feeling, so to speak. Because if you were to feel that pain without the necessary complement of substance which permits you to feel, it would be just a vibration which would run through the nerve system and be sorted out and related to some previous experience of similar nature.

Feeling is possible because the vital body of man has substance within it, aside from the physical body. Many writers have erred and called this stuff a psychic body. Well, if you want to call the concrete in the wall the whole wall, why all right. But it is psychic stuff which fills the spiritual body that lets you have the reaction of feeling in the flesh. Regardless of whether there is a distinct nerve stimulus there or not, there is feeling. The sense of touch.

Q: Where is the unifying factor between the spiritual body and the physical body?

A: The center of the cell has a nucleus. And into it, out of the spiritual body, is the point of contact. Into the center of the cell. Even your modern biochemist says that you get the energy that feeds the cell structure of the human body from and through the core or nucleus of the cell.

I also have to agree on a couple of other things and that is, that there cannot be life manifest in cell structure as a composite form without light being received through one source or the other. And that source through which the light is received is, of course, the spiritual body

Q: Does the spiritual body also have regeneration of cells?

A: It is never degenerated. It is always perfect. There is only one action that can take place in the spiritual body. It can lose some of its potential impact. In other words, it can be below normal potential.

When a disease takes place or somebody gets, we'll say, an ulcer on their leg, right over that area there's a tremendously high, intensified electromagnetic field, because the vital body, or spiritual body, is throwing tremendous energy and collecting tremendous energy into that area to expel out of it the foreign structure which is defacing the physical. And it is attempting to reconstruct and bring the chemical structure back to conform to its own pattern, the perfect pattern of that body.

Q: What about someone who has a spleen removed?

A: There's still a spleen there. That didn't come away. You still have an appendix in the vital body, though it has been removed from the physical.

Q: Is there an equal correspondence between the spiritual and the physical body? In other words, for every cell in the physical body, is there a cell in the spiritual body?

A: Oh, yes. Let me put it this way. The physical body is an exact duplicate of the spiritual body. The physical body is denser, but it is just like the spiritual body, which is the prime body. It is a perfect form, and it can't deteriorate because it is constantly drawing on the spiritual forces of the universe.

Now let's get back to the one thing that's important: light. The light is there. It comes through the spiritual body. That is the only vehicle that conducts it, and it conducts it into the physical body through the gas in the spine—through the chakras, if you happen to open them up for that purpose. But don't bother playing with them. You don't need it, because in light, the finer part of the ultraviolet ray will go in and will penetrate and feed the vital body.

Now, when the healer lays hands on a person who is ill, and asks the spirit and the power to come down, he does not administer to the physical body. He administers to the vital body, because that part or function of the person which is slightly under its potential power in the vital body is fed by the power out of the hands of the healer, along with his knowing. This brings it up to normal. This will feed the vital body and immediately will cast out of the physical the abnormal, pathological deposits, regardless of what the condition is, even if it is sin.

HUMILITY

If we are to hear the instruction of the Self, or our guardian angel, and we seek to have soul purity as the first attribute, we should keep the thing which is most essential and the key to all development, and that is humility. Humility is not punitiveness, it is not hang-dog, it is not the person who allows other people to step on him; this is not humility at all.

For in humility there is power, and all of the great teachers have learned this lesson, getting themselves out of the way. Because it is in their humility that they have the authority and the power to do things, not through the will.

"Whoever humbles himself like this child is greatest in the kingdom of heaven." When you have that degree of humility, it is possible to grow, unless you stop it. And of course, you stop it when you try to figure it out.

ILLUMINATION

Many people ask, "How long does it take to go through illumination?" And I say, "How long do you want it to take? You tell me." Well, this is just about right, because they don't know it but they are setting the Law in action, and that is what it is going to take.

The first step before all else is to learn to control your mind through concentration. This must be done! There is no other way; you have to learn to control your mind.

The second step is to learn visualization, so to speak, through concentration upon a candle and so forth.

In the third step we learn to meditate, so that in this way we tap the Source of intelligence within us, and there are some things that will come up. We haven't reached realization yet, but we are now ready to make a concentrated effort so that we may realize the Christ light.

There are some strange ideas about this term, even amongst students. They immediately attach it to the Bible then to their mind it ceases to be light, because it is very difficult for them to imagine anything that has the name of Christ or any other religious thing to be a reality.

We are always talking about attaining light, and then we want to quickly go on to attain greater realization, but we don't want to spend time with the light, and it is very important that we do this. In meditation and concentration you should spend enough time with the light. Don't worry about the realization, it will come; but spend time with the light until there is no question that it is always there, so thoroughly there that it completely enhances your entire body. This is essential. And if you are looking for the tools, for the gifts of God and our Lord, it will be opened up; they will be revealed to you. They have to, because this is lifting you up totally to another level of consciousness, another level of vibration in reality, so the tools have to work.

Jesus at his baptism received the Light, the illumination. The Testament speaks of the Light descending. Often at prayers in the chapel, we find the presence of the Christ totally permeating everybody that comes to the prayer service. So when they come there with the idea of worship and the Christ force permeates this chamber, they have a certain degree of acceptance. And then when the reality or the voice speaks with the authority of the Christ in it, and they begin to feel the energy and power moving, this is a physical experience, and for the moment the emotions are raised enough so that the heart section of the individual produces feeling. And when there is enough feeling, why, at that moment their own willfulness and their own determination to do things themselves is forgotten for a moment or two, and it is right then that they are caught off base.

The teacher or priest lays his hands on and lets enough power through so that they are not thinking for a few minutes, and it seeps through and gets started. Well, actually what he is doing is drawing enough power through so that the light from within the individual begins to show itself too, along with what is going in. And when they catch a flash or two of it, there is enough conviction to break down some of the barriers, and then they start toward illumination. But they have to be caught off guard.

One thing that I want to bring out here more than anything else is that the great Lord of the Sun, the realizing of this great Being, is part and parcel of the Path of illumination. And this will not be as difficult now as it was in the days of long ago, because this is the Christ Age. This is the day of darkness which surrounds the earth in the Ninth Hour. And now we are crossing the great abyss, as it is spoken of, which is one of the great solar initiations. And we need this light for our spiritual and physical protection, that we may live out our cycle of life and be here when the peace shall reign for a thousand years.

Then we come to understand probably one of the most complex things for the average individual, and that is the subconscious and the conscious mind, which is absolutely essential if we are going to attain illumination; because now, at this stage of development we are actually laying the groundwork for Christhood for man. This is the illumination. This is the building of the golden wedding garment, as it is called. And this is the perfect blending of the two minds, when the Self becomes unified with the whole life principle, dwarfing any idea of self-achievement.

One of the things a person is taught when he enters any school of attainment is mind control, for this is the key to all spiritual development. As one gains a certain level of mind control and acceptance of Jesus and the great Light through him, he may attain the state of illumination. This is something which you all understand, and yet I wonder if you do. Some of you have experienced it, but what have you experienced? You have experienced the first seed-light, the starting of illumination. The full reality, the full growth of light within you will take a little time and a greater change. And this is what you are brought towards, the great light body which you will eventually attain down through the years.

After receiving the light, it is of extreme importance that the student should spend at least forty-five minutes to an hour each night, letting that light of Christ permeate his whole being, the whole body. And when I use the word "body" here, I mean the physical body as well. By this the dross and the effects of negation in the physical body will be removed, while at the same time the negative patterns of thinking and the limitations people have assumed will be released from the mind and thus begin to build the concept, the pattern and the framework of the new body.

With the release of negation from both the mind and the physical body, with the growing awareness of the inner being and the act of "letting go and letting God", an aspirant may move toward realization of the inner being, the Self, the real You, the only thing you can ever fully understand or know and the only thing you can ever be—the Self.

For though you may live on Mars or Jupiter or any of the extremes of the universe, it will still be only you, primarily, regardless of what the vehicle looks like that you manifest in the dense or physical world. You can never be any different than just you. You will have many experiences. You will grow in the light and the power and the consciousness of God and our Lord and Master Jesus, and other great ones, but you will never be anything else but just You, the Self. And once this is accomplished, from that time on for all eternity the aspirant will forever be realizing the existence of the Great Creator and the guidance of our Lord.

At this point of the preparation it is necessary to gain a fuller degree of mind control that you may hear the Self, that you may understand what comes through from the Mind of God into your mind, or brain—for you know you don't have a mind, any more than I do. Otherwise, the purer elements of nature cannot come through, and here we are talking about the Fire; but this cannot come through if the channel is not clear.

Q: And purity is a tool toward that?

A: That's right. Fire. It's there. It's the thing that is essential for reproduction, for the reproduction of the fertile thoughts of the mind, for the fertile thoughts of the heart—because you can think with your heart too. That is one of the beautiful things that the old mystics used to accomplish, the thinking with the heart.

If you want illumination, you fill yourself full of light. Nothing mysterious about that, because if you accept something it will come into your being. One thing you must do, though. When you find out a truth, for God's sake, stop thinking! Otherwise, that's the most guaranteed way in the world never to find out anything, because the mind is a dam that shuts out everything.

The divine has nothing to do with the physical in itself, but in the immaterial consciousness, or what we call the reasoned consciousness, there enters into the body a birth, and a flood of energy comes into the Self and the soul. This also feeds into the body, and this is what can take place with such things as when Paul gained his illumination and realization on the road to Damascus, when that bolt of lightning hit him. He had some difficulties for a few days afterwards, that's for sure, but it all worked out.

This is what can happen when we go into this sort of thing. And we never try to go into this unless we are ready to let go of the whole works and forget all about what we think. Of course, that's one of our greatest troubles—we're always thinking.

ILLUMINATION II

This lecture is to give you a better understanding of the way to illumination. One of the first things which we must understand is that there is no exact method or no exact process or series of exercises that will work with every person in exactly the same order, that could be given on a sheet of paper; because each person is at some different interval of development. A way must be found of exacting the individual's complete attention and point of focus so that he will reach illumination, so that he will do what our Lord and Master told us to do, if he will be one-pointed. In other words, if thine eye be single, thy body shall be full of light.

This is not a new thing in religion, or a new way of approach. This is merely an accelerated approach due to the fact that this is the Aquarian Age, and that the power and the force around our earth has been accelerated. This is the day of the New Heaven and the New Earth, and those things which are not in accordance with our Lord and his teachings are being cleared away from the earth. People have been attaining illumination, through the instructions of their teachers, for thousands of years, even before the Master came, but it was then a long and rugged process.

We are very much privileged in this day and age because we have the great advantage of having come to earth in incarnation at a time when things may be attained and realized in this way. That is taking into consideration that you are under the direction of an intelligent Teacher or a highly-evolved priest—one who can give you some direct guidance—and who, through his spiritual sight, can help you interpret or direct your understanding in seeking out and permitting the Light of Christ to come within your physical temple, and thus bring you in contact with greater wisdom. We also take for granted that you are not a habitual alcoholic and are not dominated by extreme negative traits, but are a person who has some control and lives an average life.

One of the first steps that must be taken, when we have set our sights, is that of learning to control the mind through concentration. This is a must. We learn to control our mind by taking such objects as the orange, the apple, the flower or some other thing, preferably something with life and color; this makes it a little easier. We get quietly relaxed with the object in front of us. We look at it and think about it and about all of its parts. We think of how it grew. We think about its color, its texture, what it is composed of, the plant or the tree from which it came, the many things which have to do with it and how it is attached to the earth. We consider its growth through the same power and life and light which we are seeking to attain within our own physical vehicles.

If we can do this for a few minutes, thinking only about the thing on which we are concentrating without any outside thoughts coming in, then we have started to learn control of our own mind and its thinking. It takes varying lengths of time to accomplish, but bearing down and working on this particular exercise is the keynote to all spiritual revelation and reality.

After we have attained this first step—which sometimes takes quite awhile, according to the state of mind or confusion or state of fluctuation of the person, or what the previous situation has been, whether there were drugs or other harmful substance involved—our second step should be that of learning to visualize things, how to visualize an object without the object being there. How to visualize an orange, to see it, and think of all its parts and the things which we learned about it before during concentration exercises, and to see them. Visualization should involve also the re-creation within the mind of the colors and the lifelike reality of its existence.

After we have attained this, then we will learn to go into meditation. This is the third step. Now meditation is not just sitting blankly or quietly and doing nothing. Meditation is not letting strange and foreign thoughts come in, or letting visitations from another world come in and run rampant through our mind or take control of us. Meditation is a distinct and scientific process and tool as used by the great mystics and occultists, and we must approach it from this standpoint the same as we do all other things.

When we have conquered the art of concentration, we have learned how to visualize using imagination and will-power to a certain extent. And now we are ready to learn to meditate, to contact and make ourselves available to the inner wisdom within us, and within the Mind of the Father.

We have been able to learn how to be perfectly quiet and lose all body consciousness, and as we do this we then think about the question or the subject which we want our meditation to be composed of. We think about how we want the answer, how we want this information to pertain to us and what we are seeking. Thus we ask an intelligent question, being careful to frame it just right, after getting quiet, before we go into meditation itself. After having asked the question—and this may be asked orally and with a certain amount of sound—we then clear the mind, but do not blank out. We merely let our minds stay alive, but we do not think.

Then in a few minutes, plus or minus, we should start to get thoughts about the subject which we are meditating on, and only about that subject; because if we do not get those thoughts, we are not under control, so we clear the mind and start over again, perhaps several times. But then, if there is a persistency of foreign thought coming in, we abandon it to start over in the evening or in the morning to come. And we persist in this until we get answers which are strictly related to what we are asking questions about. Then we are ready to start a concentrated effort so that we may realize the Christ Light within us, the Light of the Christos.

INITIATION I

One of the preparatory steps is to learn to visualize yourself in a small room alone, with one chair and a table, maybe a bench or a cot, and this room should be maybe four feet wide and seven feet high, and about nine feet long—just a small cell. As we learn to visualize this form around us and us in it, we will come to understand our mind much better and will have a chance to use the tool of concentration in a more realistic way. This room should have a door which is shut and barred from the inside. Sounds peculiar, doesn't it? But remember this: once you have reached the point where you can actually create this, visualizing the room with you in it, you can have a perfectly quiet place where you can work without being disturbed by other people in the building or the place in which you live.

This is not only for the protection of the meditation and spiritual work, but it is also a means of producing evidence to yourself of your mental abilities, for what you declare will be as you declare it. And after you have been successful with this, you are ready to go on with the actual work. One must remember that he is attempting to take on the light of the Christos, the great Son of God, and that if he has anything else in mind, I say beware, for it can have its reaction.

After having accomplished the art of building your meditation chamber so that you may produce it vividly and realistically at any time you wish, then you should sit quietly in it and develop the consciousness of the sphere of your own atmosphere around you. This is like a globe which you will fill with white light, and sit in meditation in it, not for an hour or two, but for about twenty-five minutes or so. And if you set this length of time in mind, it will work and you will know when the time is up.

This is to start with, and you will be able to accomplish much. You'll find you will have adjustments of the body and you will get rid of many of your own little idiosyncrasies. After you have accomplished this and have practiced it at least once a day, if not twice, for a period of twelve to twenty-one days, then you should, after placing the sphere of white light around you in your meditation chamber, look to the center of your sphere, which should be somewhere in the solar plexus area of your own body or temple—or at the rear of the solar plexus, should we say—and meditate until you see the center or the nucleus of the sphere of light which you have created. This should be a practice for about twenty-one days, and you will never regret the results of this practice.

Now let us get a little understanding of what we are doing. Your meditation in this visualized chamber is similar, in a way or to a degree, to life or initiation, as though you had gone through from one incarnation to another. And this represents the inner awakening, the experience we have and the revelation which takes place while in this state.

It will not be necessary to build a new chamber each time you have had an experience, but eventually through this method you will attain the illumination, with the help of someone who is a Teacher or a highly evolved priest. Through all our lives, there is a series of interludes or states of mind, for there is a continuous state of change in an orderly continuity. Actually, our consciousness is never static but is in a state of constant evolvement, in a gradual ascent. As we realize these changes, we have a feeling of movement from plateau to plateau, or of rising from level to level; but actually this is not true.

This feeling of rising from level to level takes place only because at that moment, that day, that period of time, we have become fully conscious of a certain state of change and the expanding idea of God's creation, realizing certain things in God's creation that we didn't know existed. Actually there has been a continual change which we haven't noticed, though at times it seems to us that life is a series of definite changes from one point of view to another attitude of mind. Transition from one state to another may be so gradual that it is not noticed, and then we feel we have a new revelation. This transition is a state to note, and we might call it a point of initiation.

INITIATION II

Those of us who have not studied metaphysics or some mystic teaching must realize that there are twelve great solar initiations. On the lower level there are nine. Man may not be conscious of this or of experiencing these periods of initiation, but he enacts them over the passage of time. During his lifetime he might go through one or more initiations, or he might only succeed in attaining part of one, and might take several lifetimes to complete the attainment of one initiation; but this is not necessarily so any more, as we will experience the same things but in a little different way. We will experience them through facts and philosophy which have to do with our life and the ever-moving chain of power and reality of the great Forces of God and our Lord Jesus, moving in and through our lives and causing us to have certain experiences which will fulfill the attainment of them.

Racial characteristics vary and this is why you see different teachers for the various races performing rituals and worship in a different way. These are designed to bring out something needed for development within the race itself, for this particular people. So we can say that all faiths, all religions, have a purpose, to develop the races of man and bring them into a greater understanding. Those who are seeking this find it sooner, while those who do not seek, maybe from lack of even knowing that it exists, will go from life to life, several lives, in order to gain a simple point or simple accomplishment. To those who do not seek it will not be given, except in the way of cosmic evolution.

And that is the difference between that way of life and this particular method now which carries the same foundation, the same law and regulation, but is a much more rapid way in which we may gain greater fruits in our own lives and in our way of life here; and we'll be able to help other people more quickly.

Evangelism with its altar calls, even though on an emotional basis, has done some good, because some of the people have given themselves and really mean it. We know of manifestations that have taken place, and that a number of people have gained through evangelism and the Pentecostal work. Of course, the dogma is another matter, but the altar call is a functional thing and will work in bringing a person to a greater height of reality. The trouble is, very often, that the people who are using it do not know or understand it.

Now I'm looking at all of these things from the standpoint of initiation. This all has to do with either conscious striving toward initiation, or unconscious moving in that direction through the evolution of man. One or the other will happen, regardless of what you do or what you strive to do; it will happen anyway. It may take six lifetimes for you to know that you shouldn't steal bananas, but you will learn it eventually. Now you might learn that in five minutes if you seek to know yourself.

Truthfully, some of the things that people spend many years to learn are right in front of their eyes, and are just about that simple, and because of this simplicity they don't know of their existence and don't understand. It is the simple things that have been in front of your eyes since the day of your birth that are truly the great mysteries. These are the things that can't be explained, because in order to explain them, you have to get into the teachings of those old fellows who taught the mysteries long ago, and have been teaching for thousands of years the truths which lead man into Self-confidence and Self-reality, and thus away from doctrine and dogmatism. Other faiths are needed, but we are trying to prove through our living, and to give out through our teaching, those things which will be serviceable to all mankind everywhere.

Anyone can teach the person who believes the same as he does, but the mark of a true teacher or priest is one who will teach the person who doesn't believe, and prove this through his own life and through his own work and effort and love for that person. That is the mark of the school of initiation.

There are lodges where people try to learn the uses of the law and the Word, both to manifest this in the material world and to help other people learn these things, to help man to help himself. And this is very fine, because if you don't help man to help himself, he isn't going to get anything out of it.

The initiations in lodges are usually on a material level, and always have some spiritual principles back of them, true, but they prepare you with the words to say. People are placed in certain positions and in certain patterns of function within the lodge hall, then you are brought in and you go through this little play or act. It all carries a spiritual meaning, a basic creative meaning and teaching, so that by this, regardless of the materialistic attitudes of the individuals in their private lives, they do learn something. They can't very well help but learn something, because they have followed a pattern and a group of words, and assumed this–and there is a law of assumption, you remember–and certain amounts of it will definitely have its effect.

This, in a materialistic way and, shall I say, the lower order of things, is a method of initiation; because the cosmic has a habit, once you have come into this earth and declared what you are going to learn, of seeing that you get there. And the Brothers will see that it is done. It may mean putting somebody in your path who will oppose you. It may be to marry someone who will make your life difficult, and it may be that you will have six babies who are constantly squalling. But I assure you that those people and physical things work not only to build obstructions or hurdles that you have to go over, but other things that will help you to go over those hurdles, if you will to do it. And this is the way with initiation, in the natural life sense.

Many times people have an ailment or a condition that serves for them as a hurdle to get over, because there is something within them that doesn't want to hear what is said about certain things. They may not be conscious of it always, but it exists. One of the things that happens through initiation is control of some of these things. These are objectives that you are trying to gain and the initiation, when it happens, serves to open the door so that you can manifest and gain this particular thing, as you climb what is referred to as "Jacob's Ladder".

One of the degrees of initiation is to learn the direction of the will-power, to understand it and learn its use, and then to get over a hurdle by doing it willfully through your own determination, not affected by circumstances around you. This is what you might call the life-stream of initiation to the average individual.

There is a higher form of initiation which takes place in the lower heaven world, or the world beyond. Now these are not fantasies. Let's get this home: you're living in a world of reality. There is no such thing as an unreal world. There is only one difference between heaven and this place, and that is that it is not as dense and it does not have the imperfection of this down here, but it follows the laws of creation and is just as real, just as fundamental and just as material as this is, when seen from that standpoint. It is as solid to you, when you are there, as this is down here. Life is continuous. The Master has spoken of continuous life, life eternal. There is a realistic place, where there is realistic living in another form.

The average Christian church-goer sees the path of the mystic, the occultist and so forth, as an unreal sort of thing, used only by people who wish to take command of other people's will, and to use them. But this is not so. This is part of cosmic initiation; it is part of the cosmic plan, and it is far older than any church. That doesn't say we shouldn't look to the Master, no. It says that what he was teaching had been taught and proven a reality for thousands of years before him. But in a physical manifestation and in a visible way through his ministry of the three years, and through his work and his crucifixion on Golgotha, and again through his resurrection and his ascension, he brought to us the proof that these forces were controlled by these laws.

This is the path of Jesus Christ, and it is a reality. This is not something that was for the one exception, something to prove his superiority, but he gave the Word to us–and it has worked–that we could do these things also. This public demonstration of Jesus Christ of the initiations was a physical manifestation of their workability, of their reality in the cosmic, and that these mystics, whom people had looked down upon and were sometimes afraid of, were not meant to be feared but were men to cherish and to look to for help. They are a material manifestation of cosmic initiation, and everybody goes through it. It won't make any difference whether you are black, blue, green or yellow; it's all the same thing. This is the Way that Jesus was talking about, The Way, capital T, capital W. It is a real Path, an existing path in which he manifested himself.

Now, you who are just learning, after having had some experience in life, have had many little things happen that you couldn't explain. Nobody can have lived as long as most people have without having things happen that you couldn't explain, and you get in the habit of listening. But also, through the mass mind and its influence, you get in the habit of thinking of a Way as either a process or method by which somebody does something, or a road that is made of concrete or something of that sort, like the Appian Way of Rome. And this is not what he was talking about. What he meant was that when you follow the laws and the teaching and the experience, and have made the hurdles, you come to the point where you raise the vibration of your body, then your true Being takes over, and you learn the use of the forces and powers of nature that he has been talking about in the New Testament. And when you do this, you will approach a state in which–between this world, this concrete thing, and the other–you will pass through into another world. And then you will have done exactly the same thing that he did.

There are twelve major cosmic initiations and there are thirty-two detailed steps of initiation. Nine of the cosmic initiations are on the physical level. The twelfth degree of initiation determines what you are going to do and where you are going—the jumping-off point, the last of the spiritual initiations you can experience while inhabiting a physical body. The eleventh and twelfth you experience while out of the body, but while still living here. In the twelfth, you determine what you will do when the next life occurs.

There are thirty-two steps existent in the Masonic order, and a thirty-third that is another step beyond that. There is no corner on the market by anybody; this information is known to every teacher, and to many others. These things are for a purpose; they work, and are very constructive, very creative, and they help many people. But others do go through, regardless; they don't have to be in an organization to go through them.

Initiation ceremonies start in the mind and are only acted out physically to implant the pattern in the mind of the individual. In many organizations they are portrayed for you, much as Jesus pictured these things for you in his life. There are some orders in the world today that you don't hear much about, and these have the truth with them, but they are handled as mystic orders, not for the public... Yes?

Q: Is it true that every individual unfoldment is predestined? Is there a certain time and certain date? In other words, has it all been set out—or can one speed this up, or slow down, according to conditions?

A: No. Predestination is very much misunderstood. Your path is only predestined by yourself just before you come into incarnation. You determine—when you are wise enough to want to do that—you determine it. Now, this is a general pattern you determine. Then when you get here, through your own initiative, your own giving, your own godliness or desire to follow God or Jesus Christ—or under different circumstances maybe you'd be following Buddha or Mohammed, or somebody else—but your desire to follow and to do good, to be right, to do things in accordance with creation, to follow God or Allah, would be the driving mechanism of your life. In accordance with what you do, willfully, full-heartedly, unselfishly in service, in obedience to what you know is right: this determines whether you accomplish those things or not, you see.

Now, when you get here, if you are approached by a teacher and one gives you the chance to go farther, he can help you speed up this process to a certain extent, providing you have not set a karmic debt which you have to get rid of first, or something of that sort. But even so, I've seen people get rid of certain karma, because that was the way they chose it and that is what they came back for. And then from there on they can evolve the same as anyone else.

Jesus said the mysteries would be revealed, and they are being revealed. Now, this doesn't mean violating the laws of anybody's organization. This just means teaching the truth that really exists. These organizations and even some lesser orders—and there is a whole group of mystic orders and occult orders down the line that teach great truths—there's no question about it, they have helped many people.

But now we are striking at a point where we are going directly through the center, and we seek to bring people into illumination so that they can work from there on and gain the greater light and the Self. By understanding initiation, to a certain extent at least, we get away from all of this foofaraw that has been taught, and realize that when we experience certain things, whether they are pleasant or not, we are paving the way to attainment. And if we get our minds straightened out, if we get our way straightened out and keep our eye single, we'll get there without question, because this is a guide he gave us: if thine eye be single, thy body will be full of light, period. And this is what it is.

There's one way of gaining, of seeking and attaining the light of illumination, and once you get that, it awakens the senses, it awakens the sight or the other attributes, and these are things which have to do with initiation. Now, that doesn't mean that if you muffed it at some other time, that you cannot gain things now. You can, because when Jesus came he brought the atonement to humanity. He cut off the world karma at that point for the people and the conditions that existed, so that they could go on, and we could finish up our cycle of work and attainment here.

"I am the Way, the Truth and the Life," Jesus said. So this is the Way that he was talking about. He didn't give it an ism or doctrine or anything else. This is The Way. People do not realize that there is a difference between life when they have once made a decision to live on that Way, and when they have just gone along with life as it is.

For thousands of years, long before the Master Jesus came here, it was acknowledged by the ancient teachers that there were certain steps in evolution, or degrees of initiation, the great solar initiations and the degrees of attainment. We say that we seek the illumination and then go on to seek realization of the Self. Now the illumination is talked about not only by followers of the Christ but by almost every avatar and every great teacher that

128

this world has ever known, of any race or nationality, of any creed.

It was in order to bring these things into the mass mind of the multitude of people that Jesus had not only to go through it, but to know that this change must take place. Not only was it done in heaven or in the akasha, the Mind of the Father, but it must be done on earth so that the results and the experience of these initiations could come into the earth and the earth mind, and become a reality. It was necessary for him to feel the loneliness of the garden.

Here is where we approach the confusion that people have, even right here. When they have made a declaration, and start to change, they come into this confusion, this loneliness. And this is another proof of the reality of the absolute virgin path which we travel, an absolute path of purity, as far as creation is concerned. This is the Way that the Master spoke of, where the same thing takes place as the loneliness of the garden, when a person feels this and yet is not conscious of the initiation in everyday life.

At some point in your life, you will reach a time when all things turn dark. This is inevitable, and I can remember when I went through this and approached that door where there was nothing, and no place to go but through it. It is a peculiar thing, which to me depicts a need for faith more than anything else.

The Christian church has practically denied the existence of initiations, from the public standpoint of view. They have failed to pass on the great truths regarding these things, and because of this people have been unable to identify themselves and their experiences with the reasons why they happened.

Many times down through the years, I have seen people go through terrific strife, and they were merely going through the initiation of the crucifixion. If they had known this was an existent thing, they could have taken it in stride, they would have been perfectly adept and willing to experience the things they did. But as it was, due to lack of communication of the real truth of the Christian path, they failed in some things, and in other things felt great anguish—which of course means in most cases that they will go back and go through it again.

When you start through an experience in life, and you have the inward knowing and knowledge that this is a trial or an initiation, don't fight it! Don't think it is somebody putting a burden on you. It isn't. Don't think that God or our Lord Jesus Christ has laid a hand on you and has said, "Well, now I'm going to make him suffer a little bit and see how much he loves Me." This, you know, is the conventional method of approach to the problems and trials that come along in the material world, and they're entirely false.

Many things happen in a person's life which are very orderly, although they seem to be problems. This is one of the things which I have tried to get across to you who are seeking spiritually: that most of you do not have any problems. The things which you are experiencing are some forms of initiation and therefore should be taken in stride, and you should not let them get under your skin, so to speak, because they are parts of a realistic living drama. It isn't the Master reaching down and saying, "Well, now we'll put him through this one, and then we'll take him over and put him through that one, because he did something here that he just should have done a little differently." No, no. This is all wrong. The pattern of initiation is tied up with the great solar wheel of man's evolution and his life and with his progression through the different vehicles.

The churches have failed to demonstrate or to teach this. And even though they didn't know how to take a person through this, they should have taught the reality of the truth. Now, the Mass in the church—while it is a sacrifice and the Lord's Supper is being given—is a part of the initiations which are combined into one grand drama, so to speak. A priest, when he performs the Mass, takes upon himself this reality..

An initiation is usually thought of as somebody doing a bit of hazing. Well, it isn't hazing in that respect. It is hazing in the respect of someone's personality and inner spirit, and to see where you set, where your determination is, and whether you will follow through to the goal as you purport you will.

One thing which hinders and serves as a barrier for many people is the fear that something will go wrong if they start to work with some of the exercises, or if they begin to feel some of the effects of the Spirit coming in. There's just as much consternation for the individual just starting in, who has never known that there was such a thing, as there is for the individual on a higher level, when he starts to experience the realities of the existence of another world beyond this one, or what we would call another level of vibration and the heaven world. And many times people lose valuable experiences because they are afraid.

Someone under a competent teacher should never be afraid, because nothing would happen unless they tampered with something they're told not to. Now, I've seen this happen occasionally. Usually they get thoroughly spanked by themselves for doing it, and they get scared enough so they won't do that again. But the trouble is they lose confidence in themselves and their safety when they're doing those things that they are instructed to do.

In becoming aware of the twelve great solar initiations which mankind experiences over periods of time, it is easier for us to understand the teachings of Jesus, because we have the keys that go right along with them, you see. Here is the Testament and its teaching, and here are the great mystery teachings, and they fit together and complete the picture that is told in the Testament; that is why we teach them.

Q: Did Jesus consider other paths that were known?

A: He reinstated such initiations as would not be changed, though certain things were added to them and certain things purified, I would say. Not modified, but purified. Because it is harder to live a distinct initiation consciously than it would be to take it on a more or less unconscious level, you see. There are certain groups and certain schools that go through these, but it may take four or five lifetimes to go through one initiation. They'll get through if the person has any willingness at all, but there isn't a distinct action there, a conscious action, the willful acceptance, you see, of that particular experience, and therefore there isn't the greatest grace.

There is the time when all people seem to turn against you, and you are not only left alone, but turned against by your friends and relations. Thus it follows through all initiation. Then the illumination and the rebirth, and then comes the resurrection. Now you may not have worked with the Light long enough to have experienced this entirely, except on a very primitive and lowly level of things. After receiving the light, you have a certain amount of rebirth demonstrated, and then all of a sudden you begin to realize a new life. You begin to feel a new life, and this is just a very primitive way of sensing a resurrection.

You are coming out of the old, where you were full of pains and aches, and full of fears and trouble, into a life where you have much less of this than you did before, and you actually begin to be happy. So there is a resurrection. You are being reborn on just a little higher level than what you had been living on before.

Q: What crucifixion do we go through?

A: The same twelve initiations that Jesus went through physically, we go through spiritually, although nine of them are of this earth. And these nine we usually go through physically, right up to and including the crucifixion, the resurrection and the ascension.

Now, once having set the pattern topside, Jesus had to manifest, or somebody had to manifest this physically. As above, so below. It had to be done in order to cement or set the foundation for the pattern we are now following for the Aquarian Age that is now building. And each one of us goes through this same life of Christ, so to speak, in our spiritual side. Now, everyone that experiences realization, just before he gets there, goes through his own agony in the garden. At his realization, he experiences his crucifixion, his death and his resurrection. In other words, he crucifies the physical.

Q: Do the Christian mysteries have anything to do with the mysteries of Egypt?

A: The Truth is the Truth, whether from Egypt or somewhere else. It doesn't make a bit of difference. It's all the same thing. The Law is the Law, and the Truth is the Truth, and it has all to do with the same thing. Egypt pictured it one way, Babylon pictured it another way, some other age pictured it another way. Stone plaques are found in various places, and you find the same symbolism in each case. Some of them were a little different, of course, because they were of a different time. But basically the same symbolism is there, the same action is there, basically the same truths.

Initiation is a very profound thing. You are all going to go through these steps of initiation, whether here or on some other planet or system, eventually. You'll either get it now, or—well, probably you'll be taken someplace else. You understand that the cosmic initiations are inevitable to mankind, and I'm not going to fight it. They're there, and they have to be attained, that's all. And they are attained through our living and through our works and our acts.

Q: Is an initiation a sudden jump, or is it a gradual natural evolvement?

A: It can be any way you want it. Paul on the road to Damascus got initiated like "whoop", and that was it. It happened all at once.

Q: What about Saul being hit with the light after persecuting the Christians...?

A: Well, that may be, but what did he do in lives before that? You forget that there are a lot of things that are not on the records. Remember that the old initiations—while they were just as personal and just as real as ours, and in the same way were guided by the teacher, or by the rabbi who was many times a teacher—were just as simple and direct, except that the student took a long time getting ready.

Illumination is not obtained through a sacrament, but through a solar initiation. And so it is a virtue which has been attained, and comes from the love of God. In other words when a person acquires initiation, he is going into the widest form of Christianity that can exist. He is encompassing all bodies, and joining all Brothers together, because it isn't something that comes out of a church doctrine or foundation or form. It is universal. It doesn't make any difference whether you are in this place, or any church, or wherever you are, if you really experience it, you have joined a group on that level which is universal, and you are compelled to accept all people who have experienced this. You can't help it. How could you?

We are carrying out many things that are just the same as were carried out long ago, except they are being done on a higher level now. This is partly due to the initiatory path of the evolving race of people, and that is one of the things which we seem to miss in our understanding of initiation. Initiation, you might say, has been done away with in a sense; and yet it is not done away with, because there are certain cycles of progress which will continue to be followed throughout many lifetimes and many ages. We are coming through evolution now. We were going into involution then, and now we are coming into the less dense stages of man's development and evolvement.

JESUS

L et us take a few moments to contemplate the Master Jesus. Let us see if we can feel the great pathos which he undoubtedly felt through his great compassion. Let us feel the overwhelming realization which he must have felt and known, as he looked around the world with twelve little men through which to bring the realization of the Father in heaven and the spiritual doctrine which had not been held forth for many centuries but which had been fought against so diligently. And now with the earth being in this condition, he and twelve men, along with his seventy two disciples, were all that he had to spread this Word and this Light throughout the world.

It must have been an overpowering reality. How absolutely helpless he must have felt, from a physical level. How rejected he actually was. How in reality he was bringing the earth into a stage where the illumination would actually start. He was letting from his veins the lifeblood of his experience that the whole of nature might be revitalized and replenished, that through this sacrifice in the superb and magnificent letting-go, through the crucifixion, through the resurrection, through the ascension, he was to demonstrate to this day and age the three great initiations which would be the salvation of the people on earth, and would permit them to continue their life, their way and their mission.

The true understanding of our Lord is not so much in the historical facts of his life, of which few are known. He was wise enough to know that the only way a real teacher can ever become immortal, that his teachings are held and he's sort of forgotten about as a person so that the teachings come first, was to obliterate from history where it was possible everything that was natural or human, and then his opponents couldn't find anything to pick on to show that he wasn't what was demonstrated, you see. He did a pretty good job, too. There are very few facts left, except a skeleton outline of a few things about his birth and a few things just as he started his ministry, and then his wanderings in the holy land.

I oftentimes meet people who say, "Such a man never lived. There's no proven history of Jesus." And you know I've got an absolutely sure winner for that one. My answer to this is: that even if Jesus never lived, the perfection of the ideals that he has brought, the methods and the basic philosophy of Creation that he has given and the things that this image portrays and projects—even if the Brothers above had created this man and put these things into the mass thought, the very image would be a pretty good guy to follow, because it would have the same effect when followed by the people.

He is a personification of spiritual development manifested on earth. You know there's nothing bruises a human ego so badly as to be shown his right size in relation to a power greater than he. Now he may consciously say, "I accept God in Jesus, the Emissary and the great Messiah who brought the forgiveness," and so on, and he will tell you of the relationship. But if you could look inside his head and see how big he feels he is, I'm going to tell you something: most of them see themselves standing right alongside of Jesus, and think they're about the same size. They're not that size, because Jesus is as big as the earth you tread on, and bigger. He is the preserver and the provider of the world, because he is Lord of this planet!

If you have any question in your mind as to whether the New Testament is the handbook of man on this orb or not, then you've got a problem. Because Jesus Christ came here, and he has returned, as he said he would, already; and his power and his mantle overshadows this earth and permeates it. We have a problem right today with certain spiritual teachings. Why? Not that the teachings are wrong, but the fact that they won't admit and they won't acknowledge the Lord of earth. This you can't back away from. It has to be maintained, because it is through this that you are functioning.

I have said, "Look and concentrate and meditate on your atmosphere. And as your atmosphere is set up, this will declare what shall come through it." So for the time until you get a true vision and true sight, you can think of Jesus as having an atmosphere which surrounds the earth, and you would not be too far wrong. But I'm not going any further with this to confuse you.

As Jesus came to us and experienced the great Initiations that we might be brought into his Light, so also did he experience them for the fulfillment of the pattern of the Host and so that those things which had been prophesied would also be fulfilled. For in this he gave unto the world those things which would be necessary as time moved on. This great being came here to teach us, came here for the purpose of demonstrating in the physical plane the crucifixion which every person, in different ways, must go through. He reenacted the grand play of initiation in this earth, in order to bring about to the conscious mind of the masses the forgiveness and the ladder, Jacob's ladder, the ladder to heaven.

Q: And this was the initiation for the illumination for the whole earth?

A: This was a demonstration of the initiation that an advanced being goes through, except that Jesus did it in a greater way, taking into consideration the whole human race.

If you went into some orders you would go through ceremonies in the temple that would demonstrate some of these things. You wouldn't have any spiritual experience, necessarily, but you would see the portrayal, as it was done back in the time of ancient Greece, when these same things were enacted and nearly all of the teachings were given in the form of plays. Here is where our opera and stage plays come from.

When Jesus went into the Garden of Gethsemane, or into the desert to pray for forty days and forty nights, he experienced the great aloneness, the great crucifixion in reality. Of course, the actual crucifixion was held on Golgotha, but in the desert he became crucified of the Spirit and was tempted, and then he found himself alone in the world: this is the next step. Then the crucifixion came, then the ascension. Now these are all parts of the solar initiations. He experienced and went through them all, but he went through them consciously, though he didn't have to, having had his own personal experience long ages before. Therefore when he went through these things voluntarily, he did it for the people of earth. Just as a master Teacher might take on somebody's karma, if they were important enough, so he took on the world karma and transmuted it. The earth! And so it is that the earth shall take on the Christ consciousness within its being.

If you ask a minister somewhere what Jesus did, he might say, "He brought salvation to our people. He is our savior; he caused people's sins to be forgiven." They leave out the earth entirely. You have to get used to thinking just as it is, taking both the unseen and the seen together. "And for those who sat in the region and shadow of death, light has dawned." (Matt. 4:16) The Path has been illumined, you see. Now this doesn't say anything about understanding, or all the other alibis that people can think of. This spells it out, and there could be no mistake.

Q: What is the meaning of the crucifixion?

A: At the crucifixion the Master gave his blood and allowed the Christ, the personality of Christ which he had taken on at the baptism—the whole power and personality he took on was then emptied into the earth through his blood. In the blood of man is his experience, deposited in the soul—the vibrational patterns of his experience.

Q: What was wrong with the physical condition of the earth?

A: The vibrations here in the earth and of the earth's atmosphere were were in such condition that it needed just that. He brought the atonement. He wiped away the past from man and gave him a new break, a new start. He paid the supreme sacrifice, in other words. Don't forget, a thing doesn't become a reality on earth until it is both a pattern made in heaven and then manifested on earth. I use the word "heaven" as meaning the upper level of vibration, higher frequency.

We approach getting acquainted with Jesus as a very difficult thing, because we feel we're reaching about five miles into the atmosphere someplace, trying to grasp into something. Well, that isn't where it is; it's right here. And if we can simply say to ourselves, now I'm going to talk to Jesus, and just talk to him. Say, "Jesus, Master, I'd like to ask some questions. What about this problem of mine? How do I solve it?" You know, you'd be surprised. If you expected an answer, you'd probably get one.

KARMA

The soul is the receptacle and recorder of our karma, of our debts good and bad, and of our assets and liabilities.

Through the activity of everyday life our actions become our prayers; in doing we pray for the removal of all error or karma, either past or present. Thus we have an active confessional every day of our lives. That is why, when you are getting started on the road, the Way, it is good to utilize the confessional as a way in which to keep things straight. You can get rid of a lot of things in this way that you might want to dispose of, habits and other things of this nature, through working with confession and penance. And sometimes penance is more enjoyable than you might think.

Now, we have not only the Law of cause and effect and the Law of the Word, but we also have a Law of assumption. And when we are breaking up the pattern of the past karmic form and motivation in the student, and allowing it to disseminate, then we have to bring him to the point where he assumes a new life, a new form. And if we can get him to assume this new form, the old form—from his karma, deeds and so forth—will just dissolve; because he is going out of one life, out of one level of vibration entirely, and taking on another in which he has been taught to see the laws of cause and effect, the Word and prayer.

These things are basic, and when he takes on and assumes this new identity, if he will but act on that part, then the basic internal functions will conform with the outer part of the function, and we will see him progress on, so that he will start to work on a different level entirely.

Getting rid of karma is the shedding of the mortal cloak of cause and effect. Here we have again the stored-up grace, maybe not from this life, but another, or over a period of many lifetimes. This free and unmerited love of God is the original move in what the church calls our salvation or, as the Indian would say, the gaining of our freedom from the wheel of Karma. We say it is the shedding of the mortal cloak of cause and effect.

Q: Doesn't the Master perform a function for the earth by being mediator; he's a mediator both ways, isn't he, so to speak?

A: Yes. But you see he cannot interfere with the Law of Karma, in that sense. If we let off twenty atomic bombs in the next twenty days, this earth is going to feel it and Jesus isn't going to do anything about it. He does not interfere with karmic Law.

Q: Is this why we should refrain from asking for healing of certain people we see, because we have no knowledge of their karmic situation?

A: Well, this is partly it. And then you have to get yourself to the place where the work and the Word of God become a living reality to you. And this is the only way you can ever approach this work, you see. "The Father gave unto me the Word, and I give it unto thee." When it begins to become a living reality, then you'll just start to bend toward this naturally, and you won't have any problems. But if you tried to jump from here to the other end of the room, you might have problems. If the power is delivered, the person will be healed, unless he wants the sickness very badly. And if he does, he can keep it.

Q: Are you speaking of karmic conditions, of their sins?

A: Karmic conditions don't leave quite so easily, because this is something that's been carried across in the memory of the soul. We're talking of healing the current problems, or what we might call spiritually critical diseases—all kinds of disorders stemming out of your presently existing cycle of life. When you pass and drop this shell, you leave behind all of the little things of the mortal flesh. You take with you the good experiences. And if you get rid of the others, why then, you're all set. It is only your violation of those things which carry a greater karmic debt that you will take with you.

In this path we strive to attain illumination because once we have this, with its light we can find the Self. This gives us the full knowledge of our being, of our power and ability to create our lives the way we want them. But we will not find the Self until our karma has been paid off and our debts are paid. And we will not find it until we have given up the world itself. Now, this doesn't mean that we cannot enjoy what is here on earth, because this is God's world. Man didn't make it. We have made and controlled many of the things that are on it, but we did not create the earth itself—though we have done a lot of things to it that weren't supposed to be done, that's for sure.

KNOWLEDGE

If you are prejudiced, you are wrong. If you think there is but one way of doing God's will, then you are wrong because these things which God laid down are too basic; they encompass all the teachings of man. As the text says: "When you think you know, you have not yet known, but he who knows not knows all".

This is an absolute fact, and anyone who has traveled this path any great length of time knows that the Master was the same way: simple, very simple. No great lengthy books did he write, no lengthy discourses. Shortest sermons in the world, because every word and every letter was Truth, and they brought the Light and Love to the people. But when a teaching condemns, then you have a problem because you have untruth.

I don't care whether you've ever gone to school, whether you know how to read, whether you know how to do anything; that doesn't stop you from knowing the Master of all Creation and it doesn't stop you from knowing God within. For the Spirit wearies of much reading. Let us try to understand, instead of seeking to flaunt our knowledge—which is so small, so small—in front of others.

Let us try to search ourselves to understand the simplicity of the wonders of Creation that our Father has created. To know better, to feel, to sense, to see the Light that is within us. This is all we need. For all the knowledge in the world won't do us any good when we have left this vehicle behind. Only then can we truly realize how much we depend on the infinite wisdom of the Self.

Unless we reach the point where God is a reality to us, then we have not reached anything, regardless of whether you call it cosmic consciousness, brotherhood, or otherwise. It is therefore a vain and fruitless inquiry to be asking beforehand for knowledge of any purpose regarding matter or God's universe, for the knowledge can be yours only as you have met the reality of life.

A truth revealed to you by someone else is merely a statement, merely a dogmatic or pragmatic idea, and until you take the idea and nurture it, and until it grows into the blossoming fruit of the reality within you and comes out in your function, it is not truth.

It is not that you, as a brain, have the wisdom, because it doesn't know anything at all. All it knows how to do is associate. But you as the Self and the soul really have all knowledge accessible.

Now there is one for you to chew on. If you take those words and really think about them, contemplate them, you will find something there to give due consideration.

INVOKING THE LAW

U nless we understand the basic laws of Creation, such as the Law of Cause and Effect, the Law of the triangle, and the Law of assumption, we are going to have problems understanding what Jesus was talking about in his simple way. This Law is not a dry, hard, cold thing; it has life. It is motivated through the Spirit of God. It is alive. And when you put yourself in His hands, to live and work and serve him, you'll find it works for you.

When you are taught the Law, you learn about this very simple little triangle, where you contact the Father at the top, and then come over here to the right, which is the Son portion, and make the pattern of your prayer; then you let go of it. And here at the left it comes out and is created in the Holy Spirit. Now, this is your function of the Law. All of these things represent living symbols in the Mind of the Creator.

Δ First of all, we have the Creator Who initiated it, so we'll start with the number one of three points. Now if you will notice, they are like the Awakening, Return and Feast. Why should there be three parts? Because in order to be part of the functioning Word, they must come through the Holy Family, you see, the Father, Son and Holy Ghost or Holy Spirit; because it's the only way anything really can exist. There is no other way, and we are all children of the Holy Family. The Law doesn't work unless the Spirit motivates it, and that's why you have got to feel the existence of it.

We think of the Law as though it were remote from us, that we can use it or not. It is not remote, but rather as close as our next thought, feeling or action. We can't help but set the Law in motion, so the choice is not whether, but how to use it. The Law is a true servant of the Word. It does what it is instructed to do. However, it is set in motion; action sets the Law in motion. Reaction is the result, plus a little grace. Action is what moves, what initiates, what begins thoughts, feelings, or deeds. "In the beginning was the Word."

Q: Is there any difference between the action of the Law and the action of the Spirit?

A: Yes, because the Spirit was first. Spirit had to be there, or He couldn't create, could He? It is that simple, you see.

Q: What is the difference then between using the Spirit and using the Law? And what is meant by transgression of the Law?

A: You don't use the Spirit. You never use the Spirit. The Spirit uses you. But you can transgress the Law by invoking something that shouldn't be invoked.

Q: Using the Law in a destructive way for something?

A: Well, it wouldn't necessarily be destructive, but it might be getting something that you had no right to.

Q: That would be using the Law selfishly?

A: It could be. You see, in working with this Law of God, the Word, it is all right for you to have a Cadillac, providing you're not taking it away from somebody else who has a right to it, you see.

For instance, if you wanted an accounting job, and asked me to pray for it, I'd say, can you handle the job? All right, let's pray for it. And I'd pray something like this: Now, Father, I accept for Johnny an accounting job like the one he wants, but I accept right action on this; no one must be hurt. And thank you.

Now, by putting it in this way, that may kick somebody else up the ladder somewhere, or may kick somebody out that has no business being there. But we don't know all these facets off-hand, so we use this form so that everybody is taken care of, there's nobody hurt, there's nobody infringed upon, and there's no injustice to anyone. But still you get your job.

Q: Should you always ask for right action in every prayer that you make?

A: Let me put it this way: anything that involves a number of people. Now if I were just asking for five thousand dollars, I wouldn't necessarily ask for right action, because I am not asking it from anybody in particular or limiting how it comes. It can drop through the roof if it wants to. It isn't going to hurt anybody; I'm not involving anybody in this, and it is perfectly all right.

Q: Can't you set the pattern for right action in every prayer you make, without stating it at the end of the prayer?

A: If you get this as an unconscious factor in your prayer, you can, yes. You have good will, and this will somewhat take place. But I always feel the responsibility because I know the reality of this prayer, and I will not usually request anything that has to do with people, unless I ask this. You use this right action also if somebody asks you for healing, where you have a strange feeling that this is a karmic situation. You ask for right action, and then everything is taken care of. There's no problem.

However, some people who knew the Law and the Word and all the rest of it, right down the line, have used these things for negative purposes. They were profoundly anti-Christ, that's all. They're determined they're going to run the earth and their world the way they want to.

Q: But they know they're going to lose, don't they?

A: They know they're going to pay a penalty for it, probably. But some of them get to producing their own world, and they forget their world is so different than the world around us.

Q: Would you describe such use of the Law as the sin against the Holy Spirit?

A: Just plain cause and effect. They are not above the wheel of karma, and they're working on a totally negative basis. Their whole creation is negative, even though it is using positive forces.

There is one thing we do not have a choice of, and that is the working of the Law. We can choose what it produces, but it is going to constantly produce. If we live on the level with our objective mind, in that state of consciousness, we then will have our bodies working with it. Our mind will be working with it, and the people around us will be working with it. Otherwise, the state of perfection at this point is extremely painful to those who are not working with it on that level, when you are.

The eternal laws are never wrong, and never change. It is only the evolution of the experiences we get out of them that change. It is only the things which we create and the advancement of our physical bodies that change. But the basic laws are not going to change, because if they did we would have to change the Law of Cause and Effect, and then surely we know the whole universe, our whole solar system at least, would fly apart and we would have a mess which no computer could straighten out.

The word "infallible" can only be used when it comes to the principles of creation, and the definite one or two laws of God. There isn't any question about this. And in your seeking, the only reason that you get something different from the next person is the fact that you are you, and he is another individual, and that while these laws are at the same base, they manifest through your personality, which is in the soul.

LETTING GO

For many of you, when you have had the door of realization opened, the answers start to come and you get an idea of something that you don't like, then you close the window and try to make something else out of it that you would prefer. When that doesn't happen, you say, "The Self told me so." Well, you're just about as far off the track as you can be, because you, this outer man, are still trying to give yourself the answers. And the Self is down there wondering, "What's wrong with this creature that I'm carrying; where did he get all the authority?" Well, he didn't get it, he took it. And that's one of the problems that we have. We take the authority, whether it's right or wrong, and use it.

Then you reach a point where maybe you have got your foot in the door and you begin to see a little bit of the sunshine over there, or have felt a little of the warmth, and you become aware that there is something you haven't experienced before; it's a little bit different. And you try to put one foot through and kind of go half-way. You can't do that; you have to go all the way through at one time. There is no easing into God-realization, in treading on the Way.

It's like the man who goes to diving school and gets put through all the gymnastics, the training of his muscles and all that sort of business. And when he comes out to do some beautiful work on the diving board at the pool, he gets up there and bounces up and down, and goes through a lot of motions. He goes up on the third bounce and then, boom! He stays right there. He doesn't let go of the diving board.

Now until you learn to let go of the diving board, you're not going to get off into the water. And you're not going to get into spirituality either until you let go of the earth. You cannot tread the Way fastened to earth, that's for sure. That is something you can't do.

Now all this time that we've been talking about letting go has been just the preamble of what you might call "The Great Let Go". That is when you really have to let it go, because there is no other way of doing it. And it doesn't make any difference who is your teacher; it is the same thing.

Going through these experiences reminds me of a picture where a person is seen walking down a hallway and approaching this "darkened door", as it is called. There were many doors leading off this hall and, as he went along, it grew a little bit lighter and lighter until he came right up against this darkened door. There some people would sort of back away, and start opening other doors to go in and look around. They found those doors opened up quite easily, and there were amusing things in these side rooms, very interesting things.

They'd start examining these side rooms along the hall, the path, or the Way. You know some of them really got lost in their amusement in those side chambers. But when they got down to that door, there was just plain nothing there, and it meant that they had to let go of everything and really go through. They had to really go through the "Grand Let Go".

And you know when you're talking to people on the street someone will say, "Oh, you should come over to our place. There's the most interesting speaker there, and they tell the most interesting things. You can get really wrapped up in it." And they'll tell you in detail what they have heard and what they have read of this person's literature, and so on. But nobody talks about what they have attained, or who has been healed, or who has been transformed or regenerated. You see, they got into the side rooms along the way, and they're still there and will be there for a long time—just as long as they want to be amused, believe me.

Now this same thing holds true when you first start in: the first exercise you are given as a student is to learn mind-control so that you are thinking about what you want to think about. We have told you how important it was to control your mind. You see, these little rooms off to the side of the passageway down to the jumping-off place are just like the recesses and chambers of your thinking, of your mind, that have kept you busy for so long. And I hope they're not keeping you busy now, because you're really going to stumble if they are.

All of these things, you see, are related, all the way down. This is sort of a thumbnail sketch of the approach to the Way: going down that central path of mind and the things that you want to think about. And that is when you have dedicated your life to the service of man, and giving to him that which the Master and the Father gave to you.

Now, there comes a time when you have gone into the pool, so to speak, off the diving board. You really made that third bounce and went in. That is when you let go and went through the door with both feet. Then life begins. Then regeneration begins. Then you start to realize what is really taught in the Testament.

The Way is narrow, that is true. In comparison to the whole universe or our solar system, the Way is extremely narrow. It is narrow when you compare it to all the antechambers of interesting things. But when you get on the Way, you will observe that your vision is extremely clear too, and you can see a long way off. No longer are you blinded by time nor the interim of space, nor things now present, because then you will have that long-range vision. Then you can see far away and can observe the many races, the many peoples and the many religions in operation, and see them truly, without any feeling of disturbance and without any prejudice. You haven't given up yourself totally until you can, because that is where it is.

You know, people get so used to being in gloom and in the shadows, that it is really hard on them when the sun shines all the time. Because they're so used to limiting themselves, it has become a habit. Even though they have let go, they still need to learn to enjoy the sunshine on this path. You've been so in the habit of carrying a load that, even after you put your foot on the way, you have the hardest time in the world trying to get rid of the imaginary pack that's been on your back all your life. You can't let go of the past either, and this is part of the problem.

So I'd advise you, once you have started on the Way, to look at the pack you're carrying. I think you'll find that there's very little inside it except the fact that it's hard for you to get used to not carrying it, you see. Jesus said, "My burden is light." He didn't explain that, but if you just carry the Light along with you, you won't have much of a load.

You'll find this is true all the way up the line. People have gotten so used to crucifying themselves that they can't let go of it. But somehow or other, you're going to be forced to let go of these things; because unless you do, there are going to be some people you'll want to walk alongside on the Way that you aren't going to be able to keep up with, because they dropped their burdens a long time ago. There is no place for carrying them on the Path. You may go through some initiations occasionally, or gain some greater realizations that will make you perspire a bit, but the good Master did this, and there won't be any more burdens to carry.

You have to get used to traveling light, and that's difficult sometimes, but there are lots of places you can't go unless you travel that way. I'm sure most of you have a great desire to move along at a good pace.

If you drop your burdens, why, you can go right along. And we have too much work to do and too many places to go to sit down and muddle over a lot of crazy ideas that we used to have.

Of course, you don't get in a hurry when "you" are out of the way. Unless you are on assignment someplace there's no real hurry, because you'll accomplish things sitting down as well as moving, you see. The most solid thing in the world is your spiritual attainment on the Path, the Great Way.

LIFE

The average individual has a great desire for Life. He has a great desire for spirituality, and of course most of that desire comes from within himself and from the attraction that the Self has for the Father, within Which it lives and has its being. But most people have not been informed that true life as a Christian means living as close as you can to these three principles of the Christ: Light, Life and Love; that you absorb and you live with these, and work with these, as closely as you can. Of course that may not be very close to the ultimate reality, but it will be an outstanding and out-shining example of Christianity if you do just that, as nearly as you can at the present time.

Don't try to condemn yourself for making mistakes, because the only real mistake you can ever make is if you stop trying and don't pick yourself up the next day and say, "Well, I did that yesterday, but I'm going on today." It is one of the sayings of the ancient schools that man's greatest mistake was not what he actually did that was wrong, but that he didn't pick himself up and try again. Not trying is one of man's greatest sins; and this is not a pacifier, by any means, but an absolute truth that has long been known.

Now the physical active life alone is a tremendously spiritual thing, and without life, that attribute from the Christ, you would be a pretty empty shell. Our experiences are recorded in the soul, around the Self; so you'd better live.

You know, one of the ways in which you can miss a few experiences, if you want to, is to just close yourself up. Close your mind, close your body, and just walk through life with a pair of blinders on, until something happens that takes you out. Though you may be able to escape learning for a lifetime, or even two, you're going to learn sooner or later. But if you LIVE—oh, I mean that with capitals too—then your experiences will be etched on the very record of your own being. This is why we try to lead you toward the reality of the God-Self: because only in this way can you add all the increments of the fullness of the vital way of moving and being, of life.

For goodness' sake, wake up and live! Or are you afraid that you'll find out the Truth and have to accept it? You know there's a lot of power there, don't think there isn't, but it's static when you have not lived, when you have not let the Spirit work. Don't try to figure out how you can run God; you can't do it. Or how you can run this world. You can't do that either, except through the power and the life and Spirit; and the quicker you learn how, the easier your life becomes.

It may seem strange to hear us speak of those things which have to do with this orb and that which will come after. But sooner or later you will learn, as you advance in understanding and experience, that we live this life not for this life alone, but for the lives to come. For only with preparation can we be ready and willing to play a greater role in the world in which we'll find ourselves when we return, or into whatever world we may go.

Each of our lives is actually a series of interludes or states of consciousness. Life, of course, is a continuance of all being. There is no point of mental rest—that is, no arresting of our consciousness—for we are conscious in one state or another continuously, at all times. We are continually moving forward in consciousness. Nothing is static in life, either on this plateau, or in the gradual ascent, though at times it may seem that life is a series of definite changes from one point of view, one conception or attitude, to another. These have to do with what we permit and what we accept—what we accept, too, in our mind, in relation to our being, one to another, or in the relation of our being to the Father and to the great Christ.

Life is a strange thing to watch in operation. You can sense it in the electromagnetic influences of organisms in the physical body. It will manifest as such, and yet the consciousness of it comes out of the being itself; and this is the channel through which it is brought into motivation. Actually, the Spirit is that which sets this life into motivation. And there is no question but that when we have decided what we are going to do in our lives, we will find a greater and a more magnificent fullness in this.

In time you will reach the point where you become happy with things around you because you're no longer searching for something. You'll have reached a point where you are satisfied to serve, and then you become acquainted with this little "L", life. And without being taught, you will learn how to be happy, to get a joy out of living; and believe me, you can.

You can get a tremendous boost out of living, because you know that all power and all force is with you. Living. Just breathing and living. And how can you feel this way? Because you know that as you live and breathe in the life force in the air that comes to you out of the Sun, you are taking in the Spirit, the life force that comes from the great

Christ above, the Christos. This is right from the very Mind, the very Being of God, the Creator. There is an absolute sublimity that comes with it.

Now, when you get anywhere near this point of living, you have reached something that can never be taken away from you. You have reached the thing that will let you work twenty hours a day and be happy doing it. Don't think that living is something to be learned. You've got to reach the point where you love to live, to breathe; where you walk along the street and it feels good to move. Don't you feel that power? Right down the line, you are feeling the Spirit of God move through you! This is a dynamic, moving thing. Until you've got that fire inside of you, until you can truly live, you're like a candle without a match—you get as much light out of it.

You know, what we breathe in are the tiny sparks and charges of light. I hear people say, "I get so tired out." Yes, I know. Well, that's your pattern of living—getting tired out. Now, there are a lot of times when I like to sit down and have a cup of coffee or something of that sort, for a few minutes, but it's all in the upper story up here. You haven't yet reached the point where you're not afraid of giving, and therefore you're going to be tired after a certain number of hours. You've laid it all out in your mind that: "when I get through with this day of seven or eight hours, that's my time to be tired."

You can sit and watch people move, and enjoy their movement, even with all the stupidity and that sort of thing, because it is God's power moving through them that makes it possible. It is most interesting to watch the person that God created move and express himself in this world, and whether in the slums or on Park Avenue it's all the same. They all move the same way. They all express the same thing, knowing it or not. And practically any person who will come out on the street and sit for two or three hours and truly put their attention on people moving through the Mind of God will realize things that they never knew existed before.

How can you watch the reality of life in action and movement without sensing, without picking up that infinite spark of divine Reality? You have to sense it. Just as when, if you keep perfectly quiet, you must hear. You must hear that resounding sound. Our great trouble is in acquiring the simplicity. If we can keep still long enough to be simple, if we can keep quiet long enough, we will let things happen in a normal way.

If you really want something to meditate on, sit down and meditate on life and see how much you know about it; see how much you have really lived. Oh, you breathe, partially; you have eaten, you have been from here to there. But have you lived, really? I think I could safely say that most people have lived just about fifty or sixty percent, if that. If you had really lived, you would be so free and full of life that you couldn't have done wrong, because wrong cannot exist where perfection is the pattern of existence.

Life is perfect. You cannot live it all the way and be imperfect, because life will swallow you up if you use it wrong. Watch somebody walk and see if they're just picking 'em up and laying 'em down; or are they floating along? Are they conscious of their body? Are they really conscious of the person next to them? There is a difference between living life and just existing. With life, you are vigorous spiritually as well as physically. I've seen a lot of high-tension, high-pressure people who went through a lot of lively motions and were almost dead inside. That is not living life.

You have got to feel life, and to feel it flow through you, not just up here on top—because that's where most people's life is—but in your hands and in your body, even down there in your big toe. Is it alive, or are you partly dead? Now, I'm really not being facetious; because when you are alive the Spirit moves through you, and when you are alive, you can sit there and feel life all through. You are living, living! It's a reality.

Now let us stop here and close our eyes, and then tell me if you feel life. How about it? That's a new discovery; that belongs to the Aquarian Age. Now try and keep that with you and you'll be surprised how many of your problems you will have gotten rid of. Just live this coming week. Don't exist, live! And all of these things will have passed away.

He said Life is eternal, didn't he? Well, if it's eternal, then it isn't going to stop. So you're going to have to put up with living, whether you like it or not.

LIGHT

All through the New Testament and through the ancient wisdom teachings we hear of what is called illumination and this, which is very much misunderstood by most people, is really the receiving consciously of the light of Christ within man. Now it doesn't mean, as some writers or teachers would have you think, that only when they get through working with you have you received all the light you ever had. This is contrary to all physiology and biochemistry. It is impossible that man could live without light, because light is a basic source of energy through which life manifests. And life manifests in the physical body because of the light energy from which it comes.

In studies on plant life and various other subjects, educators tell us that we get our life and our growth from the sun. But when they talk about religion, that's different; they've changed their whole idea. Light isn't then considered a source of our knowing ourselves or of our inner growth because, of course, they think that things such as spiritual growth and mind control don't take energy, so it would have nothing to do with the sun at all, or with the Christ. Well, this is pretty absurd for people to accept, regardless of who teaches them.

If you were to make a study of the raw ultraviolet from the sun's rays before it goes through the atmosphere of our earth and your atmosphere, you would find that it was a pretty deadly thing to the average growth of most people. But after it has been filtered out—and if you had control of your atmosphere you'd probably do a little filtering too it then becomes a useful thing, and you have growth. If you studied it very closely, you'd find that science is perfectly correct in that the ultraviolet from the sun penetrates the physical body only through the two layers of skin. It will go to the dermis and there's about where it stops. You get a little heat reaction below that from the little bit of infrared that exists around it, but beyond that it is pretty much stopped. And of course, you get the suntan when you go out wearing a bikini, and if you get a good dose of that, then you have trouble.

But something more does happen. From the sun's rays you pick up some part of the ultraviolet through the spiritual body, and through this it is fed into the chemical structure and absorbed, so that you get the light into the physical body again. Now there is something different about the common ultraviolet rays and those of which we are speaking. The ultraviolet that we are talking about, while it does have a part in growth, has two rays of energy and frequency—different frequencies, incidentally, which are composed of the sun's rays. One of them you don't see, but it is there and its reaction can be calculated mathematically, although this is in its infancy, as far as what most people know about it. But it is there, and it is a sort of light which you don't see very much of until you strike some resistance within the structure of the human body itself.

To this light we have given the name of the Christos, the Christ light, and it is very aptly named because that is what it is. The reason you do not know that you have some light within you is because you are not conscious of it, primarily; and you must become conscious of it in order to find it. You see, if you were taught over a period of years that no such thing exists, why pretty soon, no such thing exists—it doesn't exist in your world anyway, as far as you are concerned. But it is existent in what happens when we start to receive the Christ light or the illumination.

You can go down to the library and find twenty books on how to receive the illumination. And when somebody finds one that gives a distinct process of it, I hope they will show it to me, because I've been looking for one for about the last thirty years. Now, the reality of the light can be attained, but not through the sort of thing most people are talking about. By light they usually mean understanding, and we're not talking about understanding at all; we're talking about the reality of the Light. We're talking about the reality of receiving the Christ. This is what happened at the River Jordan when Jesus was baptized.

This is what we are referring to when we speak of the initiations you would have found in the ancient mystery schools. They would be talking about something like the eighth or ninth initiation, usually the ninth, the last one on the physical plane. But this is unimportant. The important thing is that this is the time when regeneration starts. When once you have started to become conscious of the light and you start to receive it, then regeneration can start. This is the starting of eternal life; and it is eternal, though not in the physical body.

This is why Jesus, when he came out of the tomb, said, "Touch me not, for I have not fully ascended", because his body was becoming a light body, and he was building it after he had come out of the tomb. And this is the body that he took when he arose and returned to the Father. Putting it on a practical scientific approach, we can say that Jesus did think in accordance with the laws of physics and chemistry and he didn't necessarily pull any magic wand to do it. Some things he did through the laws of alchemy, and some he did because he knew the Word and how to use it. We hear about the vehicles, the chariots and all these things. These are very simply your spiritual bodies. In the Bible we read of a fiery chariot which came out of heaven. That is nothing more than a great soul who came and spoke and left a streak of great light after him.

Light is just what it says it is, and because it is so simple is the reason it is hard to understand. That is why it is hard for us to get our teeth into the things which really happen. There are some schools that you might go to for twenty or thirty years and not really acquire any great degree of illumination. But believe me, it isn't just a matter of getting to the point where you begin to find the light within. You'd better work on it thereafter, because otherwise you are not going to be very highly successful. This is only the start of things; it doesn't mean that you have already attained your wings, by any means.

Sometimes people get a little slovenly with some of these things and don't work with them. It is important that a person not only receive the Light, but nurture it. You know how a seed is planted and nurtured? Well, this is the same thing. You receive it, then you have to take care of it. You have to preserve it and increase its strength and life. You have to give it consideration and not reach for something else until you are able to take care of what you've got. You'll get to something else just as soon as you can handle rightly what you've got.

Illumination can be had by anybody regardless of what church they go to or what "ism" they have found. This has nothing to do with it. As we read in Matthew 4:16: "The people who sat in darkness have seen a great light, and for those who sat in the region and the shadow of death, light has dawned." Why? He took on the illumination at this time, the starting of it. The Path has been illumined, you see, and no longer the shadow of death. That Light had to pass through him. He was the one through which it was possible for the light to come to the people of earth—and in this day, the way it is doing right now.

The Scriptures speak of the ancient serpent and dragon; and man for many years has held forth and created his own form of devil. There is a lack of light in some places, and where there is no light there must be darkness. But the Light shall fill the darkness, and the darkness shall be no more. Man's concept of the absence of Christ, or the Light through our Lord Jesus Christ, is his own creation, his own concept. These images of darkness come in many shapes, and in older religions they took many forms that people looked to and used.

It is said, in that hour in which ye think not he will come. This is very old, and it is true that when we are truly seeking and when we have let go and given up, this is the time when the Light comes in. It is when we have let go of all earthly concepts, when we have let go of all things and said, "Here I am", that the great Light of Christ will come in and flood our vehicles, flood our bodies, and here will be revealed the inner light, the Light that never fails. But the message that is important in this context is the fact that it is now the time.

I don't know if you can catch this thing. You see, the Light of the Christos that fills our atmosphere forms the substance of the body of our Lord. Thus, when we pass through illumination and really attain it, we move toward it to raise the vibration of our whole being, and then it becomes part of the Body of Christ. Through the illumination and the light, we energize every gland in the body, and it is at this time we see that people have their extreme ups and downs.

When you let the power of the Christ come into you, it will show as Light within you. Where there is Spirit it will manifest as light, because that is the nature of the Spirit. There is the knowing, and the Light and Life and Love. All three facets have the intelligence of the Self and of the other two. We can't possibly have received illumination and worked on it and gained the fullness of it without having a little love. Otherwise, you need to work at it some more.

In speaking of the solar initiation, what do you think was meant by the New Jerusalem in the Book of Revelation?

Q: That the body would go through the illumination?

A: Now we're getting someplace. Certainly, regeneration has set in. The new body is being built, descending out of heaven, isn't it?

Q: What is meant when it says that the twelve gates will not be shut by day? And it says there will be no night.

A: That's right. All the sources of light will be present; because if you have illumination, and all the other people have it too, they won't need much more light, will they?

"You are the light of the world." He was talking to his disciples. You have never seen this, probably, but if you could get above the physical— still in the physical world, but above the plane of the surface of the earth— at night, and were able to see spiritually, you'd see those lights. They're visible; you're just looking at something that nobody ordinarily sees. If you could get above the earth and see spiritually, then you could see here and there little dots of light and groups of them all over the globe. Living lights, just moving around like a lot of little lightning bugs.

Q: Is that why people usually stop by here at night?

A: That's right. Many of the people were guided here by the Light. Do you think if a Master was trying to find this place, that he'd have to stop and ask directions? No, sir.

So anybody that is carrying the light and bringing the light, and giving it to the world and to other people—you see, I made a distinction in that, to the world and to other people. There is a distinction. You can give it to other people without giving it to the world, and there are some who will give it to the world, but not as much to other people. Of course, eventually these two things will cohere and become as one.

When we understand this, then there will be no feeling of difference between ourselves in any group and others who are out there truly doing the work, regardless of what they call themselves or what they call their organization. It makes no difference; because there is an invisible kingdom, an empire of persons who, regardless of whether they are in an order or a church or other organization, still work and still are doing the same job that we are. Let us not be fooled by words and names. The only criterion is whether they've got it and whether they give it. And this is most important.

When you go out to a job, to a mission, or when you talk to somebody on the street to help them, know one thing: that you are not alone doing this! There is a vast empire that is with you, unknown and unseen, but which still exists, and you are part of it.

LOVE

Light, Life and Love, the three "L's", are the way in which the Christ brings life, growth and development. And it is also the thing that helps to bring on epigenesis or grace, because the growth has to be substantiated by the Life and the Light within which we live.

As we go along through the studies, we have shown Light: which strengthens the spiritual body, Life: which works through the soul, and Love: which works through the flesh body of man, not only in its relationship with man and woman, but also in its relationship to the ultimate of the Self and the gaining of illumination on the Way.

Light, Life and Love: these three attributes all work together. Now, you'll hear this: "Oh, if you only would demonstrate some love." But you cannot demonstrate love unless you are using the other two; you have to use all three in order to demonstrate love. So all this that is printed on the subject of loving and this sort of thing—you know most of them wouldn't give you thirty minutes of their time to save your life, to say nothing about working eight or nine months or a couple of years in order to learn how to really demonstrate love. In the first place, most of them have very little Light. In the second place about, say, fifty percent of them out there are walking corpses, and Light and Life don't demonstrate through this. Of course, they may cut up a few capers and move around, but that in itself is not Life that's going to come naturally and stick with you.

Because this is God's way, the Father's way of getting through to you on this plane of existence. Without the Christ, you cannot get through, and neither does He get through, except through this; because from the Son comes the Light and the Life. And it is through this that the Law, when it is given and the Word is given forth, is motivated into existence. This is very fine to talk about, but believe me, it is something that few people want to do, and there are few people who will pay the price to show any real love.

There is also the fact that when we really and truly love some one, or a group of people, it is pretty hard to say, "I love just this group of people." No, that can't be done, not by the person who is teaching truly the Word of the Christ. You have to love all people for the Life which they represent and are manifesting—no matter how little, but that they are manifesting—because it is part of the Creation. And we know that the Self is there, though this is not being manifested in the way it would be if they understood.

There are few who love people well enough to say "no" to them or to correct them, or to try to really help them, because they're always afraid they're not going to be liked after they've told them what they feel should be said. Or they won't speak up to someone who is doing wrong because they "love 'em too much". Well, if they loved them at all they'd tell them, because love is the thing that brings forth true sacrifice. And love is a thing that will lay its efforts and its desires and its wants upon the altar for the purpose of helping another man or woman. Anything less than that is not love, it is purely emotion. It is not the all-encompassing Love.

Jesus didn't have that sort of love, and he didn't tolerate it while he was on the earth. He forgave, yes. So must you. But you have to learn what true love is, the love that disregards any personal feeling between the other person and you. And until you've got it that way, you haven't got it. You have selfish love, and nothing else but that.

Now I'm not saying that man and woman cannot love one another. They certainly can, but very few of them want to demonstrate it. If they really did, there wouldn't be as many divorces and there wouldn't be as many unhappy homes as there are.

When you reach the place where you can begin to understand Jesus, when you can listen to him and feel his presence, then you can really begin to understand what love is, because you will know what it is, that it isn't this sort of thing that most people are talking about. No, it is the kind that, when it is felt, sets you into action. You're ready to get going and do something about it, not sit there and go ga-ga. That's not love; that's just laziness, plain and simple. Because the moment you have it, you cut off everything around you and become lazy. Now just think about it.

In 2 John 6, he writes: "This is love, that we walk after His commandments." And this is the kind of love that expects nothing in return. It is the kind of love that gives without expecting, and it is the tough kind of love to attain, because you know the truth, that you can't give without getting. But if you can obliterate the last part of that and really give without really expecting anything back, honestly, then you will know true love. This is the love that gives and says and does because it is right. It is truth and it is real.

You love nature, and you love the Master, surely you do, but you're here to love the people with all their perfections and imperfections. Don't leave out the perfections! And this is what you do, very often. You leave out the perfections and look at the imperfections. But see the perfections in that person. Sometimes you have to look awfully hard, but they're there; and you're giving that person comfort. That's what we're here for. That's what I'm here to teach you for, until a greater Teacher comes. That's what you must learn to do, because if you dwell only on the imperfections, that is the only thing that will have life. And this is not what we want. The first message that any child understands is the love that is given, and he gives his love back.

MANKIND

We have many young men and women coming into the spiritual work who have been brought up under the mass mind, where people feel that they are distinctly individualists. While they do, each one, carry the divine gift of choice, they still are part of the great Creative Power and Intelligence that this solar system is made of. They gain their freedom according to a plan that has been used for thousands of years. So it is perfectly natural that the student is seeking to know and understand himself according to one of the oldest and most famous of sayings, "Man, know thyself", which came out of a school other than Christianity, but which is all the same thing.

He naturally says, "Well, who am I?", meanwhile striving to know himself, and to attain true realization. Now, we're not talking about understanding; we're talking about how he has found the Self, knows it and works with it. This is a reality. This Self is the being that God spoke about in the first chapter of Genesis when "He made man in His own image."

But here comes the problem that we face today—we've had it for years, but we haven't faced it—that each individual, while they may seek their own spiritual attainment and to climb Jacob's ladder, as it is sometimes called, the ladder of initiation, they carry with them a debt, their karma. They might have attained, through much labor and much conscientious prayer, the ability to reach up to any stage of development, but still they are a cell in the great Being of the Creator. They would have to be.

Each person has a responsibility to the whole race of man, no matter where they are. We have heard many times on this earth about brotherhood, and yet in the very essence of this presupposed brotherhood we find in each person an egotistical individuality. But as man climbs this ladder, he owes to every person one thing, and that is to respect that his brother is also a cell of the same Being that he came from.

Now it doesn't make any difference what the form is, whether the person is male or female, whether of the brown race or the yellow or the white race. It doesn't make a bit of difference. That cell looks the same in all people, with the exception of the change of radiation which is caused by your thinking and your own consciousness.

Now you have a responsibility, and in my mind it is a number one responsibility—I have to say number two in a sense, because the first Commandment says, "Thou shalt love the Lord thy God with all thy heart, with all thy soul and with all thy might." And how can you love God without loving all of it? I know this may hit you a little hard, because I'm going to be stepping on a lot of egos that think they're real special.

Now, who are you? To begin with, you are a cell of the great Creative Being; and I often use this term because it doesn't carry any doctrinal reaction. It doesn't carry any religious presuppositions to set it in any one category; but it does carry with it the fact that you're a fool if you don't acknowledge It, because that is the Source that your life comes from. It does not take the name of any religion, but It does call Itself the Creator. As far as I'm concerned, it doesn't matter what It is; but I'm living in It's body, and I'm not fool enough to turn off the switch from where my power comes.

You may think me the most unholy man that you've ever heard talk about God, but just the same, I like to have results; and we know what set of switches to turn off and what to leave alone and leave on. And the one you don't want to turn off is the Source of all supply. So the number one thing that I am is a cell in the body of the Creator.

Now what I do with that cell and how I got down to this degraded state, or elevated state, or whatever state it might be, I'm not going to spend time worrying about, because I'm here. The only thing I've got to worry about is how I'm going to handle it, that's all. Now, I might have been the right-hand man of old Melchizedek himself, but if I can't use enough of this power at the present time to get out of this world the things that I need, and even before that if I can't communicate with one of my co-parts, I've surely made an awful failure of myself.

Because, you know, in the human body the parts do get along. They get along marvelously well, for the way they're treated. And one organ of the body will take over part of the functions of something else, when that organ sort of starts to lie down because the load has gotten too great. And if in one part of the brain a few cells get destroyed, why, some other cells take over the load and start to do the job. If we'd get our parade on the same basis that the human organism operates, we wouldn't have very much trouble in this world, believe me, we wouldn't.

The one thing I do know is that, first of all, I must acknowledge the Creator. Secondly, I must acknowledge every single individual alike, and I don't care whether he's a student, priest or prince; he's a cell in the divine Creator, the Source of power. And you see, if I don't cut him off there will be force that he'll draw that I can have the use of too. But when I start cutting people off of me, that's when I start going downhill.

We talk about brotherly love, but until you have something of that sort, you haven't learned the reality of seeing a real person. You've just been looking at somebody's face and flesh. That isn't him, that's the vehicle that carries him. If he's an advanced person, it is just the beast that he rides, that's all. And when you get to recognize man truly, you will look and recognize the being himself, the Self and soul, because that's all there is to the man, and this is the way you have to acknowledge it, though it may be sometimes pretty hard to do. That is all there is; there's nothing else. That Self is close to the soul, and you must learn to know this.

You know, you can fake all you want to, and it isn't going to do you one bit of good, because you can't fake this. You can put on all the appearances in the world and the other person still knows where you stand. He may be the most ignorant man in the world, but he still knows what the score is. He knows it through intuition, and he'll act on it. And the more primitive he is, the more reaction he will have to that, because he isn't thinking as much. He's reacting to your own knowledge through his primitive knowledge.

The key saying, "Man, know thyself", came out of the old school; this was their main striving. Of course, once they did this all the other avenues of service were open, and they followed whatever path they chose to follow. It is probably one of the most guaranteed ways to have a happy life, because it will be a life in which you will be contented with what you're doing, and you won't be whisked around like a chip on an ocean wave. This is the difference between knowing yourself and just knowing something about the world out there.

Many people know things of the world, even from the philosophical point of view, but they don't know themselves. Of course, a lot of times I can't blame them, because they don't want to look in the mirror to see what's there. And you can understand that, I'm sure; you have probably tried it. But if you really do know yourself, then you will know the possibilities; you will know how you are created, and how you can function.

The first chapter of Genesis distinctly states that God made man in His own image; so you must be a creator too, mustn't you? It is time to throw away the stuff that you learned in kindergarten, and what you learned out there in the "club of confusion", and start thinking in the image of the Master, start to learn how things function, really.

You have the ability to create. How do you do it? You declare what you want and then God fulfills it, doesn't He? His Word was spoken in the beginning, and it will fulfill that which you put to it to be fulfilled. Does He reach out and tap you on the shoulder and say, "Yes, James, I'll give that to you."? Don't get puffed up; He'll never do that. Here you have the Father (positive), and you (negative), and here you have the earth. Whatever comes to the earth comes through you, and that makes you responsible for your world.

Changes have been made in the earth, and they are being made, because they're still going on in some people. And you realize that what is in the mass mind and what the people radiate, that's what the earth is going to be like. Plain and simple. And that's why we fight against these wars and so forth.

What the people think and what the people do and bring into reality is going to determine what the influence of the planet will be, and this is what the Master has brought to a head, you might say, because we're coming into a new age.

When God said that He made man in His own image, He meant it, and that is what He did. Do you understand? Now, it is pretty hard to conceive of that size. And someday or other you may have the experience of taking a look at this universe in its entirety, which will be an initiation for you, or part of an initiation.

This sounds like an impossibility, probably, like stretching the imagination; but I have seen men, I have seen teachers, whose aura would fill these two rooms. This is a measly little man, a tiny speck of carbon, that's all you are. Some of you may have had the perspective of seeing this orb as it really looks and the people moving upon it? We're awful, awful small. And yet in that tiny little spot is the power to move a mountain! Jesus said so and I know it is so. Until we get this concept, we don't have it; we have neither the ability to teach nor to become a minister or a priest. To do this, you have to have the unflinching, unmovable knowing that your word is law over all matter.

Q: You were saying we descend into experience and then rise back up again?

A: That's right. You take with you the good experiences, and if you get rid of the others, why then, you're all set.

Q: Why is earthly experience now more dense?

A: Well, you're having experiences in a dense world, aren't you?

Q: Yes, but why is it more dense than it was before?

A: Because the wave lengths of vibration and frequency that are here are much denser. That works out chemically and according to the laws of physics.

Q: I understand that. But wasn't it kind of high in the beginning? What made it slow down and get lower?

A: Well, because we decided to go into involution in order to attain the experience of all worlds, so that we might be like our Father in heaven.

Q: Did He cause that?

A: No, man decided he'd like to. It was by our choice that we did it, or wanted to do it. And it wasn't an error or a sin or anything of that sort. Just a matter of experience.

The unending or the eternal life, as we call it, is the final gauge of those who can survive the last days; and those who learn to control the forces around them will survive that day. Those who do not learn to control them, with the mind and the Law and the use of those things taught by the Master, will not survive and will not be here.

God has graciously bestowed upon us the tools that man may use for a happy and capacious life. Not only happiness but a breadth of movement unconfined by anything which might be in the mass mind. Man is his own determiner—not what your neighbor thinks, but what you know—if you know the use of the power and the Word as it was given in Creation.

We are not talking of a philosophy, we are not talking about my opinion or your opinion, we are talking about the forces of nature in action. This is the use of power and force, and how it functions and how you can control it.

MASTER TEACHER

Q: Discuss briefly a master teacher. I guess he is one who "lets go and lets God"?

A: Yes, that's the real answer, but to discuss it... Well, he's one who follows the way of teaching the people from one incarnation to another. His is the way of the teacher of the priesthood. He has no personal karma himself; he takes on the karma of other people very often, and disperses it when he sees this as a benefit.

When you ask him for help, he is bound by the rules of the order, by the rules of the Masters, to give help according to the Lord of the planet in which he's working. His mind isn't worth very much, because he doesn't really have one, not while he's working under the influence of a Messianic being, at least. If he goes where mind is extremely useful, why he would take on that aspect and use it.

He has the ability to leave this body when he pleases. He is able to use the four elements of creation. He is the Fool in the Tarot, in a sense. A teacher has but one goal, and that is to bring individuals into spiritual reality. He actually doesn't have anything to want here, because he really doesn't live here most of the time, I'd say. He'd be in a body, but that is no particular criterion of where he is at the moment.

I don't know whether I've hit what you're looking for or not, but he can set the pattern in a person's life so that they will get straightened out, that is sure. In this age, he has the gift of illumination, if he is willing to pay the price for it to be given. Does that answer your question? There might be a few things I've left out, but this is basically it.

We are coming into a new form of teacher who is a little bit of everything. He must be all-encompassing, or he won't make it. He must be able to function above. The teacher now must live in the world, but not be of it. In order to produce balanced, fulfilled students to the point where he can bring them through, he cannot sit about cross-legged and praying all day. He must do something. We have to demonstrate that activity.

You can't bring them up to heaven and drop them there. You must help them to attain a balanced life. You can do more in a relaxed way, with laughter, than with a long face, as though humanity were a dirty thing. You can get to the individual in a relaxed way, because then his guard is down. If you can get one sentence in, you've done a great deal. But sometimes you must do a lot of talking to get through, to get that one sentence in.

Through lifetimes, you get trained in all the workings of the universe, until you have attained this, and then the mantle of the mastership falls. There is a difference in the prerogative and obligation. The master teacher may be a priest, that's true, but he wasn't always, necessarily. He could be a true master teacher and not necessarily have any priestly obligations, because what he taught might be strictly from the Self within, which did not put him in a place where he had an obligation in a priesthood. He might, over some periods of time, of lifetimes or lifespans, have been a priest. Unquestionably he might have, because it is a stepping stone. At the present time of existence, it is essential that he should have been a priest in the old schools.

In every true Teacher, there is always the hope that he will have some student who will become more proficient and a better teacher than he; and if this does not exist, then he is a false teacher. We've seen it in the sciences, we've seen it in music and in the arts. A true teacher always tries to perfect his student, tries to give him something which will make him outstanding. This is a natural thing, and it is a thing which we call selfless giving. Here is where the great world performers have come from, the great artists and artisans, the great scientists. And of course, in our day and age we have seen many of these people, but always they are the kind who are not worried too much about the actual material things of the world in compensation.

As a little sidelight on that, a Sufi teacher was talking to me tonight, and he said, "I have recently met so many who said they were teachers, but you know something? I don't find that their students or their disciples have reached any degree of illumination or realization. I don't understand, but my idea is this: there's a difference between a school teacher and a teacher of God-realization, a vast difference."

And there is a good criterion to go by: when he puts a price on it, that's one down; you can forget him. Don't even give him a second look, because no genuine Teacher ever put a price on anything. I would starve before I'd do that; I wouldn't dare, believe me. I don't starve, but I don't have any money either. Don't need it.

Now, this isn't about myself; I'm talking about teachers generally. I'm talking about something that it's very well time to get aired, because there are too many people being waylaid that are looking for Truth and looking for reality. And the fallacy that is being perpetrated amongst many young folks smells to high heaven. I'm not using any names, and I won't. Let the ax fall where it will, because it can only hit the guilty.

Save your time and pick up your Christian Bible, even though you're not a church-going person, and if you can't do anything else, read the four gospels carefully, and don't interpret them. Don't interpret them, and you may get something out of that work that you didn't realize was there.

Q: In some classes there seems almost too much to concentrate on, or to focus on any particular thing. What is a good way of assimilating the whole thing without avoiding any particular aspect of it?

A: Forget it. That's the truth. To memorize by rote is probably the worst thing you can do, not only for the purpose of service to others, but it is also the worst thing you can do in order to give a good answer to another individual. Because the answer which you have memorized does not fit the individual who asked that question.

Therefore, as far as you're concerned, learn really well the basic functions of the forces of nature and God, and then just go on about your business and forget the whole works, because if you have truly learned, it has left its impression on your soul. And then when the time comes that somebody asks a question in which that particular information is pertinent, you will find that not only is that information there, but just a wee little bit of something else that you learned some other time.

If you are studying mathematics, you only remember the basic factors and the basic procedure of mathematics. If you know what the force of God is, you know what the Spirit is, you know how the soul reflects, you know how people's minds function, roughly. This is unpredictable in most cases, but if you do know this generally, then with the aid of the great wisdom within you, the real teacher, the Self, you'll come up with the proper answer. You'll have the basics to work with, or the factors that you feed into the computer, and it will come up with the answer, even though you haven't studied the subject or the person. This is the beauty of studying philosophy in a true manner. It's a perfectly simple thing, nothing mysterious.

So never worry about memorizing anything, except to remember the law of Cause and Effect, the law of the Trinity, the law of Assumption; and the number-one thing that you must remember is that God comes first. If you remember these things, you won't have any worry about the rest of it, because with these four simple statements, all things in the universe can be solved. And there isn't any question about what is right or what is wrong; they all conform. Mathematics, chemistry, physics, all the rest of them conform to these four simple rules and the multiplicity of them in their combinations together. Does that answer your question?

The student, having worked under the framework of various religions, comes to the Teacher and lays all at his feet, then becomes afraid, because he's beginning to get a picture of the reality of the cosmic, which has no framework! The person who does a good job of teaching will move things gradually, so the student discovers it himself, and he never knows it was given him. He realizes it himself. He has gotten hold of something he'll keep and will put into action, and he's happy because he discovered it.

I have taught classes and have taught people individually, and it always takes about six months before they wake up to find that you've said something. Because when you have an egotistical person, there is one thing he's not going to do! He's not going to accept anything you say until his outer being has forgotten it, and then he remembers it, and then it is his; you never told him. That's the reality of teaching, and that is a fact.

Many times when you are being told how to do something to approach realization or illumination, you're very respectful to the person who is teaching you. You sit quietly with ears on each side of the head. I didn't say they were open though, because while you're sitting there looking at him, you're thinking about something else that you want to think about. Never suppose that we don't know about it, don't fool yourself. But we are not going to stop to call everybody because they're sitting staring at us while doing their own thinking inside.

You're just going to have to wait and try, and sometimes do a little bit of suffering too, because you can't do it, you can't concentrate, or you can't seem to get rid of this or that. Well, of course you can't, because you haven't been listening. You have gone through the physical motions, but someplace in there you drew a line, so nothing came in except the things you wanted to think about, then you were perfectly comfortable, but you were rejecting the teacher or the speaker at the time.

Let's lay it down basically and fundamentally: you can't go into a school and accept a master teacher unless you wholly accept him and follow his instructions. Neither can you live on this earth and have the benefits of the Master Teacher of it, the Lord Jesus Christ, if you don't wholly accept him and do what he tells you to. And if he were to do the same as the teacher in a house or a school might do, he'd say "get out". But Jesus doesn't have to say it; you get out in suffering and everything else, because you're cut off. You cut yourself off. He doesn't have to do it; you cut yourself off.

When I say, "Don't read that book now", I'm speaking as your teacher, I'm not laying down the law for the world. One of the first things to consider in teaching is that you are not teaching a subject, you are teaching a body, a body controlled not only by the habits of an individual, but of past life. In your contact with that body, you use your own forces, your own word, with forces coming from that body, to contact the spiritual body. Teaching a subject is different—moving into a subject and breaking it down to teach an idea.

But here you are taking several subjects, because there are several things that need to be acknowledged, trained out of the individual. You are doing in reverse what you teach the student to do. We teach him to forget the past, and let it die gradually and become less active, having less to do with his own personal life. If he had an experience of an extreme ego which got him into trouble, you let him forget about this, but you work on it, giving him something to do which will blow his ego up and then disintegrate it.

One who is going to teach must get in mind that he follows the basic form, and never mind whether anybody likes it or whether it appeals to them or not. We're not interested in that, because we can appeal to vast thousands if we want to put out a lot of gibberish to those who say, "Give us all the trimmings and folderol, because we can read this and be amused, and we won't have to get tangled up in the reality and be responsible for it." You can sell almost anything as long as it's pretty and doesn't give any distinct truth that gives you any responsibility; and much metaphysics is written on that basis. Confuse it, make it attractive, make it interesting so they can take half a dozen connotations out of it, and they're happy. But put it down in the nitty-gritty class and you've got problems; they don't want it.

Now, this is where it sits, and this is what we're up against. So you might just as well learn the realities and deal them out that way and forget the rest, then you'll be gleaning the real good wheat out of the harvest; because the good wheat will accept and they will come with you. The other, the chaff, will get blown away, and you will keep the kernels which are good. And this, after all, is what we are seeking.

MEDITATION

Meditation is a conscious form of reaching the Christ, so that you are halfway between here and there, and at that point you can receive from the Mind of the Father the information you wish or the state of consciousness that you wish to attain. And this is true meditation. Meditation is not sitting down, and within three minutes going sound asleep and then waking up and saying, "Well now, wasn't that a beautiful meditation." I never bother to argue with it, because they demonstrated where their consciousness was.

Sleep is an entirely different thing. In sleep usually, unless you're terribly hidebound, you leave your physical body and go just outside of it, at least, so as to give the chemical structure of your physical body a chance to recuperate and rebuild, through its natural sources of absorption of energy and the intelligence of the cell structure itself, which is a function that comes out of the soul, basically.

But meditation is a distinct determinate process of asking a question, or setting up the pattern of a question, and then going into a quiet state in which you cease to think, and listen instead of thinking—which is difficult, of course, at times. Then in your mind, or in the Self, or in the senses in some form, sometimes audibly, sometimes otherwise, you will receive the answer which you seek. In meditation the answers can come through feeling, they can come through words, or they can come through visual pictures.

But the two, meditation and sleep, are not similar at all. The body always needs a certain amount of quiet time in which the being removes itself so as to let it be quiet. And, of course, then we can be active on the other plane of function while the body is recuperating.

Long sleep is not necessary. You can sometimes gain more rest in shorter periods, and maybe two or three of those periods; but there's no predicting what the individual needs, really, because all people are different, and the actual amount of sleep necessary is determined upon, to a certain extent, by the resistance they have to life and the functions in life.

Q: If you have set your pattern for a meditation, and have actually gone into meditation and fallen asleep, can an answer come in the sleep state, or is the question lost?

A: Someone might fall asleep but, for instance, if he said, "I want to know in what way to get rid of this psoriasis", which maybe he had, and he went to sleep, the answer might actually perform the cure, in reality. He might not hear the answer if he fell asleep, but would get the results.

Or on the other hand, if he fell asleep and it was necessary that the question be answered in word or picture or something of that sort, why, it might just pass on beyond, and sometime in the near future there might come to his mind the answer to his meditation.

Now you can sit down and go into meditation and can gain a state of peace and quiet, or you can gain a state where there is no disturbance. But peace and no disturbance are two different things. Coming to a state of nondisturbance is still not meditation. Meditation requires some definite knowledge and definite ways of approach. It is not merely a matter of sitting still and being blank and seeing what happens. There are definite ways of approaching these things.

You may sit quietly and meditate, and may gain considerable peace. You may gain an understanding of some things, even things about yourself, if you can get out of the way enough to listen. But the actual attainment of spiritual, lasting quality, that something which changes you, is only existent where you, with your senses, have moved among the things of the world in action, and you still retain some understanding of those things and those people. This is a functional attainment.

The Eastern schools understand meditation. They have the information and they know how to meditate, but most of them won't come out and teach openly the whole truth and the inner workings, as they would be taught behind the walls of their own organization.

Meditation doesn't necessarily function in bringing something into creation unless the Law is applied and you declare this. For meditation is an active rather than an inactive thing. Now, some people have the idea that meditation means sitting down and doing nothing for hours at a time. Well, it is active, really one of the most active things that a being can be engrossed in, because he is saying to the soul and the Self that he is looking for information on something. And at the same time he is saying to the greater Intelligence, "Let's get it through. We have a need here some place, so I'm going to stop all the machinery and all the starting mechanisms and open a channel and let You come through. I have stopped thinking. You know what I want. I've put it in the computer, now I want the answers."

And so the person stops thinking, but doesn't blank out his mind. If he blanks out his mind, the vibrations can't come through because there isn't any feedback there. And so he sits there, and he "acts". The mind is actively alive and his whole system is functioning, and if that answer is in the Self, or in the soul through your experience, it will come through into your consciousness. You won't think it—it will be there.

Now it doesn't necessarily come out in red letters and capitals, or some specific form of writing or something of that nature. It may come out in any one of half a dozen different ways, according to your personality and what fits, and what's going to work best with you.

There are two polarities of consciousness, but only one type of meditation and one type of concentration. If you go beyond that, you get into contemplation, which is a combination, really, of both of these things.

Q: You can't go into contemplation until you have learned to meditate or concentrate?

A: No, it won't work, because you need to have absolute control. There is also the sort of semi-sleep state, when you are not really asleep nor really awake, but just kind of between here and there.

Q: In this state you wouldn't rise far above a psychic type of thing, would you?

A: No, you wouldn't, because to go above this you really have to either project yourself out or move out, one or the other. And this is not really very difficult or complicated, as far as that's concerned, once the body is clean and in shape and you have strength enough and power enough to do it. But some people try this when they don't have good clean bodies, and then they have troubles. That's always the case.

That is where the teaching of some forms of meditation, and some of the various concoctions that people create, expose you to all kinds of trouble. Because as quick as you get out of your physical vehicle or you get exposed to drugs or anything else, certain beings are ready to step in. And that's just what has been happening and why we have seen so many in this state [of possession].

Now nobody would deny the words of Jesus Christ when he spoke about casting out demons and all that sort of thing. And yet we'll turn right around and deny their existence. It doesn't make sense, and you're on the wrong track when you deny these things.

As for concentration

In Rodin's famous statue, The Thinker, we see a man sitting slightly bent over, with his head resting in the palm of his hand and his other hand partly covering his eyes, shutting out the impressions of eyesight. This is a typical picture of a person in concentration. But we must also shut out the impressions of the ears; and the reason for sitting comfortably in a relaxed condition is in order to shut out the impressions of touch or feeling. Then we must gradually eliminate taste and smell. All senses must be shut out if we are truly to enter into a perfect state of concentration.

We have seen a little boy walk along the street reading a wild west story and so lose himself in the story that he bumps into people and walks past places he intended to go. This would illustrate the complete concentration that is necessary. He is not conscious of his walking or his outer environment at all. And so the businessman cannot be conscious of the cigar or pipe in his mouth and at the same time focalize all of his thoughts upon the idea that he has in his mind.

In order to concentrate perfectly upon any thought, every degree or aspect of our consciousness must be centered toward one point. Not only must all of our five objective faculties assist in this regard, but those more subtle faculties such as that of keeping our balance while sitting or standing. That is why some lean forward and rest their elbows on the table while concentrating. We find we must eliminate all external impressions as far as possible. This means that your thoughts are working distinctly without interruption, in the purity of the pattern you have set. When we start to detach ourselves from the material world entirely, we are then approaching a place where cosmic consciousness can be a reality.

Then there is what we call divine consciousness, and this is when we pull out all the stops, get everything we learned or even thought of out of the way. And we don't ask any questions particularly, we just get ourselves and our mind alive. And then we stop all the other thinking mechanisms and all other consciousness or looking to the Self for an answer or anything else, and we open the line wide and let things come directly in, right from the Core of Creation.

Now let us take a very simple thing to concentrate on: the love of one another. And this is a divine thing, because it is only through that consciousness that you can truly attain.

MELCHIZEDEK

There are people born without necessarily any distinct parental ties, either to father or mother. This is the parentless state and is what was referred to in the Testament as being "after the order of Melchizedek". According to the writers of the Epistles to the Hebrews, Melchizedek was without father and without mother, without descent; having neither beginning of days nor end of life, but made like unto the Son of God, abiding a priest continually.

The Order of Melchizedek is not an order of celestial formation, but a pattern that depicts the parentless, endless life eternal in this work. It depicts that person who has reached the point beyond life or death.

MENTAL PROBLEMS

When the mind is not in balance, the so-called mystic powers of mind cannot be performed. A person who is not mentally in balance cannot use the Law, they cannot use the power of projection, or the power of association or dissemination. And they cannot use creatively the power of their own imagination, because these things are taken over by other forces which are in the psychic world, and then they are called mentally ill.

Many people develop states of mental illness because they have used imagination persistently without a recognition of divinity; and thus they have separated the two worlds and they have no balance. They have no control of all the forces that can and do rush in, which separate them from the external realization of the world around them.

Therefore how to sense things and to visualize is one of the last things that is to be taught, because it is felt that the person should have developed some cosmic consciousness in order to become in some form spiritually balanced, so that he can control these things, and will not be creating falsely.

MIND

The mind is the Mind of God. The brain is the prism, a part of the mechanism through which it comes. Life is there, because life is the specific energy. Before bringing an external manifestation of creation, there must be a clear mental picture, a clear conception in your mind. When it is in your mind, then it is in God's Mind, because you don't have any mind. You have used part of It, you have individualized part of It, but it is not you. You do have a body-consciousness, but that isn't the mind. That is the thing we try to get rid of when we start to master the "beast" which we ride. Each person has the power, the essence of God, and through this speaks the Word of God, if he does it within the scope, and the pattern and form of Creation.

We know that people create certain patterns in their mind, either through their imagination or controlled thinking. We know that in order for us to understand that this is a chair, we must have received instructions from someone or something that this particular form is called a chair, and that if we go over to it and sit down, it will hold. Now this is a form, and every time this form comes up in our mental mechanism, we recognize this through association of vibratory form.

Before something can come into manifestation we must first have a pattern and form in mind, or in the Mind of God, for it to exist on earth; because the form, the geometric form and its relationship to mind, of line and potential strength, determines the possibilities of its use, both in the physical and spiritual, or mind-aspect, of this creation

Now, we do not draw the line between heaven and earth, because there isn't any. We do not draw a line between spiritual and material, because there isn't any. They are all existent in one space, or what you would call space. But they exist there because of vibration, the difference in frequency of that substance and its state.

Our experiences with radio and other modern scientific achievements have demonstrated many of the higher laws of spirituality to us in a better way than we could have imagined. But few people out here in the world who talk about vibration, or "vibes" and all this sort of thing, even know what they are talking about. Something has been experienced which they call vibration, but they don't understand what it is. They don't understand how they themselves are broadcasting stations, because if they did there would be a lot of things they wouldn't do, or take the chance of doing.

Many people are very sincere in trying to help others, and yet all the time, while they're making certain physical efforts and giving certain physical service to other people, they are doing things which have just as much effect in the opposite way. And I am not talking about sins, now, I'm talking about things just in living and thinking alone that have more than outweighed all of their physical actions of trying to help somebody.

It's awfully hard these days, even with all of our scientific equipment and all our scientific advancement, to get people to the reality that they can sit in a room and shut their mouth and do almost as much good as they could if they talked, providing they understand how they function. Now, this is not an opinion; this is a reality, a scientific fact.

Q: What about the effects of thoughts? Say a person sat around and thought evil things all the time, but never actually did them; then another person went out and did them. What would be the difference?

A: Thoughts are things. You can influence a whole lot of people in the area, just by being with them, and if you have evil thoughts, it's a very bad vibration.

Likewise, when you have good thoughts and keep the Master in mind, and when you are really functioning on that level, you can do an awful lot of good without saying a word. This is what the Master meant, partly at least, by "Thine acts shall be thy prayer in this age". You see? You're just like a broadcasting station. You're giving off all the time. If you give off negative things it has its influence, that's all, and it surely can disturb things.

It is essential for all leaders, all teachers, whether of Bible class or otherwise, to get to the point where they realize that if they are going to do any true thinking, they don't start with their opinions. They must let loose of everything, because otherwise, they have already set their minds and will not get a true thought.

Now a stubborn person is nothing more than one who has already determined what he is going to think about, and save hell or high water, he's going to think that way, and that's all there is to it. So never argue or debate anything with a person who has made up his mind. Let him go on and bang his head against the wall, then talk to him. Because the hurt that he gets will make an opening so you can speak to him, and then he'll listen.

I'm sure you've seen some of this happen. But you've got to wait until he has stopped running his course. And when he has had a hard enough thump, this will give him something to put his mind on and then you can inject a little truth that will sink in. It will slide by, you see, and it will get home. This is a point, you might say, of material cosmic consciousness; because he is so engrossed with something else that he really has no opinion at the moment.

The average intellectual is not interested in finding the answer. He is only interested in finding something which brings up a controversy, where he can express his intellect and intelligence, and so draw some attention to himself. Man has not been taught that his word carried, and would reflect in the actions, and would produce in the world around him that which he spoke and that which he thought.

If you look at the advertising field and the psychology used in the upper level of advertising you see a great many things that are taught in metaphysics, many of the same principles are used, and some that are even in the Testament. But the reason for it is that it will get them a buck. As long as it gets them that, they're not too big to use it. You show a person how to make two or three thousand dollars and he doesn't care what he has to do to get it.

"If thine eye be single, thy whole body shall be full of light." They are not looking at it from the standpoint of illumination, but they have another goal, and believe me, their eye is single! They get just what they go after. There is nothing existent in this world that is not created and that is not set into motion by the thinking and the actions of individuals as a whole. No matter what it is, it is not set and it is not possible to have unless someone thinks of it that way.

As long as mankind lacks the ability to handle the powers and forces of Creation and work with the Creator that gave them, there will be wars. But you can have wars and rebellions and they are not going to change a thing, because every change has got to start from the ears up. That's where the changes of the world start, and they don't start anyplace else; because right there is where you have to start to learn to control yourself. Once you have controlled yourself, then you can start to control your thinking and your word and actions in accordance with the creative way, and these things will be a reality. But they can have all the uprisings they want to; nothing happens until the things from the mind have changed. That's where it has to start, and it has been that way all through history.

Nothing can happen until you get to the Mind that can open the way to the reality of the power and force of this universe. If a handful of people with enough mind-control, who knew the truth of this and had reached mastery, sat together, they could totally protect a city. But it takes complete selflessness to do this, no thoughts for yourself. No objective, no fear, no disturbances whatsoever, because otherwise you're doing something for yourself. You may go ahead on the altruistic basis of anything, but if and as you do so you have in mind that you're protecting your own skin, then you're not reaching the epitome and level which is required for true altruism in that respect. A dozen words, spoken by one who knows and has no particular purpose for himself, can move a great deal in the world.

Now, you can have an understanding of the Law and the Word, and can see why it is scientifically correct, but when you go to use it, if you have any idea that you are doing it yourself and that you are the creator of it, it isn't going to work because you won't be able to let go. You're going to still be hanging on. And the reason so many people are able in this day and age to have prayers answered is because in this time things are much more powerful and there is more energy in the atmosphere than there was, and therefore prayer works much easier than it did before.

So many times we fool ourselves with our own mirages that we build. You can't misuse something without having to repair or rebuild it, and you have to rebuild a mind, a brain, just the same as you rebuild anything else—that is, not rebuild it, but you have to clear it out. Of course, you don't have a mind anyway; there's only One that has that. But from that portion which you are using, you've got to clear out the debris before you are going to get good action. And the moment you get that mind and your thinking straightened out, and as you get through to the Master, completely through, no one between you and him, no "ism", no philosophy, nothing—when you reach the point where nothing stands between, then you begin to realize that you are alive. And that is when you really start to move in the right direction because you do not fear the presence of God or our Lord Jesus Christ.

Jesus recognized his divinity, and that made it easy for him to express and give for the sake of the world in general. This gave him one thing which most of us miss and shy away from—maintaining the divinity, the purity of our own minds; and here is the seat of all our trouble anyway: in our minds. If we can clear this up and get hold of this one idea, get hold of the fundamental fact of what we really are, and not stand and revolt against it the way most of us do, then we'll find that we will get something good out of what normally would be a struggle.

MYSTIC

A part of the unseen will become seen in this age, with being able to see those that come to teach and help us. This will happen as the bodies of those that remain here adjust and expand. We will then be able to control our own bodies and to control the things around us. This is the time for the return of the Christ.

If we truly understood it, we would look with great concern upon ourselves when we receive the gifts that we do from the earth, of which our Lord is Master. This is one of the great mysteries, or at least what are called mysteries; because as I have said many times, a mystery is only a mystery to us because it is right in front of our eyes and we have seen it and known it since birth, practically. It is a mystery because it is so simple that all peoples have seen it but have not recognized it as a reality. And this, of course, is true most of our lives, in all things that have to do with religious or spiritual matters.

Those who understand the work of mystic orders – not the occult, but the mystic orders – do not denounce the work of the Master Jesus nor belittle the work and the power of the Christos. And this is true of every mystic that has lived for the last two thousand years and over. For they have constantly been trying to re-establish the ancient work which has been torn down by the present-day churches, those which deny the existence of the greater Order of which the mystic is a part. For he is a member of the Brotherhood, and by that I mean the White Brotherhood; not some physical organization, but a greater one.

A true mystic, a person of true divinity, is one who is true within himself. He will look at both sides of any question, unprejudiced. Until he does that, he has not reached the point of being a true God-man. Because if you have prejudice, then you do not have wisdom. Under no circumstance can wisdom and prejudice coexist. And logic is not wisdom.

NEW AGE

(New Heaven & New Earth)

For a long time you have heard me refer to the New Heaven and the New Earth, and the fact that as the sun and the power of the Christ comes into earth, there will be a constant expansion until we reach the level where the heaven world has come down, the psychic world has enmeshed and come into conjunction with the earth, vibration-wise, and then we'll have a new vibration on the earth.

Now some years ago, it was pointed out to me very clearly what this new heaven and new earth was, that it is a change of the relationship between the molecular structures, in that we are becoming less dense.

Having come to the New Age, we have entered a way of life in which we can no longer move and act in the way we did in the past years of history, for that was another day. Now we who are here on this earth must go forth knowing consciously that our acts and our deeds shall manifest the same as our prayers would have manifested before. We are citizens of that new race, that new risen world into which the Light shall spread; and it shall be in accordance with the teachings of our Lord. As long as we remain part of the heavenly reality, so will the regeneration and the rebirth of that reality within us take place.

When you have received the Light your body does not feel as heavy as it did before. You could not do the same things you did before and get by with it, because the matter was transmuted. If this is going to be a new heaven and a new earth, and the psychic world is going to unite with the earth—as it is—it has to be less dense. Your body is going to become less dense and therefore you will see more than you see now.

Q: For many years now we have heard of the power and force of the New Age. When does that start?

A: About 1890, in that neighborhood. Of course, this could be—give or take maybe thirty or forty years, as far as that's concerned, because we're talking about man's concept of time. But actually there is no time; there's only a period or state of vibration, in reality; and that is how we see, through vibration.

Electricity, the electrical science rather, came into its full bloom in this age, in this time. And then we started to investigate the other sciences more deeply, and we find that the electrical science itself is

191

almost a fundamental science alone, because we have now traced it and are using it in conjunction with chemistry and physics; and much of the mathematics that we now use in calculations is based on the electrical theory.

We are also beginning to reach into the field of science which has to do with the physical body and its bio-chemistry, and we are beginning to realize that man and his whole vehicle is based on electro-chemical interchange, rather than just the fact that he eats food and that food goes into the cell. The food builds up certain electrical reactions and then the cell is filled from the vital body itself. This is merely potential reaction; action and reaction. Of course, we know the laws of cause and effect are absolute, because these have been mathematically and scientifically proven. And we find it in the Bible too. So if it follows through the sciences and it follows from the Book, why, we have a pretty good reason to believe it.

In this age, man must know the world he lives in, the scientific law of prayer and the basic laws which the beautiful creation of God, this world, works with. This means he must become conscious of the unseen, at least a part of the time, as well as the seen. For a part of the unseen will become seen in this age. Jesus said, "All of these things that I do, so shall you do also, and even greater than these"; because he knew that 2000 years later, man would have evolved to a greater state of being, with greater powers and greater possibilities. He would be living in a world where there was more force, more energy in the atmosphere that he was living in; and in the last decades ours has increased tremendously.

Many things that are not being seen.

We are looking for somebody to come down with a two-wheeled chariot and five or six horses, but because we can't see the horses and the chariot, why, of course it couldn't be there. You can remember some people predicting the end of the world. They did this in all good faith, but they were not taught to understand the basic principles, the basic spirit and truth of the creative power and how it works. Jesus taught the principles openly in his time. Those things which the world was not ready for and could not understand were preserved for this time, to make it ready for the Christ and the new body of man, taught in the true science—the science of life, beauty, health and brotherhood, the teachings of the Fire of the Spirit; for Jesus worked with the Spirit of the Creator. The Spirit of Christ must burn out the dross of selfishness in

192

order for us to become simple enough to be as little children in God consciousness and habit, when we rise above our material selves.

Our problems in this era are different in nature, and require something different to solve them—entirely different and much tougher than the people of this earth previously experienced and which were presented to historical man in his long chain of evolution. In this crisis there just might be the coming of the end of something, but let me relieve your mind: not the end of the human race, only the end for those that do not learn to use the creative power. This hazard exists only when men fail to know or experience the realization of the great consciousness, and the realization of the existing power of creation and how to use it. It is absolutely a must for each one of us to be conscious of his smallness, in order to be conscious of his greatness.

Now that we are entering a new age, an age where Man is the theme of creation, we are entering the time which Jesus predicted when he said, "I will be with you till the end of the age." He meant the New Testament teachings for the age that we are now in, and it is not a flexible thing but lays it on the line, and that's the way it works. It doesn't make any difference whether it is the Roman or Greek or any other church you are dedicated to, it is only that you must understand these laws and how to use them.

OBEDIENCE

Obedience is not a matter of doing what someone says but of doing what is right, even though they are not able to see all the ramifications of it. It is obedience to the laws of creation, in reality, because no obedience should be inflicted on a person which is not in some way traceable back to the basic laws of creation. If you have given a true order, it can be seen to be founded there.

But obedience means obedience to the laws of creation, which the individual doesn't yet have the wisdom to follow without direction. So on the lower level we bring this out in another way, through following direction which they understand to a great extent because they get something from it when they follow it. And that is a freedom that they get by being obedient, in that they are relieved from the responsibility of following the laws of creation, you see.

And, if you want to go back that far, disobedience is the action of the rugged individualistic soul, you might call it, wanting to follow only its own creations, rebelling at its captivity in this system. And nine-tenths of the disobedience, even on some of the lower levels, is reaction from what you might call soul personality, and things that are carried out of the past up into this life.

PATH AND PRESENCE

No one seems to truly understand the passage in the Bible that says, "I am the Way". Recently I heard a couple of ministers talking about this as though it were some sort of celestial highway. Well, it is, in a manner of speaking, but that doesn't make too much sense when you're teaching a class, and it is very difficult to put on paper, but we can try. To begin with, I want to repeat that although we study about power, force and energy in many ways, this is something that we do not generally relate it to.

Everyone knows that wherever you go, whether you're consciously trying to or not, you leave your tracks behind you, not only by what you say, but by your presence. If you ask somebody what presence is, they may say, "Well, it is the spirituality of the person." but they will avoid explaining what it is. They never come back to the power, force and energy. For some reason or other, the intellectual person avoids this, because he is avoiding the state of reality.

"Presence" is a good enough word, but it tells you little except that you are there. Now, just being there could either be derogatory or it could be of great value. The presence of Jesus Christ was of great value to the world. But the presence of Lucifer at the temptation in the wilderness certainly was of no value except that our Lord in his temptation was demonstrating one of the initiations; and there are a lot of people whose presence you don't particularly care for.

What we mean by presence is the radiation of your being. And we are so prone these days to keep away from this idea of energy, of your being; what you radiate! Now, when you speak of someone's presence it doesn't appear to put any responsibility on the person that you're talking about. But when you say it's his radiation, that puts the responsibility right where it is—from him. Because he is responsible for his being and what he gives off.

Jesus Christ said, "I am the Way". Now, he had traveled this way before. He had traveled the route of the great initiate and master—he was one when he came here. What we mean by The Way is exactly the same thing, only it has other deeper meanings too, because he said, "I am the Way, the Truth, and the Life."

To begin with, he was telling us one thing: that he was traveling this route which we are going to travel, following the way that he was traveling then, by that same path, that same electrical path that he was leaving behind him, as well as the Word. He meant: "I have walked this Path that I am describing to you; and the things which I have done on this Path, that is the Way. That is my way, by which I am leading you to the Father."

Now, the Truth was in his words and in the teaching and the Reality which he gave forth. The Light he spoke of had to pass through him. This is something which I don't think can be described, but he was the Christed one, the Messiah. He was the one through which it was possible for the Light to come to the people of earth in this day, the way it is doing right now. He laid down this Path and this Way to lead us to the day that we are now in, and to accomplish this goal that we are now striving and working toward. The light comes through him to anyone on the earth, because he is the Lord of the earth, so it must come through his body to reach us.

If a bloodhound were on someone's trail, how would it know where to go? Because of the vibration, and the power and energy left behind from that man. He left a trail. Now, let's not avoid realities; don't try to cover it up with fancy words that excuse people. That is why theology goes so far off the track, and why it is not understood by a lot of the people. They cover everything up with a multitude of words, and yet they avoid these vital words: power, force, and energy. Reality. And we have gotten too far away from it. We have gotten off the track of the reality.

Jesus laid down the way for a two-thousand-year period, pretty close to that, and this way is being extended with some things that have a new tactic, or a different application. He said all the mysteries shall be revealed. In other words, we're going to cut off these performances in the temple with the pageantry, the enacted mystery; and the plain, simple reality will take place. His journey toward Jerusalem and Golgotha was filled with these things which would have been revealed in pageantry before, but through him they are revealed in the reality of life. This is what he was talking about when he said, "Follow me": follow what I have shown you, follow what I have told you, receive through me the Light which I came to reveal.

Q: Is his the easiest way to follow, while the other ways would still be there but his would be strongest?

A: Well, because he brought this path into existence and projected it out as the way for that coming time, and due to the fact that he lived every act of it, it became. Because he was designated as the Messiah, he took on the Christ and brought it to earth, you see. This was a mission of the Father which he took on, with His Authority. When he said, "The Father gave me the Word, and I give it unto you", he was commissioning directly from the Father to us the Word. And in following the initiations, this was therefore what he projected for mankind on this planet.

Q: Would you say that he also considered all the other paths that were known?

A: He reinstated, so that these initiations are not changed, but with certain things added to them and certain things purified, I would say. Not modified, but purified; because it is harder to live a distinct initiation consciously than it would be to take it on a more or less unconscious level. There are certain groups and certain schools that go through these, though it may take four or five lifetimes to go through one initiation. They'll get through if the candidate has any willingness at all. But there isn't a distinct action there, conscious action, with the willful acceptance of that particular experience; and therefore there isn't the greatest grace. The reason the grace comes to us as it does is because we enact it, live it, right down the line.

Q: We hear it said that there are many paths but just one Way. Well, it seems maybe the paths are getting shorter.

A: The paths are there, but we must remember that with a lot of the paths, a lot of the organizations, churches, mystic orders, and so forth, many of these things are race religions, or racial teachings. They had a purpose and there was a need for them, but that need has been pretty nearly fulfilled, and therefore it will not be too long before they will no longer find a need in the world, and they will be supplemented by the enlargement, reeducation and coming into a greater uniformity among groups. There will probably be certain groups that will come together first, certain churches that will come together. They may not have total unity, but they will work one with another, you see.

We have no quarrel with any other religion or any faith, but we do have to keep in mind what we're doing, how important it is that we learn to think this way so that our actions and the trail we leave behind us will be sufficient and strong and in the right direction, in the right methods and procedures that will be used to lead people directly to the Christ and to the Light; a method and process of illumination that will work for anyone.

All you have to think about, if you want to put it graphically, is to take the time that Jesus came on earth and passed through the initiations, and how he lived while he was here, what he did, what he taught, and the ancient teachings. And this is The Way that he produced, that he projected when he said, "I am the Way."

PEACE

People speak, not of real peace but a peace which is dickered for with the moneychangers, who trade for peace in the courts and in the temples, rather than working and accepting it from its source, from the Almighty. None of their peace has been very successful, because we have not preserved the temple for the worship of God.

There is no place and no time now to trade for peace. It must come through the power of the Spirit, and the Almighty God must move through men and women or there will be no peace. It has to be within your minds and your hearts or it cannot be, for otherwise it will be the peace that has been in the past, which comes from the negotiations of man, and which is not lasting.

"Thy peace shall be thy shield". This comes under the law of non-resistance. If you don't resist, they can't reach you, can they? Because they, of themselves, cannot operate in your world. Therefore, they need your strength to reach you. Action and reaction.

POWER

We have oftentimes spoken about radiant energy, which is a physical force but it is also essentially a part of consciousness. The brain is an organ whereby this essential consciousness is released and put to work in the field of your own personality.

The Sun is the dynamo of the sky, or the battery through which the universal life breath is concentrated, and from which that life breath radiates into our solar system. It is the foundation of all physical activities, all properties of our solar system; and it is the source of power of the universe, dominated and working through our consciousness out of the great Sun, the Christos. This is the Way and Path of the power of the Father, the all-encompassing Source of power.

There are electromagnetic fields of the earth which are all around us and in the air. But when the Light of the Christos comes down, or the Power of the Father comes in, whichever way you want to speak about it—because you must remember it isn't directional this way—it is from one stage of vibration into another. The coming down or the calling down are merely figurative words which are not descriptive.

Man can release power with very little work, but he must have an absolute and conscientious understanding and a sincere letting-go of his own being, knowing that this power and force will work through him if he doesn't try to do it all with his will. If we could but release this power as easily as we release the power in an explosive, and as systematically, we would accomplish many great feats. But you see, we still haven't come to a place where we are looking at the unseen part of life and the unseen world as being a greater part of this creation than what we are looking at with our physical eyes. For the force and power within man, the human being, his vitality, his magnetism, are far greater than that of any force he has released through engines or through his atomic devices.

We have power and energy manifesting through the human mind and body. The brain would not have any power of its own if it were not for this. No amount of food put into the body could furnish enough energy for the brain to keep alive. The directed brain contains all the forces of the universe, many types of which may be released, both seen and unseen, known and unknown.

This is the day for man and woman to learn the use of the wondrous forces that we've been left with, which God has put at our disposal, and the knowledge of these forces gives man the control and the use of these powers in his universe every day. Man must experience the realization of the existing power and how to use it, because if you once learn to use these powers and these laws, you will not have such difficulty, even with your own personality.

Down deep within each individual there is a striving and a yearning to understand the powers of nature, because somehow we do not think that this God or this Creative Being, as a Mind which has created this universe, has forgotten us; and we'd feel terribly hurt if He did. When we get the overall picture of things, we find we are extremely small, and yet the power and the Laws and the force wrapped up within each of our own vehicles and our own minds is tremendous. It is enough to move many other particles, and determines the path in which we are going. It is enough to bring us to the state in which we will be free of all these obstacles which we have created for ourselves in the past, and so find that freedom which we seek.

In the ancient temples of initiation it was said: "All the powers of nature shall deem themselves happy to obey your every desire." No ifs, no ands, no conditions; whether you're good or bad.

That was a little shaker. You have to learn that you have command. You have to learn that you are working with the powers of Nature and that you must control them. The people in this room, if they all had their consciousness and understood what I'm saying, if they sat here together and were of one mind, and an earthquake started, they could stop it just like that.

Now, power is nothing more than the ability of energy—or a combined group of energies—to do work and overcome a load of something. And that reminds me of the force of the Christ when it really does some work. It's properly named "power", because it is manifesting that right along, every day, and especially when it changes the nature of some folks.

You have your greatest power when you have reached the point where you know you can't do anything except through "It". Why do you suppose the most ancient of all symbols is the perfect circle? One of the first symbols that we are taught is this simple symbol of God, and that one circle tells you the whole story. It defines the epitome of mastership. I won't go into that, but it defines what you need to know. What is that? Nothing! When you know nothing, and when you know you know nothing, you have learned it all. This is the truth. It hurts the ego, and it really whittles down your superfluous physical being, especially after you've got a couple of Ph.D.'s; that's for sure. But this is where it is. I have given you in this little bit all the wisdom it is necessary for man to know, providing you can work at it.

PRAYER

Many of us have prayed and had no answer, and therefore we could not use prayer with assurance and confidence in the power of the Word which Jesus passed on to us from the Father. The problem has been how to establish real confidence in the laws that govern the power of God and the forces of nature, and in the authority of the Word. When we are taught the inner truths that our Lord taught, the knowledge increases our confidence and faith so that we can use prayer to solve our problems.

Learning to use prayer is a way that you can get across the border into the other world because, even without the understanding, prayer in itself very often is functional and will work, even with those who do not know the Law. And that is because they are going to live by the Law anyway, regardless of whether they know that prayer works.

We generally feel that prayer is something pretty intangible, but this is not so. Prayer is a practical thing. It is not only a matter of the control of your mind and understanding of the Law, but it is actually a scientific thing too.

Now let us go back to our old definition for the law of the triangle or the law of prayer, and the way of doing it. You get in contact with the Father, make the pattern of what you want to manifest, then you toss it over your shoulder and say, "Thank you, Father"; know that you have it, and go your way out into the world. You feel it, you know it, and it is there. Now this is what was set up, this was in the understanding and thinking of the Father in creation. It traces itself all the way down through into matter; and this is the law of prayer, referring it to the Trinity.

When I say toss it over your shoulder, I mean you toss it over your shoulder and turn away from it. You don't think about it. Forget you said it and go about your business, and you'll get results. But don't turn around and look to see if it has happened yet, because if you do, you've got a new prayer.

After having made the prayer, make yourself accessible. Try not to do it yourself, but make yourself accessible so it can be brought about. Conversely, one must not be too presumptuous and attempt to instruct these things or materialize something for himself, at least not at this particular stage of his development.

When we come to the point of letting go of the prayer, here, of course, is the pitfall for some people. We have successfully had a good prayer up to this point, and we say, "Thank you, Father". Then we need to let go and walk away from it. He'll take care of the rest. But usually when they get just about three steps away from where they issued the prayer, they look back over their shoulder to see if it is coming down out of the thin air, so to speak. And the chances are it won't be, right at that minute. Then next morning they'll get up and wonder if they did a good job, and will go and start all over again. Well, of course, if you don't believe it yourself how can you convince the Power Upstairs that that is what you really want? These are things we are usually not conscious of and have to look out for; and then there is the ego and things of that nature that sometimes get in the way.

Man must not, with his consciousness at the present time, consider himself a modern Aladdin who can rub the lamp and have his wishes fulfilled by the Cosmic. Often we, in our finite, limited and frequently selfish consciousness, honestly believe that what we want or think we need should rightfully be ours. Well, maybe it should; but are we willing to open ourselves up so that we can receive it? Can we take care of it after it is received? You have to be careful what you pray for, because when you get something, you're going to have to take the responsibility of it.

Sometimes our lack of knowledge of cosmic principles may cause us to ask inadvertently for something which is in violation of what we should have. We must ask for right action in our statements. First, because it may be detrimental to our good if it could injure someone else. Second, man must be in proper relation with the Cosmic and admit his humble station, and not be vain enough to dictate demands, until he has become a selfless being who knows of his own right.

Now when the majority of people pray, it's: "Father, give me this. Father, I'd like that." You know, I wish we could stay on the other end of the telephone line of prayer and listen to the "I wants" that come up, and I think we'd be pretty well disgusted with the lot; because you hear very few prayers that say, "Father, it's such a pleasure to live in Your world that You've created." How many people think of giving thanks for what they have received, to say nothing about what they are going to get in the future? Just for the privilege of living and feeling the joy and exhilaration of life, this is something to be thankful for. But as a rule it's a process of, "I need; gimme; I want"; and of course the majority of these prayers never get answered.

Then many prayers are said by people who don't know that they are saying them. People pray for things that they don't know they're praying for, and that they don't want, but they get them just the same. One of the things that we need to learn a whole lot more about is the unconscious or subconscious prayer. We have a great many problems because of the things we choose to do which the soul does not want, and neither does the Self. In other words, the animal wants it, but not You.

Have you ever listened to some prayers? "Oh God, oh God, I am such an awful sinner. Oh God, I have been so wicked. Oh God, we are people fallen from the Garden of Eden." My answer is, Oh God, how can you stand us, if that is the circumstance? I think it takes more patience than I've got, if I were in God's place, to listen to that all day, because you never hear one thankful note out of them. It would have to wait for Thanksgiving to do that, when they've got their eyes on the turkey.

You know, unless people start to change their tactics they can pray themselves right into hell. Did you ever stop to think about that? I'm not kidding with this. If you repeat those woes long enough, you are really going to have them. You could pray yourself right into hell; and if you had created the right kind for yourself you'd find it, believe me.

Now what about these other statements of negation that you've been issuing forth? "I can't do it", and "I just wonder if we'll ever get that far", and so on. How do you think you're praying? Because that is a prayer. And how many of those did you issue today? How many of these prayers did you say? And tonight when you go through retrospection—and I hope you do—I want you to chalk those down on the red side of the ledger. They are liabilities!

Jesus said that thy words shall become flesh, didn't he? What do you think he was talking about? Just on special occasions, on Sunday, or when you get in a prayer group, or something? No. This is an everyday deal. And the sooner you and every one of us finds out that every nasty thing that we've accomplished in our life has been done by misuse of the Word of God, the sooner you're going to have peace on this earth, and the sooner you're going to bring it there. That's the bare truth, without any window dressing. And remember, your actions, day by day, are your daily prayers; they will be fulfilled.

Prayer is done not only through the sound of your voice, but then there is the sound within. If you can't walk down the street and keep yourself from being run over and still give a true prayer, then you just haven't made it; because you can pray and give voice inside without making a sound outside—unless somebody standing next to you has spiritual hearing, and that wouldn't matter anyway.

Don't get inflated if once or twice a prayer has been answered, after about forty-five minutes of hard work and trying to get yourself oriented so that you could get it to work. It only takes about fifteen seconds if you're really functioning. And during those fifteen seconds you could clear the atmosphere and clear your mind, make the prayer and be on your way, without any stopping.

Now that is prayer, but it is within you and you are totally conscious of the fact that the Word of God must manifest in this way. Because if you are not convinced, then you don't know and you haven't found this to be true yet, you see. If you don't understand how to use it, with your own mind and your own heart and your own feeling, then you're going to have trouble.

You can go on and say all the prayers you want to, but unless you have felt the existence of God there, or the Master, you're not going to get any answer. You're just praying up a blind wall. Of course, the laws of percentage are with you so that you're bound to hit something, sometime or other.

If you are thinking while you pray, though sincere, you are just composing and there is no feeling in it. As long as you think, you are not praying. You have to get God all inside so there is nothing else there, then you can pray. This is when you have it. It possesses you, you don't possess it! One of the greatest prayers is being quiet long enough for God to speak.

Where most people fall off in their prayers is reaching the consciousness of the Father at all. When you reach that consciousness, you will know it for sure, because your whole being will respond to it. You will feel it, and there won't be any question but that you have reached the state of consciousness where God is going to answer!

If the reality isn't alive in you, how can you expect to reach That which you don't believe or which you're not even sure exists? Now you have got to be able to reach an actual conclusion within yourself that this really exists. This proof can only be gotten through you, not somebody else; and until you have proved that within yourself, you cannot really reach God

You know there are more people who break the first Commandment and don't know it than you have any idea of. The Father should come first. When we pray, the Father's name should come first, even when we are asking for intercession from Mary. It should be an automatic thing that the Nameless Name comes first, and then all these other things. Now this should be ingrained into us so we wouldn't think of saying a prayer any other way, because otherwise this is a violation of the first Commandment.

Now, prayer is an active thing. You don't have to be set in the corner, you don't have to go off into some great open space, nor to sit cross-legged and wear a certain robe to do it. And you don't have to have started either wings or a halo. It has always been our contention that if you can't sit on the curb next to a drunk and reach God there, you haven't got it; you'd better start over again. Because the person who needs to step into the sanctuary or a meditation booth in order to reach God hasn't got much God inside of him—in his consciousness, at least.

We sometimes use written prayers. Now, repetitious prayer has its use, but not for teaching people how to pray. Repetition is useful where a great mass of people are after a uniform goal and they want to accomplish a specific purpose. That is like setting down a formula and asking everybody in the city or country to wire their house a certain way so that it will light up at the same time every night. Well, you'd get some results that way. Uniform prayer, absolutely uniform prayer, works because they are conforming to a uniform striving. But to the individual this is a different thing. For members of an order, the form of the order overshadows this, and it will work. But for the average individual the repetitious prayer is less effective.

There is another point where we need to reach a very definite understanding, and this is the formation of what we are expecting to accomplish by the prayer. You notice I didn't say, "what we want", I said what we expect to accomplish. There are prayers that can be used to accomplish something that has nothing to do with material things of the earth directly. Perhaps indirectly but not directly.

There is much that we need to accomplish which can be done by prayer, if we have gotten to the point where we are convinced of the Creator and His existence. We can use prayer for something in our own development, if we are looking to find the Master Jesus and really become conscious of him. This is a prayer of beseechment, so to speak, a prayer of need. And here is where the old law of chemistry comes in, that Nature abhors a vacuum; and it will be filled, providing we have made ourselves specific in our need.

But don't expect God Almighty and our Lord Jesus to always be mind-reading. Many people think because they are praying to the great Creator or the great Intelligence of this whole universe that they don't really have to be too fussy about what they say. That's where they're wrong. They have to be more specific in what they say there than they would if talking to another individual, because the other individual probably couldn't produce it anyway, but with Him it will be produced if you've really gotten there with this consciousness.

Q: How would you pray for someone having a legal problem?

A: If I felt that they were not guilty, then I would use prayer, and I'd ask for right action in this, just to make sure that I was on the right side of the fence. I would use a prayer of positive motivation. Whether you're a defendant or plaintiff really doesn't say whether you're right or wrong. It just means that one started the action before the other, that is all. So you have to do this from the standpoint of right action.

Q: What if somebody asks you to give them a blessing or pray for them?

A: You have a right to give anybody a blessing; there's no question about it. Pray for anybody. Just warn 'em though, it'll probably come true.

Q: What about praying for groups of people? Like getting in the habit, when you ride on the bus, of making a prayer of right action that each person will be brought closer to knowing God, and bring what is needed to each being?

A: Now, this is a different thing entirely. This comes in the category of another form of prayer. This is partly a prayer of contemplation, and it is a universal prayer. It is actually an opening of yourself as a universal channel for mankind, you see. You know none of them personally, but you see the good in them, and you are praying for their upliftment. There's nothing wrong with it; it's very beautiful. It is part of the system of "prayer without ceasing", where you pray automatically; just as getting the Law ingrained within you is another phase of prayer without ceasing.

Now prayer without ceasing is a form of constant consciousness that God is here. I stand in the shadow of Jesus. I feel him, I feel his consciousness. I'm in the grocery store and he's with me. I feel the reality of what the other man is looking toward, and I feel the response to that consciousness, you see. This is the prayer without ceasing; "O Father, let their light be shown." You've never seen them before, but let their light be shown. This is the upliftment of the nation. It is the way that many teachers will feel.

This is compassion on an upper level. It isn't just being tolerant or something of that sort; it is compassion as a whole, the feeling for the race of mankind. And this is something that comes, this is the stuff that saints are made of, because it is done without thought of themselves or without thought of any return, without acknowledgment or any of these things. You do it strictly because you want to help, and so you take on the image of the Master to give the blessing to them; and you're conscious of this, feeling the reality of what is called "altruistic giving". Absolutely no thought of yourself. It is just a moving out and extending your feeling in giving the blessing.

Now let us go back. We've talked about how to pray, to bring things into manifestation, reaching to the Father, building the pattern, letting go of it, and saying thank you, then forgetting about it. In praying, you have not only asked the Father for the fruits of this prayer and not only has the Father heard this prayer, but the other laws that He also put into action in the Creation are immediately going to take form. So not only did He hear it, but so also does all creation hear it. When you call on Jesus Christ in prayer and you say, "Jesus, let there be peace", not only you and Jesus hear it, but so does all the earth!

PROBLEMS

People have problems; they're so worried about one thing or another. The problems they are worried about don't bother me a bit, because the real problem I'm worried about is something they don't even know they've got. And nine times out of ten, it can be summed up in one sentence: "If thine eye be single, thy body will be full of Light." Really, it's right there. This is where the cleansing process starts to take place and one gradually becomes fit to come to the Way and the Truth, as he surely will if he wants to serve.

I presume many of you have gotten rid of your problems, but if you still have some, don't let them be the main objective of your life and breath every day, because they are not going to enhance your journey at all, nor help your soul growth either. Forget them. If you have a problem, go to the chapel, give it to Jesus and forget it. Why should you carry around a minor problem? If you must have a problem, please have a major one (laughter) and you'll gain a lot of growth out of it.

Many of you worry, "How am I coming along? How do I look? And oh, I have this problem and that one." Sure you have. You've manufactured them all. We create things in our own mind and make them problems. God Almighty did not bring you into this world with problems, unless you had built up an awful background before, in another life. But even these can go.

God never created anything that He didn't give the answer to; and you have the answer within you. You have the answer to the problem or otherwise you wouldn't have the problem. You see? Because the answer must come before the problem can be created.

If you look at it very closely, you will find this is so in science. There has to be an answer to something before they can find a problem to work on. Looking down through the halls of time you'll find that the old wise men taught mathematics long before Professor Joe Doakes ever thought about it, and they knew the answers. So after Joe Doakes found out about this, he started to create the problem, and he created many of them. Of course, it is true he's finding the answers to many problems, and that he gradually gets a little closer and closer to God Almighty. And whether he knows it or not, or even wants to, he can't help doing so because this is God's creation, not his or mine or yours.

Now the closer you can get to simplicity, the more complex the problems you can handle, because you won't get chased off into one of the many channels or branches of your problem and get up a blind alley, and not be able to get out. Each one of your problems is a blind alley. They don't exist in the Mind of God, therefore they shouldn't exist in your mind. And because they shouldn't exist in your mind, you are in error when you accept them.

Man is infinite; there is no limit. You only limit yourself. What I'm saying is that if you didn't want problems, you wouldn't have them. Primarily, when you have a problem, you have somebody's attention, don't you? It's a rough thing to have a nice sunshiny life with nothing to complain about, and to have to go on and be happy each day. Isn't that the truth? Oh, you can always get some good out of any mistake you make, yes, but it isn't necessary to make a mistake in order to grow.

One mistake you do make is that when something happens or you get into difficulties, you don't go to a priest or teacher and tell him about it and say, "I've pulled a boner; will you give me a hand? I want to get rid of this thing." The student is reluctant to come and tell the truth so that he can get these things straightened out. If he would do this, it wouldn't make any difference how many times he'd stumble; it's whether he's going to get up and go. That's what counts. He would be able to do things a lot easier, simply because he unloaded each time, instead of keeping it within himself, instead of holding it inside and letting it ferment and then setting his teeth and trying to fight it down. You don't have to stand there and fight something day and night; get rid of it, then you go out and start clean.

When you sit down and think about it, in reality it is often fear that is holding you back, nothing else. Fear that you can't do it, fear that you are going to have to do what somebody else says, fear that your ego is going to get hurt, fear that somebody next door isn't going to like you, fear that you're going to fail in a test or something of that sort, fear that you can't get close enough to things and get enough Light, fear that some of your old friends are maybe going to say something a little derogatory because they don't understand the way you are following; fear of yourself! I can go on down the line with a list that long, and they are the foundation of what's holding you back—fear of this, that, or the other.

Lift up your consciousness. And always let prayer work; do it the easy way. You'll find that the way set out by our Lord is about the easiest that you've heard of. Jesus gave the answer to all problems: "Come, follow me"

PSYCHIC

There is no psychic body; there is only psychic "stuff", a transmitting substance. It has no exact formation, or no exact laws under which it functions, and no law under which it reacts. It just reacts to everything you picture in your mind. That is why psychic sight is of little value.

In the spiritual world we have form which flows over into the psychic world and there is held in abeyance. Here you have some simulation of law and order. You are not looking at or through something, but your sight is transmitting from another plane.

Psychic phenomena tends to distract one's attention from the spirit and from understanding and knowing Jesus Christ. That's the detriment of it—not that it's evil, it's just a detriment. People get caught up into looking at what they are seeing, and this is why they get distracted from the reality. They don't even believe themselves half the time, what they see with their own eyes.

I once saw a man putting on a little demonstration. Each person in the room wrote a sentence, a question or anything he wanted to, put it in a numbered envelope and sealed it. Another individual took the envelopes and shuffled them up like a deck of cards. They put a blindfold on the psychic and he just ran his fingers over the envelopes, told you what was contained in the writings within the envelopes and answered the questions, told the name of the person who had written the question, and did it as easily as I sit here reading a lesson. He could see with his fingers, he really could.

Yes, well, don't get any ideas. That is not a spiritual accomplishment. It is nothing but phenomena. He is taking the power of God and using it in another way, that's all. You can pull ten thousand of these things. They're real, they happen; sure they happen, but it's nothing but just a performance. Nobody gains anything by it. It's just an experiment, like you'd take a little bit of lead and put a little bit of steel in, and something else, and you'd heat it up and wait to see what happened.

If you want to, when you have nothing else to do, watch the fantasy of the psychic world. But when you do it, know that it doesn't mean anything. If anyone from above wants to get to you, no matter where you are they'll get to you. But don't go off on a "sightseeing trip". You don't want the psychic manifesting? The psychic world can't go behind the veil. It's only when you reach into it that it can be operated.

It has been a mystery, which has been substantiated throughout the years and demonstrated in the spiritualist movement, that persons could pass over and after transition show themselves as they had been on earth. They knew nothing beyond, and thus rebuilt bodies as they had been on earth, and reappeared thus.

When these persons have gone through the lower strata of the psychic world, when they've been there long enough, they may keep some aspects of this body form in order to appear so that people can understand them. Otherwise the individual drops the shell and moves in the Self and atmosphere of his own, and he can function through it totally. He can speak from this or move through it.

Forms appear as light emanates, and then disperse and break up. This is the emotional side of things, and when they function in the desire world, or when they function in the psychic, we do not have the consciousness of such functions. They have the emotional reactions and this is how obsessions take place. When people give over to negative emotion, this leaves them open to obsessions.

After the being has been there awhile and has assimilated knowledge, when he develops true feeling instead of emotion, gradually he will build a vehicle on the other plane, with the help of the hierarchy there. The small white light you might see appear is a person ready for incarnation, having shrunk down to this size so as to inhabit and not disturb. But a person living on the higher planes would be quite a good size.

REALIZATION

The reality of God-realization, the realization of the Self, is the last door to go through. From there on up it is not a matter of initiative, it is the evolving of the individual himself, or the world he chooses and the path he chooses. There are two branches that he may follow, but he has no choice over them consciously at all: he may follow the path of mastery, or he may follow the path of sainthood.

As the light which exists within the body comes into the consciousness and we accept it, we then draw greater light from the spiritual Sun, the Christos, and it becomes one with us as our consciousness moves up the line and the dross is burnt out. And the very fact that we understand and sense the new world around us gives us what the theologian has called the unity with Christ. Because in order to do this, to have this rise of consciousness, it is necessary that we should have gone through and been in accord, in tune—or technologically speaking, have been in a synchronous wave vibration—with the Lord and Master Jesus Christ, and thus we have reached unity with him.

This is the realization that, while the consciousness of Christ is on another level, it is acceptable by us and, when we assume that, we reach it. Our assumption is possible because the existence of the light raises the vibration of the physical body, thus releasing the vibration from the Self within us, and so raises our consciousness and lets us become conscious of a higher level of reality and living.

It lets us become conscious of another sphere, another world. That is why our finer senses develop without sitting in circles or going into trances, or any of these things. They develop because these senses are common material senses on that level. They are not supernatural; you couldn't function any other way.

So realization is becoming conscious of other worlds, and revelation of the existence of life in other worlds around us which are in another time, or those events and those forces which have not yet reflected into the dense form of this earth. Thus we have unity with God.

This is what the old metaphysicians mean when they speak about this plane or that plane. These are not "planes", they are worlds, because they are globular. They have to be, because they are in the form of our Father. We are told God made man in His own Image, and this He did.

This is why man can go into suspended animation, because if he can lift his body-consciousness and his self-consciousness into another plane, he can live there, and the body will function on a magnetic field level, and the flow of the Life-force will be slow because the cellular structure of the physical body is at a point of static action. Static action is living, while not functioning outwardly, but functioning internally within the cell in the same way that you are doing as a whole body. Therefore you are in suspended animation. You have suspended the animate world, at this level.

There are too many people who think that the attainment of spiritual ability and spiritual sight is a thing which comes haphazardly just because you want it, but it does not. There must be distinct self-discipline in everyone's life before they can attain any great amount of spiritual understanding and realization. And what we are talking about is not this picture-book proposition that you see in the bookstores. You may read books from now till the end of your life, and you would not gain realization through it; because this is a functional thing, a real thing, and it requires the cooperation of students and teachers or they do not get it. It is a matter of self-discipline and involvement of the individual. If you want to know, ask the person who has been there, because he's the one that can tell you—not through somebody's supposition or opinions.

When you get close to the point of realization of your own true spiritual being, you will learn that when we say realization, we're not talking about what you know. We're talking about realizing, seeing, working with it! And when you get next to it, you will learn one thing: that you are going to quiet that mind of yours that you thought knew so much, and try to get past what you have built through the technological forms of mass mind, so as to get to the Self which is in constant tune with the universal reality which has all answers. And when you do get it quiet, then you will reach the realization of the true God Self.

This process of gaining the greater realization may go on for many, many years, or for a lifetime or two. But the akasha is open to you, and it depends on just how much you get rid of yourself and how much you are in control, you see. It works just like any other electrical circuit. If you can become absolutely quiet and negative, so to speak inactive, the force will flow to you. If you are seeking something, a particular bit of knowledge, and set this up and don't try to think, it will come to you, once you have reached this state.

It is just like being a sponge. A dry sponge will absorb water. The water is always there, the knowledge is always there; it is according to whether you can absorb it or not. That depends on how much you can get your own little self out of the way. You, of yourself, really don't know anything, and you will find that out before you get through. I'm not speaking as a personal thing; this is general, you know. Of course, if the coat fits, why, that's all right; put it on.

This is one of the great solar initiations, in reality, and without that you would not come into the place where it would be possible for what we call going behind the veil. In other words, your total consciousness then is aligning itself with the cell of the body of the Father; and that's putting it in a rather primitive way, but this is as close as you can get to it with words, at least. You may strike a greater realization later on, for which words wouldn't be of any account.

And there's another thing, that after a person does come through either illumination or realization—I don't mean "through" realization, but that the door has been opened—it doesn't stop there! He hasn't learned anything; he has just started to learn. And this is what we must impress upon the minds of students. They haven't learned anything yet, they have just started to learn. Now they have to start to really work upon the Self. They've got to really work for the Light. This is what they need, because they've had just the original opening of the way, and now they've got to start taking it to themselves in their consciousness, really.

This has not been put across yet, and I want to see it put across, because we have too much misinformation in that way, or too much misguidance, should I say. It isn't willful; it is just one of those things that happens in the course of transferring information from one person to another. It doesn't help to write this down; it doesn't click when you do.

We must use the term "the door of realization has been opened", not "gone through realization", in order not to misinform. Because the door has opened you have not reached Messianic consciousness, nor learned all there is to learn. And that is not where it stops. You have just begun, and from there on, you are really going to learn something. You have accepted the gifts from Christ. You may not know how to use them yet, but you have accepted the responsibility of them. We must be cautious with the terms we use.

It may take you the next ten lifetimes, but you'll get it. Or it may take you the next fifty years, according to just how humble you get, how much humility you can really attain. That will determine a great deal of how much you'll get out of realization, because this is something that has to come, and it only comes when you really get next to the Master. And you will learn that when you do start to experience, you will find yourself in a new world which you never knew existed. You will walk paths that you've never walked before, believe me. I've been a long time on this Path, longer than you can conceive of, and I'm still having some wonderful things revealed to me.

REBIRTH

When you say there is "a fine-looking man" or "a very beautiful woman", what do you mean? What makes them beautiful? It certainly isn't the decaying flesh that does it, for this person, no matter how old he is, is on the way to the grave; he is dying day by day, getting ready for transition. And until he is reborn, he knows not the Spirit, nor can he know or see the kingdom of God in which he is living. He does not know the world around him, for his eyes have not been opened, and neither has the Spirit moved within him.

Now, don't misunderstand me; we are not talking about an altar call. Oh, that would be easy, if we could put on an emotional appeal to God, an appeal to enter the Spirit, if we could come up to the altar and confess our misgivings and our misdeeds and the rest of things, and have the rebirth. That would be beautiful; I'd go for that, because it would be a much simpler process than what we go through today, and what we have gone through for fifteen thousand years and more. For unless you know the reality of the light within you, you do not know God, nor do you know Jesus Christ!

It seems we take this word "rebirth" with a grain of salt. And I don't see the expression of thanks, and the gratitude toward our Lord and the Father in heaven, for the opportunity of coming into the reality of this new birth, this rebirth. Jesus said, "Lest you be born again, you may not enter the kingdom of heaven." It was plain and simple, put in that many words. Those who sell this short can really cut it off, and I have seen some do it.

All persons who come into the Way will know that it is through their devotion, through the absolute acceptance and giving up of all of their own likes and dislikes, that they can reach the point where they can accept the Light of the Christos, and they will start toward that glorious rebirth of themselves. Not merely a new spiritual sense and consciousness, but a real true rebirth of their whole being, and their body as well.

The very purpose of the spiritual development and cosmic unfoldment we are striving for in these higher levels of life is not to make ourselves appear outwardly different, but to bring about that great rejuvenation from within, and that attunement with the higher forces of the universe which will bring us a degree of immortalization, the everlasting life which Jesus spoke of. We know that we cannot make ourselves immortal in this physical body, except through attaining the total body of Light, for the flesh cannot be immortal in itself. But the Light, when it is transformed into that ever-glowing, ever-moving body, can be. This is the rebirth.

The body is corruptible, but natural in its purposes. The soul, on the other hand, is incorruptible. It is immortal totally as it is, because that is its natural purpose, form and way, the way God created it. But we can develop and bring about a greater degree of attunement between the corruptible outer self and the incorruptible inner Self, that will tend to make the two more balanced and more harmonious. We can bring about the rebirth that our Lord spoke of, and thus some of us may even reach that degree of purity in which the Light will cause our bodies to be transformed.

REGENERATION

Regeneration takes place during periods of initiation, and it also happens from three days to nine months after starting of the light. We are not usually conscious of this, though we see it going on as part of the continued action and reaction of illumination; and this is what builds the light, the light body through which man might become the son of God. It is the regeneration of the physical body and the charging of the vehicle.

If you didn't have the Life Force present, there would be no life at all, and there would be no regeneration of any kind in the body. There has been regeneration going on right along, or you wouldn't be here now, because you'd have broken up a long time ago and disintegrated into the earth.

Some scientists have said that we have something like—what is it?—500,000 explosions an hour, cellular explosions giving off energy? I'll have to look that up. So we have regeneration going on now, but not to the same extent as when we have become completely filled with the light.

When the body gets filled with light, we are starting into illumination. Then the countenance and the entire personality begin to change, because everything else is being flushed out. The negation and the decay is flowing out of the body.

Regeneration takes a lot of power to rebuild, reorganize and bring back to its normal pattern the structure of the body. The appearance of the light in our being is not the same as going back to health, or becoming normal again. It is not a state of becoming well; it is a state of becoming as the spiritual body is. Actually the regeneration, with illumination, is the uniting of the spiritual body and the physical. Then it becomes as a prism to the Christ light and the force of Life which some call Nous.

It is a new body, just as we've talked of having a new heaven and a new earth. That is what Jesus called the "golden wedding garment" which we put on to receive the great Father and the Master, when he comes.

It gives the privilege of eternal life, for it is after this full attainment that death is no longer a factor.

In our work with the Testament we have read that "the bride and the bridegroom cometh". This is the secret of the proper unity of the soul and the divine consciousness on the one hand, with the mortal body on the other. This is the time when regeneration really takes place. This is the fulfillment, and at this time we are preparing for those things which are beyond.

REINCARNATION

In an organization of any kind where we are trying to unite our efforts to help man, and a group of this nature builds up the sensitivity and the vibration that they do, at times they start to see things. They start to have revelations, and they sometimes hear names, such as those from the Bible, which arouse their curiosity. Then along comes a foreign entity from someplace or other—probably from the borderland of earth, someone that's been stuck there—and pipes some little statement to them; and they get all excited about it. They'll come to me and say, "Well now, do you think that I am Joseph, that I was Jesus' father? I heard something like that the other night when I was in meditation."

Well, I'm not going to laugh, because it's not laughable. It is humorous sometimes, but I never laugh, because they're serious. This is probably one of the first things they've heard, really, out of the world beyond. Well, then I have the job of showing them how and why these things happen.

Q: *What do we mean by a "nameless wanderer"?*

A: Those who are seeking to serve wherever that service is needed. We're not saying, "Well, I was Caesar in my last incarnation, and therefore I have a place in royalty." No. Now that name, whatever it might be or was, has nothing to do with this life and its station or its service. If I had been Sir Launfall in King Arthur's court, it's no sign that I'm a spotless wonder in this life or if I'm even supposed to be. But I'm here to serve, just the same.

There are those of us who know they have lived before. And there are those of us who are willing to return into a flesh body to serve man and to bring about the things that are necessary for his good comfort and his good life, in accordance with creation. I would not shut the door to any who think they can attain the heights, for all will learn something and gain some help and some advantage, even though it may not manifest until their next incarnation.

Q: *Why do some people seem superior to others?*

A: We begin each incarnation where we left off in the last, and a little higher. If the last one ended with high aspirations, with no hatred, no injustices or cruelties, then early in this incarnation this higher development has to manifest, regardless of the station in life, the environment or outer education. In this sense we are not all born equal, because our present life is due to a great extent to what we made it in our last incarnation. There are those who start early in this life to over-come the bad effects of the last incarnation, and finally end this one in a much higher state than they came into it.

We speak of "traveling from infinity to infinity". Well, that's the incarnation after incarnation on the earth. It's the perpetual plan of eternal life, isn't it? It's the plan and the way and the pattern of life. Past experiences have become amalgamated into the reality of what we are.

We pray, "remove all negation from my conscious being". My conscious being is that part of me which manifests in the physical world. In this body, of course, there is a consciousness, because it is part of the memory of the soul itself, and this is what makes it function. It functions as it does because of our long years of experience, you see, and with the experience we have brought forth through many incarnations, whether here or in another place. This is the reality of the many systems in our body which we do not necessarily remember at all, but which must function from the memory of the soul itself and the record in the soul.

SCIENCE AND RELIGION

There is one thing which you can bank on. If any faith, religion, cult, or anything of this nature, won't stand scientific probing of the normal healthy mind, and if the facts which are given you do not coordinate with the basic facts of science, then you'd better look again, because I think you will find in what you are being told some particular facets of fallacy.

You've seen how everything in technology has to be in accordance with God's Word and Law; otherwise one or the other is wrong, it couldn't work. But to bring something down to cold hard science doesn't belittle the greatness of Jesus, or of any person, or of God Himself—just because we have a scientific reason for it. The general contention of most teachers seems to be that as soon as you have a reason for something and it is proven to be scientifically accurate and correct, it is no longer part of your religion and faith. And they seem to feel that your faith and knowing—the beauty of it—is cut off, and that you have lost something if you have broken open a mystery.

To me it is absolutely the opposite, because to see God in action and see what our Lord has done for us here, and to see how precisely it works, how precisely these things and orbs function, gives me a greater joy, a greater confidence, and greater faith in God and in our Lord Jesus Christ. And it all works continuously without having to be wound up each day. In other words, you won't lose the beauty of God or our Master just because you know how it works. Why should you? Every complete particle of matter is always in motion in our universe, and so it is completely imbued with spirit.

No matter what happens in this world, if we dissolve a mountain, the energy that's released is still here and it is still accessible and will be here continuously, because this is the form and pattern of creation, and that isn't going to change. We put things into the test tube and dissolve them into their atomic form, or electronic form sometimes—usually atomic form in the test tube—but that isn't changing anything. The basic elements are still here, they're accessible, and that's it.

Q: You're not just dispelling this, so to speak, into the astral plane?

A: No. You're releasing energy, period. And removing the vibrational pattern, changing the vibrational pattern, if you want to come close to it in technological form.

You don't have to try to do everything. You don't have to take each thing and learn to develop that particular thing, one after another, like learning mathematics, addition and subtraction. After all, one of the greatest material sciences is mathematics. It is the bible of the scientist, isn't it, really? Because at the foundation of all these sciences that you have created—and you have; man has created them—at the foundation of them is mathematics.

Mathematics down at the root is only addition and subtraction. All mathematics is built up of just that, various ways of adding and subtracting. And anyone who has gone into empirical mathematics, equations, knows that you can start with any group of factors and find any determined value that you wish, to a certain point. Mathematics is a science of the Spirit, because it is the science of geometric form.

There are in mathematics many proofs of this particular function of matter. If you are acquainted with logarithms you know what a logarithmic curve is. If you have ever used anything in drafting or design and the movements of things, you know the curve of acceleration. Well, this is exactly the same movement that we have in the force which gives us grace. There is no other way of interpreting this grace because, if you do, you belie the very foundation of all matter and all force.

At the foundation of all teaching, whether it be of Jesus Christ or others, the Law of cause and effect is the basic motivating law which controls the movement of force and matter, whether it comes from a generator or it comes from your own "generator", where you are propelling this force. There is cause and there is effect, and it is inevitable. It has never changed and it never will.

Thus if you were to look at grace from the standpoint of something given free of charge, without effort, something contrary to the mechanics of the universe, you would then have a broken law. And if you were to break one law in this universe, it would fly apart. You know this would have to be a fact. As soon as you break the magnetic field between atoms, the molecule flies apart. The laws must be inevitable because, if they weren't, matter would not stay as it does. You would not be alive if the Law was broken, because your body would fly apart too.

This brings us to a point of understanding of the laws of creation as taught by Jesus Christ and the Apostles, and other teachers. These laws and these systems of function were taught. You have only just certain things at the foundation of God's creation, a certain two or three Laws; and all the other things you find are the creation of man, not of God.

We can console ourselves with one thing. Science says that if you test this under a certain condition, and test it again and again under similar conditions, and you find that "x" number of tests give you a specific result of a general nature, that this is permission to write a hypothesis on, or derive a formula, or any of these things. And this is accepted as a scientific fact.

All basic formulas are extremely simple. You can sit down and reason any one of them out, if you have a childish mind. But just get that beautiful brain of yours going, and the mind, and there's no reason why you can't understand plain and simple scientific arithmetic. It may take you twenty years to get to be a mathematician. The only thing is, it may take you twenty years to get to see that you don't know anything in the first place until you stop thinking about it, and then you begin to know something. Now that's the truth; that's no paradox.

The Word which was pronounced at the beginning of Creation was the first soundless sound, which caused the aggregation of power and energy in the body of the Father. If I were to start to teach a theory, and I said we were going to propound a new theory, and the foundation of this theory is, for instance, seven thousand, five hundred and thirty eight, and its various uses, we would call this a factor in mathematics. But if our whole mathematical formula or thesis was written on the foundation of this number, this would be the key to the whole form of this phase of mathematics. Consequently, it would be the way of creating a system for the solution of certain problems, wouldn't it? And our factor would be the same as the Word given by the Father, because of one thing: all integral answers would be dissolvable by the factor, wouldn't they?

Well, all parts of creation are movable, and all creation takes place within the body of God from this Word, His Word. Now you know that wherever a factor is used, if that factor is removed from the functioning formula, your whole formula disappears, because there is no interrelationship. This factor is the foundation of your premise and your formula, and it wouldn't work without it.

No matter what you build in the way of a mathematical system, there are certain premises and certain factors which motivate the whole pattern and function. Likewise it is in our Creation. The Word of God still resounds throughout this solar system. And whenever we accept this, and the fact that we know that this Word will be functional, and we declare it and use it in accordance with the Trinity, the three great Forces, we know that the results are going to be there.

SELF

You come into the earth with the Self and with the soul—which is really a shell of the Self because it is that part which has been partially crystallized by your past experiences. As the blood moves through the body and begins to infiltrate all of the system, it records its potential reactions upon the sheath or outer surface of the Self. This is why, when you are initiated, illumination comes first and then the God-realization comes second, because you have to have light within the temple of the body in order to find the Self. And from the light which is within the temple you activate the forgotten memory of the soul, or the Mind of the soul, as you might think of it. As you activate this, and draw closer to illumination, the soul becomes more or less translucent.

If you were to ask, where is the Self situated? I would say, in the spiritual body of man; because it couldn't be any place else. The physical body and the materials composing it are too dense. But it comes partly into the physical body within, should we say, the sphere of observation into physical matter, because this vital or spiritual body is basically there, and that is what holds the physical matter together. Therefore the denser part of the soul or the Self shows through when you are able to raise your consciousness to that level.

The soul and the Self are very simple things. I usually don't like to get involved in this unless I have a class of ministers or advanced students; but we'll take it just the same. If you were to look at the Self you'd see light scintillating out from it. Now this Self is the cell of the Father which He has cast off and given its freedom to move, to think, to be intelligent and to follow the laws of Creation. But during its experience in many lifetimes, it has taken on the vibrational realities of these lifetimes and experiences, which are of much lower vibration and frequency than the cell of the Father and the intelligence within it. And so it is denser in form than the actual Self.

The light comes through because it doesn't usually get dense enough to hinder the light. But into the experience, into the soul, is incorporated the experience of your past life, the same as it is incorporated into the Mind of the Father. This Self, this "you": that's all there is of you, there will never be any more, and there will never be any less, except for the potential reality which you carry with you.

The soul and the Self carry the record of your experience and that will go with you wherever you go. But your greatest reality will be when you realize that, as you come and go out of this life, wherever you go, you are building into that soul and Self the personality which will be in touch with the earth or wherever you have been living, and that personality will live on as an example and a way, we hope, for man to improve himself wherever he may be.

All things work together. You can't separate anything, because the Self in man is only a cell in the great Being of God, of the Creator. There is all truth and all reality there; and once you have found it, you can fold up the books and put them on the shelf because you won't need them any longer. You'll only use them for reference when you want to keep a thing on a certain level or within a certain framework. But the truth is there; all truth is there. Just be careful that you don't get your mind in the way, because if you do you may get the wrong answer.

You have the mind of God, and you use part of it. And when you drop it right there, you will be able to use it, to understand it and to function with it; and you will keep your ego down a little bit too. Out of this working with the spiritual side of things, there comes a time when one starts to realize that his word does do something. And this is a very great day. And then he finds out that the mind, which he thought he had so much of, really is not the most important thing in the world. Because he has started to have some light, he has started to understand the soul and what was in it. And here, of course, we come to the place where man starts to awaken, and where he starts to realize that he has another source of power and another source of information that is very universal, very universal. This is the awakening, the finding of the Self, the becoming conscious of it.

It is then that man truly is able to stand in the shadow of our Lord Jesus. There and then he starts becoming the image of the Father as he was created. He goes through many reactions of all kinds. He has an entirely new perspective of life because he begins to see that there is some reason for life, that just learning how to perform with many of the sciences is not all there is to it. Or that just being a good healer or a good preacher is not all there is to it.

You wake up in the morning and look at the world around you and everything is a little sharper. Everything is a little more vivid. You will begin to realize that just living life has some real opportunity in it.

You hear people talk about the zest for life, and most of them haven't any idea what they are talking about.

The Self is a cell in the body of the Father. It is situated in man's spiritual body, basically, but it can be seen through the physical when the veil between the two worlds is removed, with the attainment of God-realization.

Q: Why is the solar plexus so-called?

A: The center of one's Self is like the sun. It is the reflection of the great Sun—the Christos. Here within is the end of all those reflex systems, so what we are like is very much like a galaxy. The Self is the sun of our body, of our universe. And I've consistently called this your personal universe.

As consciousness grows, you become more conscious of the Self until you become conscious of the whole and start to work with it. You want to function as a God-being, so you work with the Self and get acquainted with it, so that it really functions for you. And when you have reached that state where your consciousness—that is, your outer consciousness—has amalgamated with the Self and you no longer think about it because you just work through it all the time, you are the Self, and that's all there is to it.

The Self will work through the heart or the mind, either one. You know as well as I do that there is one way to get a person interested, and that is to listen to him, isn't it? Well, you just try listening to the Self and see how much it will talk to you. It works just exactly the same way.

If you don't like something, change it. There has been no limitation put on that. Once you learn to be master of yourself, you have the full authority and wisdom to do these things. But first you must be master of yourself, and you are master of yourself only when "you" do not exist. Until the time that happens, you are a body with a Self inside of it. This is the story of self-mastery in its entirety. In these few things you have the total key to self-mastery. You can take any one of these factors and meditate on it, and work with the Self, and you can find many ramifications of God or Creation.

SILENCE

From this point on we only begin to tread the Path of cosmic consciousness. All below this is nothing but a projection of words and our interpretations. From here on, where we express ourselves within ourselves and our experience is the only expression we have, here is where cosmic consciousness starts.

That is one of the reasons why we keep saying, when you have a spiritual experience don't say anything about it unless it is to the teacher who knows how to keep you from losing what you have gained. Don't talk about it, because the other person doesn't know a thing you're saying—not a thing. He couldn't; and you're only blocking his way because when he has a like experience it's going to be different. Basically it may come under the same category, but the experience will be vastly different.

When we come into dedicated service, we are stewards of the mysteries of God. We no longer may promiscuously talk about everything we have learned, for it is this which has lost to many the greatness and the sacredness, the reality of the mysteries. It concerns me that in this day and age we have lost the reality of the sacred mysteries which we study; we have talked so profusely of them every day.

And yes, they mean something to us, but they have become so common with us—though this is good in that it has helped to ingrain within our consciousness the greatness of truths which are taught in the Testament, and those things of the Christian mysteries. But one thing which we desperately need, as all mankind needs this day, is to be able to hold certain things sacred within our own hearts, within our own bosoms—to hold these things sacred as stewards.

You must not talk about the advanced work around others so that they will hear. And it isn't because there is anything that is underhanded, but if you start telling people things that they are not ready for, you're going to have problems. They'll have problems. So don't cause other people to stumble; this is not good. They might stumble because they were not ready to hear something, or you said something they didn't understand. This is not good for you or for them either, so let's understand this. And again, if you keep things to yourself, you'll have more when you get through than you would if you talked about it.

Talking probably causes one of the greatest losses in the world for any student. Each one gets his chance to learn. When it comes his turn, he is given the opportunity and he will have the chance to learn, the same as you do. But you wouldn't try to teach Greek to somebody who hadn't yet gone through the primary grades.

One of the facets of teaching those who have just begun spiritual work is the use and administration of silence. This is good for the student because in the course of following certain patterns and rituals, we grow so accustomed to using the audible sound. But underneath this there is another sound, which is the "soundless sound". This is the Voice of the eternal pattern out of the Akasha, sometimes called the Voice of Silence.

And this Voice of Silence is very powerful because it is the Mind and the reaction of the Spirit of God, the personality of God, working in the silence. It is there all the time, but only as we attune ourselves to this does it start to speak to us in that deep undertone which many of us have not learned to listen to, and where we have sort of been side-tracked because of the great stress and drive that we have had in material ways. It is now time that we step up.

We have been taught many of the physical forms and patterns, but now we must learn how to teach ourselves, because from here on in, it is not as much a case of someone teaching you as it is of you teaching yourself. Some of the lessons which you will learn, when you get the full comprehension of the work, are pretty profound, and the only person that can teach you is You. Now this calls for a higher form of work and a more serious, quiet working by oneself in unity with the reality of creation, the Godhead.

It is one of the most difficult things in the world to get an individual to know that he is a perfect twenty-four-hour-a-day broadcasting station—and I mean it just like that—without ever opening his mouth. When you are "on silence", you are broadcasting the most powerful waves of any time during your living life, because all of the power is going into the broadcasting and not into your yammering. So you are increasing your broadcast power. And what are you thinking about? What are you saying to yourself? What are you accepting or rejecting? These things, totally, you are broadcasting. So don't think that you have to speak to broadcast something.

When you reach that consciousness you will truly be able to take possession of your life, because you will not be sending out anything except what you want to be received. So don't deceive yourself. They may not know who is sending it out, but they're receiving it just the same, even if they don't know it. And the odd part of it is, it is really more effective than when you've been speaking, because there is no resistance to it, as a rule. You see? So during your silence, you are the most effective speaker, and are being heard more profoundly and more strongly than the person who is teaching the class.

Believe me, the closer you keep to the reality of no sound at all, the more liable you are to listen to the celestial music through which it comes. And it will manifest itself, but you have to stop trying to direct everything. The Director is already there and He will take care of it, I assure you.

SIMPLICITY

People don't want to understand simplicity because it brings with it the responsibility of the understanding, which is going to cost them something. It is going to cost them their way, what they want.

God has made—and our Lord has made—things so simple, so extremely simple that they are almost totally gifts. And if you put yourself to work on doing things for other people and entirely forget you, you won't have to worry about the score sheet at all; and you won't have to worry about that problem you brought with you, either. Do you know why? You won't have time to give it any life, because you'll have given all the life you had today to somebody else. You haven't had time to keep it alive. And when you stop keeping the problem alive, why, it will soon die like all the rest of the things. "He that keepeth his life shall lose it, but he that loseth it for my sake shall save it."

The child, as he grows up, is going to assimilate from others the understanding that he can't see, that he is not a spiritual being, and that he doesn't have any of these grand and glorious gifts that Jesus told us he could have and could use. The student who has learned all these unchristian things must be uneducated to get back to the place where he was as a child, so that he can function spiritually.

That's just what it amounts to. That is the whole sum and substance of spiritual teaching, to get you back to a place where you were when you were a baby, to function the same as you did then, and then you are an advanced being. "Unless you be as a little child, you cannot enter the kingdom of heaven."

The Master, when he was twelve years old and was with those in the temple, told them many things which caused them to wonder. Now, of course, he came into this world with that consciousness and wisdom, but why was it so easy for him to understand? Because he approached the things that he knew with the simplicity of a child, and therefore he could understand.

Our great difficulty and task today is to pick up a book and to read it with that simplicity. If you stop looking at the Bible as a book that can only be approached by a priest or a minister, you may learn much from it, especially from the New Testament. It is an informative book, a handbook for those who would like to learn more about themselves and the universe they live in. It will teach you how to use the many things you come in contact with every day, and how to control them. It is a record of the Law. It is a record of some of the mysteries and predictions for today.

You have to start everything from a useful base, and the first thing that's necessary is to get simple enough to read and understand in a simple way, the way a young person understands it. If you can't accept things on that basis, then you have a problem, because you will not find truth any other way. Just take the essence of things. The essence of things could be put on one sheet of paper and you'd have all the fundamental truths of the universe right there. But you get a lot of five-dollar words, and you will have something to argue about, and you will be thought a very intelligent person.

You ask about the mysteries: the reason they were called mysteries was because they were entirely covered up by their simplicity. Now if you want to really know God, stop thinking about trying to know how to do it and just act on it. Take a few simple little statements out of the Bible, six or seven verses out of the New Testament, or you could take six or seven Buddhist statements and just act on them; live by them. Don't try to figure it out, though.

SIN

One church speaks of venial sin and mortal sin, and another goes into three types. Well now, what would be the difference whether the error or sin was a little one or a big one? It would not matter except for one thing: the little one has got less energy, and the big one has more energy. Therefore, down at the very core or up on top of the ladder someplace, the archbishops and others must know that there is an ingraining and etching on the soul of the experience to be gotten rid of.

If I were to place sins or errors—call them what you may because none of the words seems to be descriptive in my way of thinking—I'd say that about the worst error that man can commit is to misinform somebody about his God. Now this isn't in the books, but this is my angle about it, because when you cut off the Source of the light, it is pretty hard to have any light. And if you get a misconception of your Creator or the Christ, it is pretty hard to get the light there. It is hard to understand Him or to understand yourself. And down through the ages the maxim, "Man, know thyself," has been taught, because when you know yourself, then you can know the reality that exists beyond the physical world, and that the visible world is unimportant compared to that of the invisible.

Once you knew yourself, then you had the tools and you could function. And this was your way of salvation; because if you don't understand why you did wrong, then it is pretty hard to be able to overcome sin, isn't it? I have a great deal of compassion for these people, because they don't know themselves and they don't know what they're being exposed to. They usually do the things that they do, not of their own will but because others have attached themselves to them, and that is why they commit the errors that they've committed.

If I don't get across the message to you and I permit you to stand in the way of other people, then I am wrong; I have done something which is wrong if I let you step in somebody else's way.

Now, it is these things that are the barriers. It isn't when you break house rules or sneak in after hours. That isn't the great sin, such as when you get in the way of other people and prevent them from raising their vibration. It's always the little thing that is the great offender. Don't stand and rebel at the teaching you have accepted, because that hurts everybody, not just yourself.

I hear people say, "But you know the things I've done, the misery I've caused in the past, and the number of people that have gone haywire through my actions." And so on and so forth. This immediately builds up a barrier, you see, and he's got another whole lifetime of things to overcome. But he doesn't stop to think—and of course he hasn't listened either—because he is still trying to do it. He doesn't stop to think about what Jesus did on Calvary. That is what he went to the cross for. That is why he was crucified, to eliminate that. So you look at your past and say, "Now that experience was entirely wrong, but there is this: I know I've been forgiven, because that is what Jesus did for me."

We are told that, "only as he looks at the past as a shadow of holiness can he gain the perfection and the function,"—the function of the Self in God, as you look at it and say, "Well, that's an experience I had. Yes, I got off the beam and had a really bad experience, but there were some things I did that were good."

One of the most detrimental things to anyone is that while he is hardheaded in listening to any direction or instructions he is just as hard-headed about forgiving himself for what he has done. This statement of "let go and let God" isn't just a matter of things that you own, or money that you have, or some girl friend or boy friend, or anything of that sort. It has to do with your own errors, your own—as the church would say—"sins" of the past. You hang onto those things just as ruggedly as if they had some value. And I've seen people work for five or six months to try to let go of a bad experience, and they'll fight like little tigers to hang onto that, you know.

Well, that is what Jesus went to Calvary for, and that is what we celebrate in the holy days. But if we'll just look at those experiences as something we went through then but know that it hasn't anything to do with now, then we will gain the perfection and function of the Self in God. You can't tie yourself up to an old life and then turn around and expect to function in a new one, because you're not living in the new one yet. You're not living in that new life until you've let go of the old. And there's no other way of doing it.

SOUL

The soul is probably the most neglected topic of the whole metaphysical field, and yet, when you come to think of it, this is the whole kernel of what you're working for. Because the soul is the shell or the perimeter, so to speak, of the Self. And it is the recording wire on which all your experiences are recorded. It is also the place where the motor system has all its records, so your heart will beat, your lungs will breathe in the air and vital forces of the universe, and so that you will remember—even though you don't physically—the entire past incarnations and cycles of life which you have gone through since you left the womb of nature, or the womb of the Father.

This all-encompassing record is less known and less talked about than any other part of the human organism, and yet we go through all kinds of sad experiences and of joyous experiences for the sake of just getting in balance with the true Self. Now this is expressed in many ways. There are Sanskrit, Latin and Greek terms and half a dozen others, so that after interpretation one hardly knows whether they are talking about the soul or the Spirit.

The very first point that we discover about the soul is its divine nature—that it is of God, so to speak, and that the body is made for the soul, and not the soul for the body. Here is a great error that is made by some teachings. The soul is not made for and is not the product of the body.

With certain spiritual experience, you may see a rim of light around the Self, and you won't probably know what it is; but that is what comes from the body of God, the Creator, coming out through the soul and its experience. And so consequently you see it brighter here and in more detail around the edge, just as you can look at a man's body and see the emanations from him, or the aura, if you look carefully or if you have developed sight. What you see is the periphery of the soul body around the Self, that marginal part like the shell of an egg.

Q: Is that the experiences of your past existence?

A: Its density is the experience.

Q: How does a human soul differ from an animal?

A: The animal has a group soul. He's part of a greater number.

Q: Is there a single being over that group?

A: Well, shall we say it is part of the Host, the hierarchy, that takes on this job.

Q: *Essentially what's the difference between the soul and the Self?*

A: One is the living recorder and the other is the living "Liver".

You carry with you from life to life the record of your beautiful deeds and some of those that aren't so beautiful. And this is why you need to receive here on earth, consciously, the Light of Christ within you, because this then brings you to a point where you can approach the Self, the real You. You can call it You, you can call it the Self or the God within, and you'll be right in all three. And the soul is the shell or the sheath of that Self, that "You".

From what we have seen we know that there is crystallization around the Self, and this is the record of your lifetimes. You have carried these things with you for centuries. These are your experiences. You couldn't learn to pray without ceasing unless you had a soul, because there is where the automatic mechanism of the physical body exists. This is the computer which runs the physical body. It is an automatic system. Slight impulses come, stimulated by chemical reactions, through motivated electro-chemical reactions.

The old Masters said, "as above, so below", and we've seen that this is evident. Like the God-Self and the soul around it, so do you stand right now in your physical body, for around you is your atmosphere and the shell of it. And when you become conscious of this, you can control what comes in or goes out, as some of you have experienced. Then if you will consider the earth and its atmosphere, that is another example like the body itself and the atmosphere or the shell around it. You can go all the way down to the atom, if you want to. It is an unbroken chain. It is a creation out of One Mind, because it is a single thought. Or should I say one of three thoughts?

It is the soul that we seek to emancipate, to cleanse, to renovate with light and with our own actions; and then we are free, and we'll get true guidance. This is why the individual who has delved into the psychic—and I'm not saying there isn't such a thing as psychic sight, because I know there is. I have worked around too much of it; I know it's true. But if there has been no light and they haven't found the Self, and it hasn't been cleansed, then the things that do come up from the Self come through all the rubbish and the records of negation and error. And this is what we call psychic perception, in lots of cases. This is misguided intuition because the true answer has to go through a false

246

filter, so we are misinformed. But when the illumination and the Light of Christ is there, when you've found the Self and the soul, and when you have paid the penalty, then what comes out is straight goods. There's no coloring to it. It is the cold factual truth, and will not err.

A thing we have to be careful of in reading many of the books on this subject is that we don't form definite opinions from them, but use them as information to gain our own state of consciousness and the realization that the soul is definitely the storehouse and vault of knowledge of our past lives.

SPIRITUAL DEVELOPMENT

An old tradition says that when you are ready, the Master will appear; but it meant that you had to be ready through study and development, not by merely sitting in a chair and waiting. A second law to think about is the metaphysical law that when the time is right your mission in life will unfold and the Master who is to lead you in that way will come to you. This means that when you have reached the proper cosmic development, the Master of that plane will show you what your real work or purpose is to be in this life, aside from the giving of glory to God and following the ways and the dictates of our Master Jesus.

When you will reach that sphere of vibration, in this life or the next, is something I cannot tell you, for each plane of consciousness or sphere of vibration has its particular field and dominion of activity. Each of us will do his best, and the work on earth in one of those fields will fill us with great satisfaction. We may spend ten incarnations doing all kinds of things before we reach the one real plane or level of vibration in which we are to outshine ourselves and do our greatest work for humanity.

The only way to reach that sphere of vibration more quickly and surely is through study and development, in order to move forward from one plane to another as often as possible. Those who do not study or seek spiritual development may take several lifetimes to go through two or three of these levels or spheres of vibration, while those who are studying, working diligently and following the exercises and the instructions, and who are gaining the spiritual attainment, may go through two or three of these planes in one incarnation. God, in all His mercy and grace, has His way of giving us those things which we need at the time that we need them.

We find persons who expect that the spiritual development going on within them should constantly burst forth with some sort of outward material manifestation. It never dawns upon these persons that the higher spiritual, higher psychic part of development may be going on within them to such an extent that no outward manifestation of any kind is made, and no outward demonstration is possible unless the Cosmic sees fit, unless the hierarchy sees fit, or Jesus sees fit to use this particular time or this particular way to demonstrate a thing. It they do see fit to do this, then they will use this as a channel and for a special purpose.

I use the word "attain", but actually you can't attain anything. There isn't anything to attain; it's just a case of your becoming conscious of it, a matter of you letting go and letting the thing flower. It is like an encased rosebud. When you open it up, or the sun opens it up through its action, it will flower out. It doesn't have to get any of the qualities; the qualities are there. All it has to do is let them unfold and be shown, because until this is shown in the material world, it doesn't fully function. And if you don't let this be shown, the spiritual color, the spiritual realities of your being, you're not yet complete; and that's very simple, right to the point.

The nerve centers, which in ordinary man remain dormant, are awakened in the body of one who has put his foot upon the Way. The barriers are burned away and the formless cluster of cells takes on a definite form. Bit by bit the mechanism for contact with the inner school is built, the inner way is substantiated, and the Host becomes our teachers. The incorruptible arises out of the corrupt and the Christ body is reformed.

You have been told about how a person, when he begins to seek earnestly and diligently, goes up into a mountain, and people actually do put packs on their backs and go up into the mountains, because they are seeking something and hoping that they will find it there. Well, it's a beautiful place, of course, and they're getting a little closer to nature and all that, but I assure you that you can find it just as easily here as you can out there. It's just according to how much dedication you want to put into it, and how much time and how much work you want to put into it, as to whether you attain it or whether you don't. You're going to have to do the same amount of work up there that you do here, so it doesn't cut any ice in that respect. Of course, I always prefer being up in the mountains to being in a dirty street, that's natural. Everybody would enjoy nature and its beauty, a tribute to the Creator, and we can't help but acknowledge that.

If you start up the mountain with love, you will find the hand (yod) will be extended to you by your fellow travelers. And there might be some amongst you who have had that experience in certain organizations—that you found the hand of friendship or at least a passing acquaintance and mutual understanding. And you might even take in a dinner or walk on the town, whether you'd ever met the person before or not; but here is the hand of friendship, the sign that you both have reached a mutual point.

Many people write about what they call holiness. There are things which have to do with holiness which have nothing whatsoever to do with things that are usually attributed to it. Holiness is not a thing in which we have a figurehead which sits on a throne. There are many great people that you pass on the street without noticing, and some have greater holiness than those who have been so portrayed or who have perpetrated themselves as spiritual leaders in many of the churches and many of the groups.

We must first eliminate from ourselves all of those traits of character which interfere with a broad and universal comprehension of cosmic attunement. Now what is "cosmic attunement"? Well, it's a state that takes place when you've reached a point where you have nowhere else to turn; you've been beaten down to the place where you're willing to do anything. And perhaps you haven't got a dime; nobody will talk to you, there's nothing to eat today, and you're desperate because everything you've done has failed. Then you're ready for cosmic attunement. That's right. That's just about the only time you can lead a person to it, because then he'll stop and listen to the words of Jesus.

It is only when we begin to define the reality that the keyword for attainment of anything real is "service", and it is only when we have learned to do things without expectancy of any reward from either the material side of life or the spiritual, that the really great attainment and greater consciousness is developed. You don't develop consciousness by sitting down in meditation alone. It takes a physical base of action in order for it to be a thing which sticks with you.

In our striving to gain spiritual attainment, we have sometimes failed—naturally and humanly so—to recognize one thing, and that is that we only really attain this through our personal service and our lifting up of other people. Now, the teacher sometimes has to do various things in the way of discipline, but the real key to spiritual attainment is through our lifting up of other people. In this great lesson which our Lord is teaching us, he implied, "I have glorified Thee. Now glorify me, Father, so I can give unto them."

You will notice that it is those persons who see the good in other people who move ahead. It is they who advance. The ones who give selflessly in service and find the least fault are the ones that come through into the spiritual attainments secure, solid, and with a great deal of reality. We have experienced many great blessings through our Lord and Master, but there is always that living up to what we have experienced and the gifts we have been given. And if we fall short of being grateful, of thanking God and thanking our Lord for what we have received, then we fall short and will not develop in the sound and secure way that we should.

Gradually and slowly as our eyes are uncovered, and we start to see the immensity of this creation, the timeless depths unto which it goes, we become a little awed. We wonder what it is all about. Why are we doing this? Well, cheer up. There isn't anybody who ever lived, and who has attained any real consciousness of the Christ within them, that hasn't looked at this and said, "I wonder where it goes."

But there is one thing I can assure you, that if you will follow the ways of Creation, and if you will make service your objective, not only in work but in thought—and here is one thing that we have oftentimes missed. You might turn out a good day's work. This is fine, we all need it. You can turn out a good day's work but do you turn out a good day's thinking? Ask yourself that, because it is not only the labor of your hands, it is the labor of your mind and your heart that determines the nature and the vitality and the power of what you represent. You could turn out a good day's work and destroy more than you had built, and that would be a little foolish.

There is a saying that you have to climb the ladder, but if you are going up, you must help somebody up onto the next rung below you, so that he will help to lift you up.

Rain and storm must be, in order to keep the atmosphere cleansed and things growing for life. In the beginning of understanding you had a beautiful day, because things were working in accordance with creation and were in perfect order. When you start to work with self-acceptance, and with realization, if something does not go as you wish, you think it is all wrong. But very often the things that seem to be hindering you the most are helping you the most. Everything is in perfect order. If we had accepted all as wrong, the prayers would never have been answered. But the blocks and obstacles are right instead of wrong, because they assist nature to work its way through, till many facets draw together in the right time and place to actually bring about the desired result.

Know the objective and know the result you want. But, for God's sake, DON'T KNOW HOW! Because if you have your mind set, you're just clogging up the machinery. There's only one thing I might add. First comes the illumination, the true illumination. Then comes the realization of God. Then comes the Way, the following of the eternal path of Light.

SPIRITUAL HEARING

We tend to take on things which are very beautiful, very right, very good, while somehow missing the reality that we do not function here in just a visual way, but there is another side to our nature which also has life. If we keep this separate from the life in the material world, then we open the door to a great deal of problems, of trouble, of misunderstanding. But when we let the Spirit move, and when we listen—but this is man's great fault, he does not listen. He cannot keep his mouth shut long enough to listen to the voice of the Spirit; because if he did, he would make few mistakes.

The hierarchical head of a church or organization may be called infallible, but only if he is a realized being and a master of the arts would he be infallible. It wouldn't be through any lineage, but because he'd got a direct connection with the Mind of the Father where no mistakes are made; and this is his only source of infallibility.

You must learn to listen, all the time, and if you listen long enough, you will start to hear. You will start to hear the reality. You will start to hear those from the other side, of the Host, and be able to receive instruction which is greater than anything you could get in the world, I assure you. But you can't do it if you close both ears and have your full consciousness on the material plane. You must function on both, that is essential.

Learn how to listen, and when you need an answer it will be there; it will come to you. You don't have to fold your legs up under you and go into deep meditation and put a blanket over your head. All you've got to do is shut your mouth and stop thinking and you'll get the answer. And learn to know that you don't know anything, and then you'll really become a wise man. That is the gospel truth right down to the cold kernel.

One of the standard questions that comes from a great number of students, and maybe you have asked it at one time or another, is that the first time they see something or they see somebody appear, and they've tested it to see if it's real and if it can take the sign of the cross, and so forth, and it does, then they'll come back and say, "But, Father, it disappeared in a few minutes and didn't speak to me." And I say, "Well, did you ask a question?"

Q: How would you do that?

A: How would you ask the question? You'd ask it, of course. But they felt they were separated from this being, because he was "out there" someplace and, "Well, I don't know how to get out there." You know what I mean? Why, you just go up there, that's all. And what is seeing? Being able to see into that world.

Q: You said that God renders to a person according to his highest conception of God. Well now, can you set up a form for the Master Jesus to render through, to a person wanting to make contact with him?

A: You mean is there a way of contacting the Master directly?

Q: I'm not saying directly. He's awfully pure to be thinking about that. But could you set up some kind of a channel he could work through, so that you could bear him?

A: Oh well, this is done very simply. It isn't really the setting up of a channel. You raise yourself up out of your material consciousness and your body—raise the spiritual body out of the realm of the physical. But just before you do this, you ask the Master to come in for a purpose, and then you move out of your physical body and you have no problems.

Q: But what if you're not ready to do that?

A: Well, you can if you have good enough faith and prayer. It's possible to draw him to you. That's the way it's more easily and safely done, let's put it that way. You can ask him to come in and a great many times he will.

Q: But wouldn't that hurt him? He'd have to get dense, wouldn't he?

A: No. All he'd do is just project his own image; you could see it. Most of the master teachers don't use a solid form, but you can see them just the same. But what I'm driving at is this: that we fail to realize the greatness of the Master's work. This is what holds back the consciousness of the cosmic for us, because we have our consciousness nailed down to such a small finite sort of thing.

Somebody will come in and say, "You know, I saw one of the Apostles." Or, "I saw one of the ancient priests", or "one of the great teachers" like Mohammed or Baha Ullah, or some of the others. Sure, they saw him, but that being didn't come down here himself. He projected his image down here so he could speak through it. Because it is too much work to develop a physical body to come into here—or even into a spiritual body dense enough to do this so that it would function. So he just projected the image and spoke through that.

And sometime you yourself may contact one of the White Brotherhood who may teach you some specific things. There's no question in my mind but that it may happen if you stick to the Path properly, and you'll gain a great deal from them. But they're not going to come down to your dining room to do it, because they have too many things to do.

There are many things that happen in the way of demonstration and that sort of thing, but don't try for them because, if you do, you're going to have problems yourself. They don't come by trying, as a rule. It is possible, if you have had a premonition or a forecast of such a thing, that you can make yourself ready to receive, then if you can keep your mind quiet, you'll be able to receive.

Sometimes you have to get down because you have broken contact, if you get too wrapped up in your own thoughts, your own abilities and your own trying to solve the problems or trying to help. And sometimes it takes a physical getting down too, on the knees, in order to get yourself mentally down to where the power will flow to you, and the Master will come. But you can't expect Him to come to you if you think you're on a level with him, or that you are going to do it, because it won't work that way. You have to have the ability, there has to be that attraction and you have to be pretty negative to Jesus in order to get him there; then it will be filled. You have to feel your inferiority with the Master, and feel much need of this, and it will come.

And I want to make a remark about this one thing, because it is such a reality. It describes the movement of power, no matter where you are. There isn't a light in this house that would work if there wasn't a draw between the positive and the negative. And it's the same thing with God. If you get too positive about it, I guarantee you won't feel the presence of God very quickly. You'd better get negative about it. You know just how much you need Him, and just how inferior you are to Him, and then you'll be sure to reach Him. I don't like the word "inferior", because that carries some other connotations, but you've got to know your relative position and how much you need Him, and then you'll find Him.

One of the problems and one of the hurdles that every student faces when he comes into a church, an order or a group, and starts to work with the Spirit and follow the voice of the inner man, is that he sometimes opens himself to the voices of others who are on the other side. And if he isn't careful, he will soon be telling you that he is the special messenger of God Himself, or some other thing which is designed specifically to make, well, a fool of him, so that he will become ridiculous and the truth and the word which has been given to him will go for naught. I'm not saying revelation doesn't come across the border, because it does. That is proven many times. But not by entities of this negative type.

And there's another thing I hear from people who come around: "Well, now, I used to do astral travel when I was dropping this or that or something else." Of course, the only kind of travel they did in that condition was in their mind, and that isn't astral travel.

Then there are those who have entered the religious life but are still listening to the mass mind. They are still thinking of those things outside. You know, all demons do not have horns, and all demons are not of a subterranean nature. There are many "demons" walking the face of the earth as perfectly normal individuals who are far from being a part of God. And in the performance of their duties, whatever these might be, they've got all sorts of special information to impart to you that they claim comes right down out of the seventh heaven and the archangels themselves, and these can be most degrading and destructive. I've listened for more years than you can imagine to these people that "have no error, and never had an error and have never sinned, and have always been right".

These are the things which we have to make sure that we understand so that we can rightly qualify the reality from the unreality. And we may hear an inner voice, through the activity of our own being, that is not just a matter of the Self speaking alone, but a voice which will come to us exteriorly, with a distinct instruction, a distinct understanding of the reality.

There is no such thing as the possibility of an individual or an organization giving away or selling sacred Truth. This is a fallacy. I might stand here and spend the next four hours explaining to you the work of a Master, and you would go away twice as ignorant as when you came. And I would be four times as ignorant for trying to do it. Divine wisdom is something that comes from within you, and it is not of the brain, it is not from books. It is experiencing the combination—and I'm going to use a technological explanation here—it is experiencing sound and vibration, frequency of vibration above the sound level, simultaneously. Now, that's one for you to take back and meditate upon.

Sound, like light, has a certain frequency, and it is caused by vibration. Sound vibration does not always produce sound out here. The lower part of that cycle is not in the audible scale. It is the absence of that sound which is below the line and to which you don't even give consideration, but the absence of that sound will draw cosmic force.

From some of the great ones, from some of the Brothers and others of this sort, we all, if we haven't shut both eyes and ears, will get spiritual guidance. If we don't think we know it all or that we can disregard the Source of energy and power of our life, why, we'll get that guidance. You can call it spiritual guidance or direct guidance; you can say that somebody was talking to you—and they were, because you don't have to separate the spiritual world and the physical world at all. You can say that "somebody was talking to me that didn't have a dense body", and that's perfectly true.

Only when you have closed your ear to divine consciousness have you misstepped. But open that ear and you will rise above all things, and you will fit in what is received where it belongs in the lifestream. You will be the creator of your world, but only when you listen without reservation and the ego doesn't stop your hearing. Listen. Don't talk, listen, and you will take on the reality of the shadow of our Master Jesus Christ.

SPIRITUAL SIGHT

Y ou don't develop spiritual sight, you have it; or you might say you uncover your spiritual sight, as Paul felt scales fall from his eyes. Somehow in this earth we have been so wrapped up in the visibility of reality that we have failed to recognize that the invisibility of reality is actually that which we should be most concerned with.

We have been trained since childhood to think from a material point of view, so perhaps we have never fully realized the other essential aspects of creation. We have been taught that unless we can actually see, feel, smell, taste or hear a thing, we have no right to believe that it exists. This teaching is, of course, false. This fallacy has been universal, although in recent years there have arisen a few exceptions, and out of the many schools some of the great teachers who have come to earth are gradually but slowly bringing some great workers into the field. We can sense, and many of us can see and follow these five senses – six senses – through the many levels of vibration.

We have been so trained to think from a material standpoint that it is very difficult for us to acquire the wisdom or consciousness that there is more to the unseen than there is to the seen. And that in those vast realms above us in vibration, there exists a most wondrous creation of our Lord, of our Father in heaven.

You may not accept God, you may not accept Christ, you may not accept anything, but still you're going to have to learn that thirty percent of what you call physical vision is not physical vision at all, but spiritual vision. So I'm sorry, you're stuck with it. You can't help it, you've got to acknowledge it. It's there. Have you ever sat in a room looking right straight ahead of you at something and swore you saw somebody coming in the door, or swore that somebody was coming down the street, and then you looked and they were not? Many of these things happen. This is the spiritual part of your vision. And regardless of whether you believe it, it's there.

If you look for them with your physical eyes and cannot see them, you doubt the existence of these things. If you listen carefully and hear nothing from your physical ears, you may doubt the existence of certain sounds. You may think according to the way you have been taught to think, that this is impossible. Your doubt and skepticism seem perfectly logical and reasonable to you. But doubt must be cut out so one can see, because as long as there is doubt you cannot see.

We know that with the coming of the Light and the accepting of it, these spiritual senses give us the true picture of Creation, and of the ways in which our great Father in heaven has created this universe, this solar system, not only the visible but the invisible. This is not an impossibility when we are aware of more than one level of consciousness at a time. Perhaps if you are able to concentrate enough and to keep your mind under control, you will be able to reach the door between these two worlds.

As the earth and the psychic world amalgamate, as they mix and blend together, beings in the borderland of the earth and in the psychic world will manifest themselves at times, so that things you will hear should be checked out; because you will not be sure at times whether you are getting it directly from its origin in the Self, or whether it is coming from someone who knows less than you.

Remember that all the things you hear and see are not totally true. This we must observe very closely if we are to keep our feet upon the path that leads to the realization and the understanding and the familiarity with Jesus Christ, our Lord here on earth. There are many things which you will experience; some of them will be good, and others untrue. So this is the way you must work.

Until you have the Light, the Christ Light, here within you, you will never be convinced that there is a spiritual body. Couldn't be—you couldn't see it. It is impossible to see it within yourself unless you do have that Light to see it with. A psychic could see the aura, and parts of it. Some people with a great deal of psychic sight can see some things about it. But to see their own, that's another thing. This is one of the toughest jobs, to know yourself, to see yourself just as you really are.

At the point where spiritual sight develops, we are no longer hampered by the psychic influences, the motions of desire, and the tearing down of forms by the desires of other people or ourselves. Then we learn the Truth, that absolute Truth that we can only know and find through cosmic consciousness.

STEWARDSHIP

The steward of a household is one who metes out the wealth of the household to those who need certain things, materials, money and other things, as they are needed. He guards them to see that they are not misused. He puts them in a safe place where they will not be tampered with, and watches over them with great care—a good steward.

This you should take a lesson from and watch over the truths, watch over the mysteries as our Lord Jesus brings them to us, and as you are taught them. For in the tremendous impact of so many things that have been learned in a short time, many have failed to hold them sacred, to guard and watch over how these truths are used, how the sacred writings are used, and to treasure them. To treasure them because you have been given the privilege to know things which for generations past many millions have never had a chance to know.

This is where we lose something which is of great value and great importance to each one. For in accordance with the sacredness in which we hold these things within us, and in accordance with the revelations that are brought and the way we hold and regard them, just so will things be given unto us. It is all right to share them amongst your fellow students, but don't take them on the street and cast them out where they may be stamped on. Let them live and be nourished and be allowed to flower into that fineness and the feeling of reality in the heart of one who has dedicated his life to the glory of God.

We talk about the Testament, about the Master, we learn the mysteries, and this becomes rather common. Then we get to the point where we feel that nobody else is any different. We hold the divinity of everyone, surely, but don't give to others these things which they cannot use properly. For this too is the duty of the steward, to apportion out that which is of his Father's kingdom, of his landlord or master of the household where he is working. And you, being stewards of Jesus Christ, it is your duty to apportion out in accordance with the ability and the skill of those to whom you give, the spiritual skill, the spiritual know-how, the spiritual understanding, so that within yourself you do not lose the sacredness of these things, for there is that fine feeling that one develops from it. Like a person moving their hand over a finely-woven piece of velvet, it has that touch to it when it has been held sacred within your life, within your thought.

Within the heart of every individual there is the kernel, the seed of eternal wisdom. And it is those things which we hold sacred which will bring to us the reality of God, the reality of the Host, the reality of Jesus Christ, in its living, dynamic form. As the vestal virgins kept the sacred fire burning in the ancient temple, keep that same sacred fire burning in your own being, your feeling toward the truth and the Lord Jesus Christ.

Be happy with the association of our Lord, and say, "I'm going to follow this and work with it," and keep that as one of the gems within yourself. Do you know the way it was given to me once? A teacher said, "If I gave you a ten-carat diamond, I know very well you wouldn't tell the rest of these people about it; because you'd be afraid somebody would take it away from you."

But you see, these words and the things of a spiritual nature that we experience are not valued like some jewels that we might get. And these are jewels, because never again, in your whole life span, if you live to be two hundred years old, will you ever receive that which you received on the twenty-eighth day of August at six o'clock, or four o'clock in the afternoon. You will never receive it again, and you never can, no matter how many eons of life you come back to. That is done, it has been created; those words have been fixed. They are finished when they are given to you, and it will never happen again. You may at some later time hear similar words, but they will not carry the power, they will not carry the same gift, and you are not then the same person to receive them. A similar thing happens when a student tells his teacher, "All right, Father, OK." He's just heard it go by, but he hasn't really accepted it. Now there is no way that that person can give the same message to you again. That gift is final. You will never get it again, because it will not have the same power, and it will not have the same exact connotation.

And you know, maybe that is what you needed in order to truly gain God-realization. Just maybe that is what you needed. That might be the golden key that would open the treasure chest, and you may have thrown it out the window. Because there are times when things are just that profound and that perfect that they can unravel, unwind the whole panorama, and things can be gotten rid of so you can go on.

So don't always blame the teacher or the person who is giving it to you. Here again the same thing is working out in you. "Well, that was so-and-so, and he and I have differences," and so forth. You know, you could meet a man down on skid row who might give to you what you needed for your total salvation on this earth, and he might have "half a jag" on too. It doesn't make any difference actually whether you like him or whether you don't, or whether you like your teacher. So don't tell me you don't like a teacher or a priest, because he may be the person that you need, in order to overcome your egotism and your partiality and all the rest of that bag of tricks, so that you can receive. We are not concerned with compliments but with action.

SYMBOLISM

L iving symbolism is probably one of the most important studies that you'll ever have. Without it you cannot understand the Bible and you cannot understand spiritual philosophy, because all of these things are written on a foundation of symbolism. Without symbols you would have no creation, and nothing would exist in this solar system, because symbols form the pattern and the function of the entire solar system. Now I know this is a rather strong statement but it is nevertheless true, because you could not follow out the first chapter of Genesis if you didn't have one simple symbol, and that is—what would you think? The circle! God said in Genesis He made man in His own image, didn't He? And what is the image of God down at the visible level?

In the solar system you have more or less the uniform shape of the Self. The Father said, "We made man in our own image." Man was made in God's image; but man is the Self, isn't he, and the soul? There you have the symbol in action, because there God is extending Himself. And what happens when you start to extend yourself?

Q: There is a flow of energy.

A: Why, sure there is, only there is this form to begin with, so this is the only form you can extend. If you are in a physical form and you wanted to project yourself someplace, you'd have to extend this form, wouldn't you? Well, that's living symbolism, because you are following distinctly the creative form in the material world as well as above.

You know the Being that created this thing is a pretty good Architect and He knew that if He didn't keep similarity between the earth and man, that man would never be able to live on the earth, because the forces would get terribly confused if He didn't keep the symbolism the same. Without symbolism you can't teach about God and Jesus Christ. It is the mathematics of the universe. It is the languages of man projecting forward.

Symbols are not just lines put down on paper. They are things through which you live. They are the movement of life! You can't live without them. Every day of your life, you move through symbolism! It has to be.

At the foundation of this, our solar system, there are three prime symbols, and we will go into these rapidly. The circle symbol is known as the Father. Many different races, many different societies in civilization have used this same symbol to represent God, the First Cause. The form of the circle follows from the unity of God in this universe, right down to the microcosm, to the cell in the tissues in your body, down to the atom. And there is no change; it is exactly the same form from the macrocosm to the microcosm. God is the circle in its completion.

When you talk about God in the solar system, then you put a dot in the center of it, and this is the symbol for the Sun. The sun disc, as used by the Egyptians, was not a symbol of the everlasting God, but a symbol of the manifestation of His power and the giving of light, life and love to all living things, in line with man's understanding that sunlight was the sustainer of life.

We have pictured three symbols, the circle, the triangle and the square: or Creator ○, Mediator △, and Creation □. You can take these three symbols, and you can find the mathematical formula and can build the outward form or structure of any building. You'll find where they fit. You'll find that the triangle, which is a symbol of our Law, is also a mathematical foundation of trigonometry. And this again is the form; because when you do a mathematical equation, you are setting up a form through which forces may move, and this is what you're doing too when you work through the Mediator, the Christ.

The very mechanics of this world is founded on symbols. The triangle is the foundation not only of trigonometry, but of crystallography. Symbolism is the foundation of physics. It is the foundation of mechanics. An engineer, a chemist, and so forth, has learned to use the symbols of mathematics and of the universe in which he lives. Now, he uses it in an outward rather than in an inward manner, but he still is a creator from this standpoint. In his mind there is a pattern of what he is designing or is going to create.

The triangle represents the Law, abstraction in mind, the foundation and pattern in the heaven world, between God and His creation. I've often said that if you want a prayer answered, you go directly to the Father and get yourself in tune. You make the form and then let go of it, and it would be created here. This is the Trinity, but it is also the Law in action.

We should always keep in mind the laws of the spiritual and material triangles whenever a manifestation of cosmic power is to occur on the earth plane, and demonstrate here on this earth the spirituality of the Cosmic being brought into physical manifestation. We must remember that these symbols with the point downward represent such a manifestation. God in great humility, manifest here on earth. The opposite action has to take place up there, before it can come in here, doesn't it? So the reality is just the opposite of what you see on earth, or what the world teaches.

The triangle represents the number 3, and the square represents the number 4. The circle represents 9; and a multiplicity or combination of these numbers gives the universal number of 12, which is the number of the division of the zodiac, and so forth.

Nowhere in creation can you get away from "three". It can't be done. God the Father, God the Son, and God the Holy Ghost. Why? Because it is present in all forms in all of those levels of density, spiritual density, you see. And it is the collating Law which motivates, holds all together and gives all life. This is the great mystery that cannot be explained.

The third symbol is the square: materialization and manifestation. Production. And you'll always find, even in ancient alchemy, that the square, representing the four elements of creation— that is, fire, air, earth and water—is also used entirely in working with dense matter on the earth plane.

This is not only a square, but it is a cube which has dimension. It represents the creative elements that produce down here on this plane— that is, the plane on which we stand. These are the fundamental elements of creation, and it doesn't make any difference what philosophy you study, you'll find them there just the same.

In the seven days of creation, you will find various aspects of the four elements, and you'll find also the three parts of the Trinity. This is really the representation of creation, an existent reality. This is a symbol in the Mind of the Creator. This is the way He created it.

When I say the illustration of the Tree of Life depicts a pattern in the Mind of the Father, you don't understand it because I've put the pattern of the Law on a flat blackboard. When I put it on the blackboard I cannot put spirit into it, so you cannot feel it. But when I talk about it you can feel it, and then there can be an existent pattern in your mind. Then it is yours; it is not mine any longer, you see, then you can accept it. That's what I mean by living symbols. All of these things represent living symbols in the Mind of the Father.

These three forms, the circle, triangle and square, are more than just symbols on a flat piece of paper. These are distinctly forms which exist in other worlds. They are part of the creative All of this particular solar system. These symbols for the Creator, the Mediator and the Creation represent the only three forms that exist in the world, the material world or otherwise. These you cannot change. Somewhere we have to get the connections between the blackboard, the written page, and the reality. We have to get the symbols and the words off the blackboard, off the written page, into action. And until we do, we haven't learned anything.

Symbolism is the mathematics of philosophy and it is very important, because if you don't know the ABC's, how can you spell a word? How can you know the answers? These are things that we have to work with all through life. We will pick up books with symbolism in them. No matter what church you go to, symbols are used either in direct visual signs and words, or in the rituals. It is impossible to perform any sacrament that hasn't to do with symbolism.

Also in society, in the physical world, symbols are used. Certain rules of etiquette are accepted as symbols of good breeding and training. These things you will find opening up a new world to you when you begin to think with symbols, along with the basic wisdom and understanding of the teachings.

Q: Is there any symbolism for grace? That is, how could we explain it in terms of symbolism?

A: Well, there's a mathematical symbolism, and that is the acceleration of the logarithmic curve that is existent in mathematics and logarithms. In most any math book you'll find it—the acceleration of figures, and that's a reality too. And another is the geometrical affair where you draw a little square, project little arms off the side and take a compass and start going, and you'll go right around and project a spiral.

TEACHING ADVICE

You cannot teach a person anything just by repeating words and telling him something. You can only motivate something within him so that he will investigate and accept what he has found, but you bend his investigation toward the way in which he will find the truth. There are ways of getting things to people, but these are things that you have not been taught and may never be taught as far as this time around. But there are things which you must learn, because it is important to convince yourself first of all. You can convince nobody of anything if you are not convinced beyond the shadow of a doubt that that is so.

Keep your own personal diary, not just a notebook, a personal diary to keep those things which come to you which are profound. Put them there because they are your book of wisdom. And if you do not put them down, they will float away into nothingness and you will forget them. You can study and study and still you will not know. I can teach and teach and still you will not know. The only thing I can do is to motivate, stimulate within yourself the wisdom of the great Being that is within you, and the channel of it, to open it up so that the wisdom can come to you which you can assimilate and see that it is true.

For no book ever carried wisdom. Books only carry knowledge of wisdom existing in other people, and that cannot be yours. It must be your own wisdom that is gained. And until you learn this, until you listen and until you function on this basis, you will never learn anything.

When you are teaching and have gone through reading the lesson, when you have discussed the subject and covered the principal attributes and principal parts of this subject, don't drag your class out. Now, this doesn't mean stop the class short, but if you've covered it, if you got it across and if you don't get any more questions, cut it off. If you are ten or fifteen minutes early, cut it off. Don't keep adding something on just to teach for an hour. You've got it over, as far as you're going to get it over anyway, so quit it and let them go away with this in mind, the important parts of what you are teaching.

We're not in a conventional school, necessarily, in the evening classes. The objective is to get the things across so they will stay with the individual. Get in your important statements.

If you have to use them during the class, all right, but then rally them up again just before you quit, and bring the important statements out last so they will stay more decisively with the students when they leave the class.

Now this is good psychology and it's good teaching practice. It is a practice, if you'll notice, that is used by advertisers. They are interested in results; and I think teachers, those who are teaching Bible or philosophy or anything else, could learn an awful lot from the advertisers. I don't go along with their advertising, but they know how to get things to people's minds, believe me.

Let me show you something else: when a person speaks loudly, you become quiet, don't you? Normal reaction. So when you teach a class and you see that the minds are not open to the truth, you speak loudly, and they become quiet, so then the truth seeps in, quietly.

Most sectarian groups, in their teachings or dogmas, stress one particular point of the teaching of the Master Jesus or whatever faith they are following, some one aspect of man's development of his life. And what they teach is good, but it does not contain all the tools needed in life. A person is left adrift with just half a map and a big ocean to navigate. He finds he does not have the tools to navigate this big ocean, to build his temple from the cradle to the grave and beyond the grave. For don't forget, most people are following a teaching that believes in eternal life, in an unbroken chain of existence.

In other words, the whole story has not been told. It looks many times as if there were a definite effort to keep back the simple truth that would let their students be free. They have sold him just a part of his heritage. For with one breath, they will tell you that when you are ready for the truth, it will be given to you; and in the next breath they will say that the inner teachings, as they call them, are for the few. And again, that a person cannot understand until he is ready.

This shows rather inconsistent thinking. If a person is not going to understand a statement or truth, if he has not reached that level of understanding, then why worry about trying to cover it up? Why not just put the advanced teachings, or the truths, into print and make them accessible to those who are ready for them, and the rest will take care of themselves? Jesus taught all the great principles openly in that time. Some were in parables; and those things which the world was not ready for, and which were to be preserved for this time to make us ready for the Christ, were taught in allegory.

When teaching candidates for the priesthood, the alchemy of the sanctuary is not taught; alchemy is assimilated. Thus you will teach an aspect of something here which is not complete and you will teach another aspect over there, and it is not complete. You do not give complete statements in any of these things. But when they come together then you will have a fact in your mind, not through somebody's words! You understand what I'm saying?

It is the same thing as we do with spiritual exercises. I cannot teach you unity with God. Nobody can! Only because I know it myself can I talk around it in such a manner that my consciousness can be transferred to you, so you can accept it in your consciousness. That's why no two students are the same. You never teach any two students alike, but you teach the general over-all patterns, the tools. And we never say, "You do this!" We will say, "If you do this, this will happen." It is distinctly your choice. We may say, "Well, whether you like it or not, this fact is so." But how you accept it will tell how it will work with you and how your results will be.

So actually, if you boil it all down, we never teach you anything except the tools. The facts are all up to you, because the facts are what you will experience. That is the way you will react to them—which is a good thing to meditate on, incidentally, when you haven't anything else to meditate on.

UTILIZING TIME

When you get into this work of spiritual teaching, if you get into it, learn to evaluate your time. Time is a precious commodity. At least, it is a good tool for using your life efficiently to gain your objective. I don't say there's such a thing as time in reality—there isn't. But you can use it the same as you use a yardstick or a carpenter's rule.

And it is the same with people. You will help a person to help himself, yes, but when you find a person that's willing to help himself and help somebody else, then you put a little extra time to it. Because most of the people who are only willing and interested in helping themselves are going to be selfish in other things too, and they are not going to be the people that will put forth the effort to accomplish greater work.

Now, we want to help individuals, this is true. But set your time up, do your work in such a way that you can multiply yourself, you see. Now, this is a creative pattern of function. You are not only helping one individual over here, but you're multiplying your own divine intelligence within other people. And as you multiply where you can really pass this along, where you can really give it to another person who will take and use it, then he will create others, who will create others, and this multiplies. This follows the creative pattern in teaching, and it is important.

You've only got so many hours in the day, and so many days in the year; you have a job to do and you haven't long to do it in. It's like when a fire breaks out—and it has. You don't go and grab your smallest cup or pan; you grab a bucket as big as you can get hold of, and you get as much water as you can to pour on the fire. That's what I'm interested in doing, getting as much water to pour on the fire as I can. And that means recreating in others the reality, so that they can pass it along, and heal, and put other people in that same shape.

SPEAKING IN TONGUES

Speaking in tongues is a gift of the Spirit, that is true. And do you know something? It is one of the greatest con games in the world. Well, this is a subject which could take quite a lot of time to get into and really answer. The day of Pentecost, of course, was when the disciples all started to speak in strange and foreign tongues to one another.

And people do speak in tongues today. It is a beautiful thing, but it opens the door to a lot of shenanigans too, because as you probably know, there are occasional fakers in the profession and art of carrying religion to the people. Now, I'm not saying that there are not preachers and priests that are really doing a magnificent job—no. I'm just saying that when you go out into the world and start to meet other people, just because they have a "reverend" to attach to their name doesn't mean that they've just come out of the pearly gates, by any means. I'm going to tell you, it's no cinch to live up to that title of "reverend" if you are really being one. It's not that easy to manifest.

But the more we seek to live, to move and to be in His shadow, the more the glory of God is manifest. Now when a person speaks with tongues through this manifestation, through the existence of this condition, then you have a reality. Then you have a spiritual manifestation of His Word made manifest, through His glory, the way that the glory of God is manifest on earth. Otherwise, it would not be. Do you understand what I'm getting at? Because this is something that you cannot express in words. I'm just making a stab at it, that's all. I'm trying to give you an impression that your own being will pick up and bring into your world and show you the answer.

Those who have served with me at the altar have heard me speak once in awhile, but I want to know who is speaking before I deliver any of it. And it doesn't matter if anyone hears me or not, because I'm not particularly interested in being heard. Most of the value of speaking in tongues anyway is the sound that is projected and its effect. Your understanding it doesn't make too much difference, as long as you know who is giving it. Of course, that isn't going to be very good ego-food, it isn't going to feed your ego a bit when nobody else hears you. But it has happened.

I'm not saying it's wrong to speak in tongues. I'm saying, don't do it unless you know what you are doing. Don't deliver anything unless you know what you are doing, because you are responsible for what you deliver or give.

Occasionally in some of these things you'll get some foreign words or some strange tongues mixed in, but don't get excited about that. If it comes to you strong enough, let it roar. It is of the Spirit, of the Holy Spirit, and don't ever be ashamed because it is there. But don't try to put on a performance! And this happens. Here are some of the pitfalls that people get into, even in this type of work.

There is a category of churches which draws almost entirely upon this as if it were the Holy of Holies. God bless them, at least they're doing something, and it isn't forsaking God. At least they do acknowledge, whether they understand or not, and so they're gaining something. But it is solely the Presence that we are interested in, you see. Because when we have the Presence, this is the whole; this takes in the whole function.

TRANSITION

The act of feeding and clothing people is a humane thing, I grant you. It's necessary and we should continue it to the uttermost. But what do you know that's going to help you later on, after you're no longer able to feed and clothe and do these other things? It's up to you, but remember, we do not work on just the earth plane alone.

There never was an order or group, under any of the mystics or the great teachers, that didn't prepare or at least start the preparation of a person so that when he moved across through transition, he would know what he was doing; because after all, this would be a pretty meaningless life if there was a complete stop at the time of transition. We haven't thought enough about some of these things, and I don't think we've come close enough to the reality of Jesus Christ so that we can gain some of this wisdom in meditation.

Q: As you go through transition do you go through another awakening, and return to the Father?

A: You don't always return to the Father right away.

Q: Eventually?

A: Well, some of us are roustabouts, you know. We tramp around places. But you do have an awakening when you get on the other side, and unless you have prepared yourself for that, a very rude awakening sometimes. Now, if you were going to choose, what kind of a heaven would you like to go to?

Q: Well, I like it here. Just clean it up a little...

A: That's pretty good. But of course, that would have to dissolve, you know, after awhile. Because you'd have to get back to the reality of things, to where you wouldn't have this type of structure or this type of earth to live on. But if you wanted a house like this one, why, it wouldn't take long to build one like that there. And you might want something else tomorrow.

Q: You can set up what you want?

A: Oh, they'll set it up, probably. Now if you're a good Baptist and you've been going to the Baptist church right along you'll probably have a Baptist heaven, you see. But if you don't go there with a preconceived pattern of just exactly what it has to be like, you'll find what you need. And you will be picked up by the Brothers and pretty well taken care of.

Q: What is it going to be like?

A: It's going to be everything that you need that you haven't been able to accomplish down here. You're bound to do this to complete the cycle. We've got to accomplish that which we weren't able to accomplish down here.

Q: I thought you'd have to come back here until you've been able to get what you needed.

A: Yes, but whatever you've attempted in this cycle, you will accomplish there. You will never come back to earth or any other place again at the same stage of development that you left it. You don't come back at this level. You come back at a different level, because you've learned the difference while you're there.

What I'm trying to get across to you is to stop trying to separate what you call the material world from that of the spirit, because it is nothing more than another form of density, that's all. If you stop separating these things, then you can move over into that other reality; because you've got to know and expect that it's there before it will be there for you. Do you understand what I'm talking about? Death is not the leaving, but the being reborn.

You've got to learn to listen to the Spirit. If you learn to listen to the Spirit, then you can get to the place where you know it is, it exists. And it is part of the Mind of God. It is the personality of God manifested. You must get to the point where this is a reality; because if you don't, you will not know and will not be able to manifest there the way you should.

You have decided to serve God and work with the Brothers for the rest of your time, not just this life, of course. That doesn't count, because there is no termination between lives. This is a sort of continuous thing. How long do you suppose it is between the time when you breathe your last breath and the time you open your eyes on the other side, and find out you're alive? You couldn't bat your eyes more than five or six times. Do you think there is no place beyond this earth shell? Well then, you've got another think coming. I've been there and I know. There's nothing like firsthand information if you are going to guide somebody else someplace.

So let me tell you something, if you have any idea of getting away from anything, you're all wrong. Because you can't escape life; that's something you can't do. It won't work, because there's just as much life there as there is here, only it's a little more vivid there. So you'd better settle down to one thing: it doesn't matter a bit what you like or what you don't like, or how big your egos are; it's going to hit just as hard.

It is a case of one thing or the other: spend a few hours now and save yourself a few thousand after you've gotten rid of the body—a few thousand months, a few thousand years. Now, that's what it amounts to, because unless you really have control of yourself and of that mind, you'll think somebody turned you into a comet, believe me. But you'll wear it out eventually because you cannot die and you cannot get away from it. You cannot stop it, so you have no choice whatsoever in any way but to live. The only choice you have is, do you want to live easy or do you want to live hard; do you want to make it easy on yourself or hard on yourself? Of course, that's your choice; I can't stop that choice.

You'll say, "Did I spend all this time in my life and all this misery for nothing?" Yes sir, that's just what we're talking about. We're talking about the poverty that you've forced upon yourself, all the way down the line, the things you've failed to understand. You couldn't find out and nobody understood what you wanted to know.

This does not refer to the petty things of life, but to the larger and more universal things. Such things as temporary and passing anxieties or even our passing angers or distaste—these things do not leave any definite or indelible impression upon the individual passing through incarnation, and are shucked off when he shucks off this vehicle.

The soul is the overcoat of the Self. It is the part that you take with you, and when you go through transition, that's about all you have left. And because the finer bodies are still tied with a silver cord to the physical, a person who passes through transition should not be embalmed or cremated for three full days, until the panorama of life has passed in review, before it is released by the snapping of the cord.

Q: What about someone dying in a fire?

A: Well, if the individual is in an explosion or fire, and does not emerge from it, then you'll find a youngster will be born and maybe live for five or six months or so, and then pass over without any particular reason. This is because they want to come back to the earth and pick up the records that are still left here and take them, so they can take them on in retrospection. In other words, they are fulfilling a cycle. It might be five or six months, or it might be five or six years, depending on whatever the cycle should be.

We teach that when a person goes through transition, let them go. Don't keep on talking and thinking about it. Cut them off so that you're not holding them to the earth plane. Let them go, because holding on only tends to keep them closer to the earth plane itself, because of the drawing. That's why the great teachers, when they write something, very often refuse to attach their names to it, because they don't want their names kept over ages of time. Otherwise somebody will be forever referring to them, pulling them back.

Q: Does the way the body is cared for have any effect on what happens to him after he leaves?

A: Well, it's nice to get rid of it soon, because it has some of your consciousness in the flesh, naturally. And then you're not so apt to be tied to it in any way until it starts disintegration, until you've gotten rid of everything.

Q: What is our procedure with vehicle disposal?

A: The best thing to do is to burn the body. Cremation is nothing new; it has been practiced for thousands of years.

Q: What happens to the ashes after cremation?

A: Toss 'em out!

Q: Some keep them in little jars up on their mantels...?

A: No! I should say not. Oh, they've done this with some people, like some of the great Teachers, but it has to be with his consent if they're to do it right.

Q: Do you go through any gradual evolution after you leave the earth? Are you still evolving on that plane?

A: You go through growth, yes, to a certain extent.

Q: Could one be a teacher on that plane?

A: Well, according to what your position was here. According to what you had attained here.

Nobody owns anything. I've looked into a good many coffins and never saw anything in them of value. I've sat with the rich, and I've sat with the poor, and the poor died a little easier than the rich did.

BEHIND THE VEIL

It is true that there is ever a veil between average humans and the illumined ones who are among us and walk the streets of earth but who are not one with man, for between them and the lower levels of mass mind and other human aspects, the separator is the blue veil of the Will of God. In this world we can see this color only with spiritual sight, but we can feel it as the wall that divides us from those outstanding souls. These people are different from all others; they are "behind the veil". Some humans are buried beneath a red veil of materiality, while others are behind this shining veil of spiritual illumination.

We have spoken of going through realization as going behind the veil, and this is true. This is the working out and the showing of the reality that when you go behind the veil you are no longer of this world. And this has a tremendous impact upon the seeker because he must learn to live a new life. Otherwise, he will spend the rest of this life searching for things of amusement, for things that please him, for things that otherwise would have been desirable but that he now finds hold no real enticement for him, for these are things of the material world and they no longer give him the pleasure that they once might have done. He will find that his pleasures and his happiness do not stem from the things outside, although he may still enjoy them.

Much has been written in certain schools about renunciation, and when you are truly behind the veil, and haven't kept two hands and two feet over on this side of it, then this is the point of renunciation. This is when you see and are truly surrounded by the royal purple, which is present in many people who have gone through these initiations and have realized these things.

Those who would become one with God must renounce forever the things which are of man as being the prime factor of importance in their life; for when the blue veil surrounds the candidate, he is no longer of the earth but of things celestial, and forever there is a wall between him and the things he has left behind. That wall seems as limitless as consciousness itself, and to the uninitiated it does not exist at all; but those who have passed behind it know that it is more solid than the thickest granite, more resistant than steel. And thousands have battered themselves against this wall of the Will of God, Whose fortress is impregnable.

Q: The first veil is the veil of the Self?

A: That's right.

Q: And there is a second veil?

A: It is around the Holy of Holies, as shown in the temple structure, in the Bible.

Q: The second veil then is...?

A: The blue veil. In Eastern legends it was called the blue veil of Krishna. It is said that Krishna, when he was here, had gone behind the blue veil of renunciation. This is something that is not fully understood, but anyone who has gone through the initiation of God-realization passes beyond, and certainly is behind that blue veil; and this is what they were talking about. But somehow there has been much misunderstanding as to what renunciation really consisted of, and those things which have to do with action.

Some people feel and believe that renunciation is a state in which we take up absolute isolation, that we are not active in the physical or the material world at all. Well, they gather that from something such as a great Master might have attained. But there are many people who have gone behind the veil who are not masters, and who have attained considerable spiritual evolvement, yet are very active in the physical world.

The Master is of a different grade of consciousness than the human, for once he has become an intelligent worker in the Great Plan, he has new joys, and the wall of mutual interest divides him from the things he once held dear. You cannot be on the fence. You cannot have the great without giving up the lesser. When man has only one purpose, to glorify God through service to His creation, then the wall will be as a curtain of air and non-existent.

THE WAY

The Way is one of the most important things, because here is where we meet all people. Here is where we meet all faiths, all orders, all works of man, for there is but one Way and one Light. There are many schools that lead to it, but when you reach this point, there is but one path; and this is above all churchianity, this is above all religions, this is above all faiths and all denominations. It isn't contradictory to them, but this Path is above them. For this is the Way of the Teachers and Masters and those who wish to aspire, and has to do not only with religions and esoteric orders and higher beings, and so forth, but it also has to do with what we are doing right now.

Many people will tell you, "Well, now, there's more than one way to God." And I have to say yes, sir, we know that. There are many schools, many churches, many orders, but they all wind up at one place, and that is The Way. This is the Way of eternal initiation, solar initiation, whether you're a Protestant, a Catholic, A Jew, a Gentile, a Confucionist, a Brahman. It doesn't make any difference what it is you're following, you are going to come to the one point where you reach the initiation of illumination.

And from that point forward you are are not a "religionist" any longer, because you lose this. You may follow one particular faith in order to fulfill your work and your way, your mission, or something of that sort; but you lose that dogmatic aspect to your life, because there is no such thing as a dogma on that level. There can't be, because there's only one Christ, only one Christ Light, and so there can be no contradiction, and there is but one Way on this level.

The Way encompasses all of the basic religions, because there are no churches in heaven, there are no creeds and no dogmas there at all. And with the exception of those that have built their own heaven there—and which they've got to get used to and get over—why, that's the way it is, and there is nothing we can do about it. There is no way of changing it. I don't care what church or sect or society you belong to, you are going to go through the same thing, period!

We learn that all things are possible as we travel this route. The longer we travel it, the more we can smile at the doubter and say, "God love you, brother; because you're going to travel the same route. If you don't travel it this time, you'll travel it the next, anyway." Because when you get to one place, then there is only one path. That is the path of

Light, the path of wisdom and of the Self. And it is not Catholic, it is not Protestant, it is not Jewish, it is not Mohammedan, it is not Buddhist, it is not anything; it is just the Way of Light. And we all reach it sometime or other, no matter how we fight to keep away from it. Sometime or other we will reach the all-encompassing Brotherhood of Man.

The Way is a distinct path of vibration and energy which you travel when you have let go of everything, and you have decided to work with the Brothers for the rest of your time. Not just this life, of course, because there's no termination between lives; this is a sort of continuous thing. The work of the Way leads within and it leads above. And the farther in we go, the higher up we go. There is, so to speak, a Lodge; and there will be a greater Lodge as we build it. No matter where you travel, those who are part of the Way will be acknowledged by others who are on the Way. This is why you are acknowledged, you are known because you are all working from that same standpoint and that same reality.

We have heard that "in an hour in which you think not, He will come", and it is true that when we have let go and given up, this is the time when the Light comes in, if we are truly seeking. It is when we have let go of all earthly concepts, when we have let go of all things and said, "Here I am." Then too, the great Light of Christ will come in and flood our vehicles, flood our bodies, and here will be revealed the inner light, the light that never fails. This is the Way that every individual must eventually take. It is the way of the Return to the true consciousness in attunement with the Great One, and the great consciousness from these higher realms.

Somehow or other, letting go of the dense world is one of the hardest things for people to do. This is part of your experience as you enter the Way. Because once you have entered it, you will no longer cling to that which we have created here. You will use it; it will become your tool, it will be useful to you as part of what you do in service for the Master and for the Great Father.

But again we move back into the matter of faith. This time of entering the Way is probably the only place in the entire structure of the universe and the archetypes of initiation where there must be absolute faith without, you might say, practically any knowledge. But knowing is there and is absolutely essential.

This is where we come to the Awakening. And we cannot come to the Awakening or our presence on the Way unless we understand the use of the Word. You cannot set your foot upon the Path without understanding the Word.

Now, there may be a number of things you do not understand fully, but this is one thing you had better know about. The Awakening is just what it says it is, and you only awaken when you put your foot on the Way. Remember the parable of the Prodigal Son, who "came to himself", and began the Return to his Father.

We start at the lowest rung of this era, which is the illumination, and it is the first particular field of work that we bend all our efforts toward. Therefore when we have taken that first step of illumination, we move toward Self-realization. And from there on we work toward what would have been previously known as the twelfth initiation, or that which can only be given beyond the earth plane. This is the path of devotion—you might say it's the path of sainthood, in a sense, though not exactly that. But this is where most of such work is done; it is where most of that initiation happens.

Remember that when you take an initiation, you will experience and work it out afterward. It is the same on this level as on any other. You then start to work at it and start to go through the experience of it, and this is the wonderful part. From the state of illumination, this becomes One Path and all people follow it, because this is the Way of the Christ, you see. It's a very simple thing automatically all is absorbed in the one continual Path.

Q: When the Master said, "I am the Way, the truth and the life", was he referring to the initiations?

A: That's right; there's your answer. There is no teacher in this world or any other that does not follow the path of initiation. It is necessary; it is the Way of God.

This does not mean merely to live a good pattern of life, but to actually live in the Christ consciousness, so every part of the mind and soul is permeated through and through with the life-force and the fire of this Being, coming from it. You are then in a world where things are absolutely mastered by the Spirit, will and mind, and are spiritualized, so to speak, so as to respond perfectly to the power of the will which comes and motivates from the Self, in full action. This is the Path of illumination and this is what we strive to attain. Because once we have it, then with its light we can find the Self.

This gives us the full knowledge of our being, of our power and our ability to create our lives the way we want them.

Q: Did they do this in the old schools?

A: When you went into one of the old schools, you were dedicated to the Infinite and Nameless One, and you were putting your foot on the Path for that purpose. You were attempting to become—you had to attain self-mastery, if nothing else. And this is what you are striving to attain as well, because that is why the promise is given to you in the early degrees, of the power and the choice of your own.

But the path of illumination is the thing that is sought first, and this is why we do not lean either to the occult or the mystic side of things, but we go through the core. It is what one old mystic called the "boot-strap" method. You pick yourself up by your own bootstraps. This is a bit rougher, but it is still shorter than going around and around the mountain.

THE WORD

Experience does not come in words.Tonight I don't want any-body to take notes, and I'll tell you the reason why. You can't possibly take notes in a lecture like this and still remember anything that you hear. And the chances are, by the time the lecture is finished you won't remember anything anyway. I'm not talking about your mem-ory, but the ability to conceive that this is not done by words; it is done by the way I give it.

You might not know or remember anything about these lectures that you receive here now, but in a month or maybe another two weeks, all of a sudden you are going to get some inspirations and you are going to have some wonderful new revelations regarding life, and perhaps some of the things which seem so trite, so monotonous and uninterest-ing, will suddenly burst forth as moving vibrant parts of your life.

All things on this level have to be taught from this standpoint so that you may conceive what cosmic consciousness is. The words them-selves may tell you nothing, but the reality within you will tell you much. There is no such thing as giving this in a lecture of words that you can always understand, until you have experienced them within. Without experiencing them, you will not understand. When you get to the reality of them within yourself, then and then alone will you begin to understand the world around you and your brother man.

When you truly know and realize that your consciousness is the vehicle and path through which the great force of God can move and function accurately, then you'll begin to understand why the minister and the priest have been given certain tools and certain things to work with. Now, everyone has been given a voice; we all can speak. Yes, but how do you speak? You can say a word, but how do you say it? Does it just go past their ears, or does it hit them right square and make its impression? Whether they accept the idea or not is immaterial. It is there. It is a living word, and it will have its effects.

If the student just sticks around for a little while, things are going to happen, no matter whether he understands or not. In other words, the truth of Christ is preached, is taught, but the existence of the soundless Word is present. The presence of the Lord is there. And regardless of whether we're instructing the individual, preaching to him or not, the Word is preaching and things are taking place.

When God gave the Word, it was given with His Spirit, therefore it was motivated.

Q: I don't understand the Word as well as I would like to. Could you explain it in more detail?

A: I don't know how to explain this quickly. "In the beginning was the Word..." Some have reached the point where they have heard the "AUM". Some have heard celestial music, the tone of this, though not while they were in the physical body, by any means.

The Word was given in the Law by the Creator and—I'm making this terribly brief, I know. The Word was given at the Creation and it carried with it the pattern and type of function of Creation and its perpetuation. This is why basically the churches have always talked about the Holy Trinity, because it is through this form and pattern which the Word now works, and because the Spirit of the Father, which carries the personality of this Being compositely, is the Word as given. It's as simple as that. There's a little edge cut off here, but this is just a short-cut way of answering that.

The Creation had to be in the Father's Mind before it became, before the Word as executing the Creation was given. Mind is the vehicle through which the form is perpetuated. Faith is the knowing and the awareness through which this thing works. Faith is the physical body, here, of the Word—it's the easiest way I know of putting it.

Q: What was the "Lost Word"?

A: The moment He spoke it, it was no longer with Him, was it?

Q: He stopped being attuned to the vibration of it...

A: That's right. Because He had given it forth in the Law which He had established, and therefore it was now functional, and it was lost unto Him. He had let it go and it had become a functional working reality.

Why was it called the Lost Word in the first place? All right, let's think functionally. He gave forth the Word, so it was gone, wasn't it? It went forth and has been resounding in the memory, in the Mind of the Father, ever since, you see, because it went into the Akasha, His memory. That's the Lost Word, because He can't speak it over again, not that Word. Because if He did, then the Creation would—if He doubted that first Word, why, Creation wouldn't have been here, or we wouldn't be standing on this globe.

Q: Do you think He could ever say another one?

A: I'm sure He has; because this is a New Age. God gave forth the Word to man. He gave the Word and He said, when you do this, this will happen. It was a contract, if you want to put it on that basis.

Q: Jesus said, "...in my name..."

A: Yes; it's a password, you might call it. Jesus was very selective, in a sense, and yet everyone had the opportunity to talk with him and work with him. And when he was speaking to a group of people, he was extremely simple. He used simple words so that they could not misunderstand him—though, of course, they did, I grant you. But at least those words were spoken so that they would live for many ages afterward, many years and centuries.

The Father spoke the Word of Creation and gave it to Jesus—the power of that Word—and therefore, as the High Priest, he had that power; and he gave the Word to us, to the people. And when he went to Golgotha and cleared the earth of the error and the disturbances that were there at the time, he made it possible for that edict to work; and therefore we have within us the right, the divine right through birth, through the crucifixion of our Lord, the power of the Word to work. But how you do use it! You have created more troubles in your life for yourself than you would want to put down in any book or piece of paper. And it has worked perfectly, without question. Then again sometimes you use the Word accidentally.

God gave you the Word. It's time you start to do a little of your own work, becoming self-sufficient, you know, through His power, His Word. You'll get much better results faster than you will the other way. As travelers on the spiritual Path, your words are eternally powerful and you'd better learn to use them the right way. You can't speak the Word the way God did, but as long as you get close to Him, know Him, sense Him, then your Word will work. Be sure to make your word clear, and be careful what you say—because it will live! So when you want that word to live, then you use it; but see that it isn't going to hamper anybody or it isn't going to be a stumbling-block for anybody.

Q: In using the Word, what is the action...?

A: The Light is the motivater of it, and the Word does it. The Light is the motivater and carrier. You want to succeed, you want to serve man— that's fine, wonderful, and these are the tools with which you go ahead. But the reality is when you become totally silent and the power and the Word of the Lord Jesus Christ is actually there instead of you; that's when it becomes a reality.

Q: What is the fiat?

A: I've heard it defined by one individual who said, "The fiat is the echo of the Word." It's a fairly good definition. If you've ever been in a mountain range and started to yodel, you should have heard the aftertones coming through.

Q: Apart from the definition, can you tell us how the fiat functions? Can you use it to move something, or to get something going, or what?

A: Yes, well, let us call it the conveyer of the action.

Q: There's a law that for every action there's a reaction. Does this happen to the fiat?

A: No, you're talking about the finality of the Law of cause and effect. Well, the Word came before this. It is the outgrowth of this that brought the Law of cause and effect into functional reality. We are saying that the Word was pronounced. After its pronouncement by the Father, it was not pronounced again.

Q: What about the Life Force, the Breath of Life, you know? When you pronounce the Word, the Spirit motivates the Word and the action. Is this in the fiat?

A: Well, the Father doesn't have the Breath of Life. He has reached beyond that: He is Life. No, the breath of life is there in your breath, that's for sure, but what we're talking about was before the life began. This was Him; this is the Reality, the beginning of this creation, as God; and I don't know where He came from, but that's as far as I go.

Q: You said the Word is the balanced sound. I don't understand what the Aum is, unless it's the Word.

A: It is the composite sound of Creation, as it is functioned. Now, this you can hear, the same as celestial music.

Certain vowels, certain sounds, represent certain things, but they will stimulate certain actions too. And they will do this through the power and the spirit existing, because He said, thy word shall become flesh. Now I believe this implicitly, because I know it to be a fact. I've worked with it. Man has a primary purpose of lifting up his whole being toward the Son. Many people make this mistake, when they say "toward God". He said, only through the Son shall you find the face of the Father.